WALKING HOME

KEN GREENBERG

WALKING
HOME

the
LIFE AND LESSONS
of a
CITY BUILDER

RANDOM HOUSE CANADA

PUBLISHED BY RANDOM HOUSE CANADA

COPYRIGHT © 2011 KEN GREENBERG

www.randomhouse.ca

Library and Archives Canada Cataloguing in Publication

Greenberg, Ken
    Walking home : the life and lessons of a city builder / Ken Greenberg.

Includes bibliographical references and index.
Issued also in an electronic format.

ISBN 978-0-307-35814-1

    1. Urban renewal. 2. Urban cores. 3. Inner cities. 4. City planning. 5. Sustainable urban development. I. Title.

HT170.G74 2011   307.3'42   C2010-904239-5

Design by CS Richardson

Printed and bound in the United States of America

10 9 8 7 6 5 4 3 2 1

Photo credits: see page 356.

FOR ETI, A CITY GIRL

CONTENTS

Introduction   1

I: THE CITY ON THE ROPES

Growing up in Cities and Suburbs   14

The Pre-War Anticity Polemic   21

Cheap Energy Fuels Personal Mobility:
   The Flight to the Suburbs   31

A Toxic Convergence: Doubts Sown   36

II: THE CITY REBOUNDING

Action-Reaction: The Emperor Has No Clothes   42

The Streams Merge   48

Leaving for Amsterdam   54

Arriving in Toronto: A Second Chance   56

Jane Jacobs' Ideas Resonate   66

A Tipping Point   71

III: THE ELUSIVE ART/SCIENCE OF CITY BUILDING

A Unique Ability to Combine Things   78

We Shape Our Cities and They Shape Us   85

False Trails and Mirages   93

A Revival of City Building   105

IV: NEW TOOLS AND TEAMS

Epiphany in Prince Albert   110

Testing a Method in Toronto   114

Taking It on the Road to Saint Paul   131

There Is a Time to Say No   143

Optimizing the Whole, Not the Parts   147

New Kinds of Collaboration   152

A New Tool Kit   158

Serial Creations   169

V: CITIES PERPETUALLY RE-INVENT THEMSELVES

Shaping Forces in Our Time   174

Doing More with Less   186

Getting Out of Our Cars   193

Retrofitting Infrastructure   197

Greater Mix and Overlap   205

Cities in Nature   211

Universities as City Builders   225

Back from the Abyss   231

Suburban Transformations   244

VI: RECLAIMING THE PUBLIC REALM

    Public Space Lost and Found   254

    The Revival of the Commons   257

    Back to the Water's Edge   265

    Urban Trails and Public Access   273

VII: MANAGING CHANGE IN DEMOCRATIC SETTINGS

    The Wisdom of Crowds   290

    Getting to Scale: Subsidiarity   295

    How the Development Table Is Structured   304

    From NIMBY to YIMBY   311

    Political Space: Mayors and Councillors   315

VIII: REDEEMING THE PROMISE OF CITIES

    Turning the Corner   326

    The Case for Empowering Cities   342

    Notes   *348*

    Acknowledgements   *354*

    Image Credits   *356*

    Index   *358*

INTRODUCTION

Think of Broadway as it follows New York City's progress from the tip of Lower Manhattan up the Hudson River or Yonge Street running north, bisecting the heart of Toronto. Consider Commonwealth Avenue wending its way west out of Boston through Brookline then Newton to Route 128 or Woodward Avenue making its way north from the heart of Detroit out past 8 Mile. Picture one of the Parisian Grand Boulevards extending beyond the Périphérique into the vast *banlieues*. Choose any familiar equivalent in another major city. Though unique in ways, the scenes we would encounter while walking along any of these streets, from their origins in the historic core out to their suburban fringes, would have much in common.

We begin downtown, where the streetscape is snug and compact. The distance from one sidewalk to the unbroken

1

2 line of building facades on the other side of the thoroughfare is short, and we easily make out expressions on the faces of people across the street. The city blocks are narrow and traffic moves slowly, stopping at frequent traffic signals. Lanes are few and tight, and drivers accustomed to the presence of pedestrians and cyclists know enough to watch for them. When we see something interesting or someone we know on the opposite sidewalk, we can effortlessly cross at a light or jaywalk during a break between cars. Cyclists and drivers make eye contact with us when we negotiate intersections, letting us know that they are as aware of our presence and mindful of our safety as we are of theirs. At frequent intervals, we can shorten our walk and jump on transit—a bus, streetcar or subway train. As we walk, much catches the eye. Most buildings extend right to the sidewalk, and their ground floors are occupied by shops, restaurants and cafés with closely spaced doors and appealing window displays. Offices and residences above the stores contribute a constant flow of people to the busy sidewalks, which are alive with pedestrians of all ages and interests. Some hurry; others stroll and window-shop. Where the sidewalks are wider, we can linger at a café terrace and watch the passing flow. A canopy of trees or awnings may provide shade and shelter. Traffic signals, advertisements and store signs are directed at pedestrians, who also have easy access to newspaper boxes, newsstands, benches, planters, food vendors and, occasionally, impromptu markets or hawkers with tables of knock-off goods.

As our walk takes us out of the historic city centre and into areas that were built more recently, this pedestrian-oriented streetscape begins to change. The basic ingredients remain— the stores, the street hawkers, the residences above—but their form and relationships alter almost imperceptibly, block by block. The roadway pavements gradually expand with more and wider lanes. Sidewalks and other pedestrian spaces contract. At intersections, exclusive left-turn lanes increase the distances we have to walk to get across the street, as do free-flow right-turn traffic lanes called "dog legs." The blocks get longer, and the distance between safe crossing points increases. Eye contact is lost to distance and increased velocity, and we feel much less inclined to impulsively cross the street to check out a tempting shop window on the other side. Slower-moving seniors, the disabled and people pushing strollers or pulling shopping carts all have to struggle to make it across the street before the light changes, urged on by the flashing timers warning us to clear the intersection. Here, the balance between drivers and pedestrians has shifted. We persevere and continue on our walk.

Gaps begin to appear where missing buildings have given way to parking lots. Our journey is becoming much less appealing. The stores are bigger, with fewer doors and windows to invite spontaneous browsers inside; many are now single- or two-storey buildings, with less discernible or totally nondescript occupancy above. We have to keep a wary eye out for cars crossing our path because the sidewalk is broken up with frequent "curb cuts" for parking and service entrances. The buildings themselves are set back farther from the sidewalk. The remaining window displays are dwarfed by signs standing at the curb or mounted high on the buildings, designed for drive-by viewing. The street may be busy, but here on the sidewalk, we pedestrians are starting to feel a little isolated. A few more kilometres out and the "walls" of the street start to recede even more.

4

The walk out of the city, from streets with lively sidewalks . . .

to forlorn traffic arteries lined with parking lots.

The roadway has become even wider. Shopping plazas sit even farther from the sidewalk—across parking lots, with no pedestrian route to the shop doors. Few trees shade the narrow sidewalk, and an eclectic mix of pavement surfaces keeps breaking our rhythm as we pass gas stations and drive-thrus at larger intersections. We are in a world visually dominated by back-lit signboards. We are clearly in another country. We are meant to drive here. The street is no longer recognizable as a shared public space; it is a single-purpose traffic artery. Malls replace plazas and storefronts are barely visible from our narrow perch on the vestigial sidewalk. The only signs we can see are the corporate logos on otherwise undecorated walls or large post-mounted billboards.

Since no one is expected to walk here, this environment has been constructed with little regard for weather. On a hot and sunny or cold and windy day, this walk goes from being merely unpleasant to downright inhospitable. Walking itself has become dangerous. Intersections are spaced far apart, and jaywalking would be much like running across a highway. And when we do come across an intersection, it comes fully loaded with multiple left turns and even wider free-flow dog legs with large radii for higher-speed right turns. There is so little pedestrian time on the signals that the streets are almost uncrossable. Now, unable to keep up with the speed and single-mindedness of the traffic, cyclists have also become rare, just a few brave souls precariously hugging the curb. Forlorn and isolated bus stops are splashed with advertising. As we trudge on through this hostile territory at the side of the road, we see that human activity has withdrawn from the street. It happens only in the private places where people live, work or shop—in separated, self-contained compounds. Big box stores and power centres alternate with office parks surrounded by their own massive parking pads. Low-density residential enclaves defensively turn their back fences to the traffic artery (the "reverse frontages" that signal surrender in this harsh environment), with blank walls and fences shielding their backyards from traffic. A little farther and there will be no more sidewalks. The public social spaces—the forecourts, doorways, café patios, sidewalk displays, where we meet and connect and that make the city feel convivial—are gone. The walk from the house to the mall is either practically impossible or completely discouraging. These last stages of our journey have been a bit like walking onto the tarmac of an airfield or into the tunnel from the subway platform: the signs and signals that exist are meant for creatures of another order. How did this happen?

This imaginary journey illustrates a succession of changing beliefs, values and practices that followed World War II. For the better part of the twentieth century, we had concluded that cities as we knew them were obsolete, and we abused them, devalued them and fled them in much of the Western world. And the city street—the most potent expression of a city's most admirable qualities—is where we now witness, most vividly, the city's subsequent demise. Two profound shifts caused this situation. First, cities and their planners started to give highest priority to the unencumbered movement of automobiles and elbowed aside all other concerns. This was seen and accepted as progress. Secondly, the very concept of the city street as a valuable social space was killed, and every component of the corpse was picked over and made into the province of specialists, who paid little

7

heed to the way their work affected the quality of the whole. The traffic engineers dealt with moving vehicles, the municipal engineers were responsible for the arrangement and maintenance of services and utilities, the transit planners determined the location and frequency of transit stops, the emergency service providers dealt with ensuring access—and so on. The parcelled-out world that resulted after a few decades of this fragmented approach to managing cities began to look and feel a lot like the incoherent and haphazard artery of our imagined walk out of town.

8

The change I've just described occurred primarily in the two generations after World War II, and by the time the dust settled, we had profoundly reshaped most of the urban environment in North America, Europe and many other parts of the world. A free-wheeling concept of the "good life" had developed, based on the assumption of an endless supply of cheap energy with no restraining governor. Every adult had to have a car for maximum personal mobility, and as these cars multiplied, they overran our cities. Although I didn't know it at the time, I came of age right in the middle of that sustained onslaught.

I was born in New York City, but as a child I lived a peripatetic existence. By the time I left high school, I had attended thirteen schools in half a dozen cities in the United States and Europe and had experienced the nervous energy of a society on the move. In my case, the relocation was not from city to suburb; it was an atypical path alternating between the two. Through this back and forth, I discovered that the "city" had become an emotional touchstone for me, so it was not surprising that I ended up studying architecture. But it was the city itself, not just the buildings, that fascinated me, and I quickly got caught up in the maelstrom of social, political and design currents that swirled around the trans- formation of the urban environment.

As my understanding of how cities had gone wrong and might yet be put right began to gel, I developed ideas for rejuvenating what I loved about urban life, and when I began my career as an urban designer, I found opportunities to put them into practice. In time, city building—a broad and inclusive extension of urban design—became my professional calling. For over three decades, I have been privileged to work in an extraordinary range of urban settings throughout North America and Europe, focusing on the rejuvenation of downtowns, waterfronts, neighbourhoods and university campuses. I have taken on the redesign of locations as large as a city region and as small as a city block.

In this book I've tried to weave my own perspective into the broader story of city revival, drawing on real examples of places, people, jobs and ideas that have contributed to my approach to city building. The result is not a story of glamorous projects realized, nor is it a theoretical treatise or a polemic laden with statistics and data. It's the personal account of a voyage to places like my hometown of New York and other cities to which I have become deeply connected, including Hartford; Amsterdam; Boston; New York; Montreal; Quebec City; Washington, DC; Paris; Detroit; Saint Paul; and San Juan, Puerto Rico. Each takes centre stage for a time. And none of them ever makes a complete exit. My adopted city, Toronto, plays a major part, too, and my ongoing relationship with this place has offered all the ecstasy and frustration of a lengthy love affair.

Along the way I have been privileged to meet and work with many remarkable people. Some are well known, like my mentor and friend Jane Jacobs. Others, while not household names, are extremely influential in their own spheres. I've collaborated with colleagues, civic leaders, friends and students—and with people who live and work in places I've had a hand in reshaping. Cities at their best provide much of what we seek in a place to call home: community, places of culture and business that we can walk to, mass transit and a wealth of amenities that couldn't be supported without a city's density. The post-war drive to suburbanization deprived us of these inherent advantages of urban living. The realization of this loss, in tandem with recent concerns about energy scarcity and global warming, has made us see cities with fresh eyes and a growing understanding that they can provide us with an unparalleled measure of sustainability. As a result of a newfound respect for their inherent capacities, cities and city building have again become our urgent priorities. They are making a comeback.

This book is first about how cities got into this mess—the walk out of the city. It is also about the challenge of turning that mess around. We face a staggering array of misguided policies, standards and institutional arrangements that still shape much of the urban environment. We need new ways of creating successful new urban places while also managing the places we have. I've tried to share here some of what I've learned along the way about why cities are worth the effort, how we can give new life to our downtowns and neighbourhoods, why doing so is a necessity and how leading-edge cities are developing techniques to realize that potential.

City building has been anything but a lonely effort. I learned quickly that no one profession—or individual, however smart or experienced—has a monopoly on what makes cities tick. No solution emerges full blown from a single source. In fact, collaborations are the lifeblood of successful city building. I have become acutely aware of what I know and what I don't know—and in a way that is the point. The city requires and demands a pooling of intelligence and much crossing of lines. It is a place where everything *is* connected to everything else.

I

THE CITY ON THE ROPES

GROWING UP IN CITIES AND SUBURBS

My first and recurring experience of a city occurred at 1902 Avenue L off Ocean Avenue in Brooklyn, where I was born in 1944 and where I returned to live twice in my youth. Many details of that place have long ago faded, but what remains with me is an enduring mental map of a small piece of the world that included nearby Avenue M, Avenue J, Kings Highway, the BMT subway (today the F Train), Coney Island, numerous neighbourhood streets, the playground that was the centre of my small universe and my school, P.S. 193.

My grandparents had an apartment on the third floor of a six-storey building, and many other family members lived in this neighbourhood of apartment buildings and private houses. Ours was basically a one-bedroom corner apartment with a very small extra room off the kitchen. When we moved in, my grandparents moved into that small room.

My younger sister, Laura, and I slept on the couches in the living room, and my parents took the bedroom. It was crowded and uncomfortable in many ways, but there were compensations in the world outside. I remember hanging out on the roof on summer evenings, collecting butterflies and bottle caps on the streets below with my closest friend, stretching the dining-room table into the living room (with several extensions) for family gatherings, watching Ed Sullivan on the small TV with my grandfather and vacuuming for my grandmother while the radio blared.

We moved in with my grandparents again when I was in second grade. My little universe, the one I could navigate on foot and explore on my own or with friends, was defined by a stretch of Avenue L between the park at E18th Street and my school at E25th Street, where my aunt was a teacher. I often walked home to have lunch with my grandmother. All ages shared the park and playground at E18th. It was well equipped with concrete tables for playing cards (mostly pinochle), handball and basketball courts, a wading pool (which doubled for intense games of dodge ball), swings, see-saws and slides. It even had a park house with a staff and sports equipment to borrow. I spent all my free time after school there. Down the block on Avenue M, my uncle's father-in-law had a candy store near the corner, and we shopped in all the small food stores between Ocean Avenue and the subway station, including my favourite, the bakery, where I was sent to buy fresh bread, bagels and bialys. There was also the unforgettable live-chicken market, with its cages, noise and smells, where I shopped with my grandmother.

This small universe would be lost to me when our family moved on in search of employment and a place of our own away from the "crowded" and "congested" city. But now, many decades later and looking back, I can see this neighbourhood had many characteristics that city dwellers now value. At the time, though, we either took them for granted or didn't have the words now used to describe them—words like "compact," "walkable," "transit-oriented," "dense," "for all ages," "mixed-use." When I returned as an adult, I was surprised to find that, physically, it had changed very little except that the Yiddish signs on some of the stores had given way to Russian. I do recognize that part of my positive feeling for this time and place rests on the fact that at a very young age, I was able to venture around the neighbourhood alone or just with friends. Sadly, times have changed. Even if the streets were safer and more human in scale, today, many parents still wouldn't be comfortable with that level of freedom for real or perceived safety reasons. To what degree that trend is reversible is a poignant and open question.

Like many others after World War II, my family was experiencing the great collective antsiness, the urge to move to the greener pastures that were opening up outside the city. I was vaguely aware of adult conversations about how the city was deteriorating, while exciting new places to live were opening up in Queens, Long Island, Westchester and points beyond. This was a time of social change, with new emphasis on the nuclear-family household, wondrous new labour-saving devices and, above all, the freedom of the car and the irresistible draw of new highways. I was just as swept up as anyone in the excitement of a Sunday drive on the recently opened Grand Central Parkway or to Jones Beach, all of us packing into my grandfather's new DeSoto. With a move out of the city, came an assumption of quality, value and status.

We first moved as a family to Fresh Meadows in Queens, a brand-new development funded by New York Life Insurance, and then a year later to a similar development on Brush Creek Boulevard in Kansas City, Missouri. These post-war housing developments were full of returning GIs and their young families. With walk-up apartments and townhouses, these developments were like halfway houses on the way to suburbia. Small, bounded enclaves that weren't exactly city anymore, they represented the beginnings of the pulling away, the sorting out of the city's varied population into something more homogeneous and controlled.

I witnessed here the creation of a more specialized world, intended only for living, while everything else, like working, happened in some other location. These new, surburban-style neighbourhoods featured their own parking lots, and leaving them usually meant getting in the car. At first, they were actually hybrids, still within the city fabric. However, as they progressively turned inward, their connections to surrounding streets and neighbourhoods started to disappear and their edges grew sterile. The layout of these projects began to reveal what I now recognize as early modernist urban planning (which I'll come to shortly): "super blocks" with many old streets removed and buildings set well back from the sidewalks of the remaining streets but at different distances, so they appeared to zigzag creating a "sawtooth" effect. There was also one small supermarket, where the parking lot replaced the local shopping street as the main community focus. All the same, this place of business was still far more modest than today's super-sized versions. The area inside the project was still walkable, but there was none of the variety found in my Brooklyn neighbourhood, and the traffic rivers on its edges were getting wider and faster. It fascinates me to look back at this development formula. As we now try to create less car-dependent "urban places" within suburban settings, we sometimes cross paths with this earlier transitional stage, though we're going in the other direction.

In 1954, we finally moved to real suburbia, to our own single-family house on Beacon Street in Newton, Massachusetts. Our neighbourhood was just inside the rapidly changing edge of older neighbourhoods where Route 128 had just been built, ringing Boston on the border between countryside and city. This place was closer to the suburban pastoral ideal. Waban Village Center on the commuter line (now the Green Line of the "T") was a short distance away, providing a quick train ride into downtown Boston. At the same time this was one of a scattering of historic or historically inspired "urban villages" close to the countryside. There was still the smell of real farmland, collecting tadpoles and fishing in creeks and ponds was within my reach. But the landscape was changing rapidly, and in a short time the nearby countryside would fill in around us with newer suburbs.

Then, in 1958, an unexpected break took place in my family's migratory pattern. My father had accepted an offer for a two-year assignment in Geneva, Switzerland.

We moved into a relatively new, modern apartment building on Rue Crespin, not far from the historic centre, and I made the liberating discovery of a city within the reach of a teenager. My world had expanded; I was no longer dependent on being chauffeured around. I had to get a bicycle licence and learn the rules of the road to pass a road test, but between my bike and the frequent tram service, I had the run of the entire city, including the nearby agricultural villages just

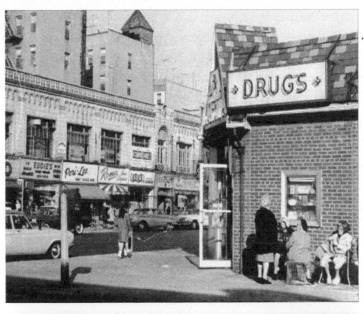

Avenue M and 18th Street, Brooklyn, to Beacon Street, Newton, Massachusetts.

outside its boundaries. I planned a multiday bicycle trip around Lac Léman with school friends, staying at youth hostels, and we also visited the Salève, a local mountain that towered over the city just across the border in France. I was enjoying the rites of coming of age with a degree of independence I couldn't have experienced in suburban America. In short, my family and I were living in a culture where the city was clearly seen as something to enjoy, not a place to escape from. Daily shopping for our household happened practically on our doorstep—at the local Migros supermarket or after a short walk to Geneva's other main *supermarché*, Coop, or the nearby street market. My mother took courses at the university. My sister and I created an impressive stamp collection just by soliciting used envelopes from all the consulates and international agencies we could get to on our own. Even as a teenager, this shift raised a lot of questions for me, not in abstract terms but very practically. How did I want to live? Wasn't this kind of life in a city more desirable than what I had experienced before, with a much more interesting world at my fingertips? This was the beginning of a revelation. What if all the things I'd been been taught to assume about the disadvantages of the "city" were only that—assumptions—and not immutable laws of progress? What if older cities weren't bad? What if they could become "modern" too? Geneva certainly seemed to have modernized while still retaining its valuable older qualities.

After two years, we moved briefly back to my old Brooklyn neighbourhood, where I attended Midwood High School. I quickly began taking pride in myself as a New Yorker, starting to hang out in Manhattan. My grandparents' apartment was crowded, but *the City* was mine. When my family moved again—this time to South Orange, New Jersey, another older suburb on the rail line built around an historic village—I was ready to set out on my own. Amherst College in Massachusetts had already accepted me for early admission, but while waiting for the school year to begin, I was a fish out of water. Without a car in South Orange, I was stranded, but getting one was not the answer. I was still tied by an umbilical cord to Manhattan and found myself constantly running there on a bus or train.

How did my own early trajectory fit into the bigger pattern of domestic migration at the time? While I was jumping in and out of the suburban pool, massive change was afoot. Our outward moves were part of a vast transformation in which cities were stretched and hollowed out and their populations drastically depleted. In the two generations after World War II, the American urban landscape was profoundly reshaped, and when the dust settled, significantly more Americans lived in suburbs than in downtown neighbourhoods. Though there had always been out-migrations (from Manhattan to the Boroughs of New York, for instance), this one was different in magnitude and kind. As the rings on the periphery now began to dwarf the centre, the centre itself was being reshaped according to a radically different vision.

THE PRE-WAR ANTICITY POLEMIC

In the aftermath of the European Industrial Revolution, a "modern movement" in architecture emerged. It came from a combination of sources and sought to break the shackles of a *fin de siècle* "historicist" approach to the urban

22

environment based on recycling the architecture and urban planning of earlier periods. The proponents of this movement set out to create a radically new aesthetic and building strategies and trained their sights on the appalling state of the burgeoning industrial city. Witnessing the horrendous living conditions of the time—substandard worker housing, overcrowding, pollution, noise, soot, poor sanitation and disease, these modern thinkers were motivated by a sincere humanist urge to eradicate such conditions.

At the same time as the Industrial Revolution had created these conditions; it had also led to an increased faith in the power of science, engineering and rational thinking to solve them. These urban revolutionaries were enthralled by the methodical logic that had so successfully applied inventive engineering to industry. Unfortunately, their naïve, unquestioning belief in their own ability to refashion cities in the image of modern, frictionless devices for living turned out to be an intellectual time bomb with a very long fuse.

As a result of these reformist impulses, a series of seductive utopian visions appeared in the early decades of the twentieth century, conceived and developed by serious and well-intentioned people (primarily architects) who'd become swept up in the hubris of early modernism. The bold visions of these brilliant designers did not stop at individual buildings or groups of buildings but extended to entire cities. Applying the industrial analogy, they asked themselves whether the city could be treated like an enormous machine. Could its primary roles be identified like the mechanical operations of the latest industrial processes and then be simplified, separated and made to work more efficiently? Many utopian theories and visions gestated feverishly in the decades prior to World War II and took flight in the energetic decades after—on both sides of the Atlantic and ultimately around the world. Their emphasis on industrialized process and mass production offered a ready answer to the problem of "the greater number," the millions who needed to be rapidly re-housed after the war. This conviction resonated with the fervent zeitgeist of an age that had become attuned to military mobilizations and massive deployment of resources. With heroic daring, pioneers of the modern movement advocated what would become the spiritual origin of "urban renewal": comprehensive schemes of slum clearance and wholesale redevelopment intended to address urban problems like deficient housing, inadequate sanitation, poor utilities and services, traffic congestion and crime.

The Congrès International d'Architecture Moderne (known as CIAM), which functioned from 1928 to 1956, was a powerful voice working vigorously to formalize these new architectural and planning principles. In its founding declaration of 1928, CIAM boldly asserted that architecture could no longer exist in an isolated state separate from governments and politics and that economic and social conditions would fundamentally affect the buildings of the future.

The group also declared that as society became more industrialized, it would be vitally important for architects and the construction industry to rationalize their methods, embrace new technologies and strive for greater efficiency, in order to grapple with the insalubrious conditions of the city. One of the movement's founders and chief spokesmen, Charles-Édouard Jeanneret-Gris, better known as Le Corbusier, often drew an unflattering contrast between the impressive, standardized efficiency of the automobile industry and the inefficiency of traditional building techniques.

Ultimately, CIAM was advocating a systematic eradication of extensive areas of existing cities, along with all their unsanitary baggage. Rejecting the form, the look and the workings of the historic city, CIAM's early attitudes about urban planning were unequivocal. Its early declarations boldly proclaimed that urbanization could not be "conditioned by the claims of a pre-existent aestheticism," that its new essence must be that of a "functional order," that "the chaotic division of land, resulting from sales, speculations, inheritances, must be abolished by a collective and methodical land policy." Out with the old—the "chaotic" jumble of streets, shops, factories and houses—and in with the new: standardized dwellings and different areas for work, home and leisure.

Five years after its founding, CIAM produced another strident manifesto, the Athens Charter (so called because the 1933 congress was held on board the SS *Patris* en route from Marseilles to Athens). The theme for this congress was structured around an analysis of thirty-four cities and proposed solutions to their urban problems. In response, the Athens Charter established the formula for the Functional City. Its key underlying concept was the creation of refashioned cities divided into independent zones, each dedicated to one of four primary functions: dwelling, work, recreation and transportation.

This division would make it possible to perfect each function in relative isolation: dwelling, with citizens housed in high, widely spaced apartment blocks; work in modern factories and offices; recreation in well-equipped sports complexes; and transportation that exploited the automobile's exciting new potential to move citizens effortlessly from one zone to the other. Greenbelts would separate each zone of the city from the others, and there would be plenty of buffering green space surrounding individual buildings—also known as "towers in the park"—for light, air and health. The city would run like an efficient machine, and by reducing "friction" and interference between zones, the modern city would create a more harmonious way of life. At least that was the idea.

The public street, an ancient urban construct and one of the most remarkable multidimensional human inventions, confounded Le Corbusier and these modern theorists. It was too hard to define. It did many things but none of them perfectly. It was exasperating to those analytical thinkers that the street weaved together so many roles—a means of access and mobility for pedestrians and people using many types of vehicles, a tool for surveying and defining the boundaries of individual properties, a way to deliver basic services and utilities, a place for commercial activities and the provision of public space for social and political life. Why not divide these functions up and accommodate each separately and more efficiently? thought the modernists. Viewing the various roles of the traditional street as an unwholesome and confusing muddle, CIAM promoted specialized "roadways," intended primarily for vehicles, and separate circulation paths and gathering spaces for pedestrians. The modernist vision untangled the complex web of overlapping activities that would be identified, later in the century, as the very essence of city life. Assuming that the city as they had known it was pretty much a goner, the modernists wondered what their entirely reworked city of the future would look like. An extreme and highly publicized version appeared in the form of Le Corbusier's *Plan Voisin pour Paris* (1925), in which he proposed to demolish most of the city's heart.

In place of the French capital's celebrated historic fabric, a field of cruciform apartment towers were to rise in a green landscape traversed by a network of highways. Streets would be replaced by a carefully calibrated hierarchy of arteries, each with a single, specialized role, related to a particular kind of movement. Le Corbusier developed his vision more fully in a more universal version in 1935 known as the Radiant City. Today, it is difficult to imagine why this kind of thinking had so much appeal in so many quarters, but the radical approach was galvanizing. Published in 1943, the Athens Charter had a profound influence on public authorities and private-sector developers alike throughout post-war Europe and eventually in America and around the world.

In America, other radical visions for the modern city were being proposed. An entirely different view—or so it seemed at first glance—was proposed by legendary architect Frank Lloyd Wright in 1932. His Broadacre City was a plan for a hypothetical four-square-mile community. An extreme, idealized expression of the newly emerging suburbia, re-shaped through Wright's particular vision of rugged frontier individualism, Broadacre City, like Le Corbusier's model, was the antithesis of the historic city. But rather than concentrating development in high-rise towers, Wright had concocted a community that spread itself thinly across the land. It was both a planning statement and a sociopolitical scheme for homesteading by which each American family would be given a one-acre plot within a sprawling pattern, linked by an extensive network of sinuous sci-fi highways and landing pads for personal helicopters.

The United Kingdom had already produced another city replacement vision—pastoral, like Wright's, and forged in reaction to the unhealthy and squalid conditions of the British industrial city. Its origins were in the Garden City movement founded in 1898 by Sir Ebenezer Howard. This movement, which was less bombastic in its ambitions than CIAM's or Wright's, also inspired many examples around the world. These would be self-contained, ex-urban communities in previously undeveloped areas surrounded by greenbelts. Each would include carefully balanced areas for residences, industry and agriculture. This vision would ultimately inspire the New Town movement, which produced a generation of free-standing, planned communities inspired by the dispersed satellite Garden Cities, like Milton Keynes, midway between London and Birmingham.

Though the anticity thinking implicit in each of these three visions was profoundly different, all of their proposed new development constructs shared certain values and biases: the belief that the mix and intensity of the existing city was fundamentally unworkable, an embrace (in the case of the Radiant City and Broadacre City) of the automobile as a means of personal mobility and the idea that functions of the city should be diluted and separated. Surprisingly, all three visions proposed similar remedies; horizontal or vertical, they solved the city's problems by dismembering or fleeing it.

North Americans bought CIAM's vision for "towers in the park," which did lend themselves to mass (if not industrialized) production, initially for large-scale public housing projects. And they did so under the banner of urban renewal. This meant bulldozing older neighbourhoods to create CIAM-inspired complexes of tall apartment slabs (spaced far apart in ambiguous green spaces) and tearing up the existing streets to create immense "super blocks." The result was projects like the infamous Cabrini-Green, built beginning in 1942 by the Chicago Housing Authority on Chicago's North Side.

The European dream of a functional city was also eventually embraced by North American property developers for private ventures based on its conceptual simplicity and commercial potential—but minus its principles of social equity, which positioned adequate housing as a basic human right and not as a commodity. The logic of modernist planning was also applied to the creation of new, single-purpose centres for government, cultural facilities, recreation and entertainment. Meanwhile and even more enthusiastically, in the burgeoning suburbs outside North American cities, planners and the development industry picked up on Wright's sprawling "frontier yeoman" idiom, building tract housing around virtually every American and Canadian city, even if they miniaturized and diluted the original vision.

Ultimately, this potent mix of European modernist town planning and Garden City and Wrightian pastoralism hijacked an unheralded and unbranded indigenous vision of the city that had been gestating independently in North America. In the early twentieth century, urban areas had been growing denser and more interesting, vital and mixed. And they had been doing so organically (in an incremental and natural way), gradually improving upon many of the cramped, unhealthy conditions that drove the modernist concerns.

As a result, robust urban environments were beginning to thrive not only in Manhattan but also in Chicago, Detroit, Los Angeles and many other cities. We catch glimpses of these settings as the backdrops to the black-and-white movies of the prewar and war-time decades. The buildings in these increasingly sophisticated, urbane locales—with great individual structures like New York's Penn Station or Empire State Building—were exuberantly and unselfconsciously incorporating complex and mixed programs. Their sidewalks were lively, and they were oriented to intercity rail and street railways (that is, until General Motors, Firestone and Standard Oil began to purchase and dismantle the streetcar networks).

Elsewhere, cities were reconciling aspects of the modernist project with a greater respect for their urban traditions and norms. We see this in places like Amsterdam, where early modern expansions took a different course than in other European cities. Dutch proponents of modernism had been less virulent in their desire to radically alter cities. There was the Plan Zuid, for instance, developed by Hendrik Petrus Berlage. This extension of Amsterdam was constructed between 1917 and 1925 and holds up well to this day as a prime example of a gentler alternative, integrating more expansive green spaces within a respectful reinterpretation of the Dutch cityscape.

The Quartier des États-Unis in Lyon, designed by architect Tony Garnier in the 1920s, was another compelling demonstration of how twentieth-century urban problems could be tackled in the modernist idiom at a human scale, with up-to-date services, generous green spaces and tight streets lined with shops. There is also the famous White City, a collection of over four thousand Bauhaus or International Style buildings constructed in Tel Aviv starting in the 1930s by German-Jewish architects who had immigrated to the British Mandate of Palestine after the rise of Nazism. The neighbourhood was proclaimed a World Cultural Heritage site as "an outstanding example of new town planning and architecture in the early twentieth century" for its unique adaptation of modern international architectural trends to the cultural, climatic and local traditions of that city.

After publication of the Radiant City plan, these intriguing (and less radical) alternative visions were ultimately overwhelmed by the dominant strain of modernist doctrine, and for a time the baby was unceremoniously heaved out with the bath water. The impact of modernist planning was captured perfectly in *Farewell to Oak Street* (1950), a Canadian National Film Board (NFB) production narrated by the late actor Lorne Greene about the demolition of an "urban slum" to create the Regent Park Public Housing Project in Toronto. It shows poor conditions in an inner-city neighbourhood with all the familiar ills: dilapidated and poorly constructed buildings and no indoor plumbing. (The area was not unlike many other, similar Toronto neighbourhoods nearby that were eventually upgraded street by street and house by house.)

The cameras show the slum being demolished to make way for a squat and stripped-down version of "towers in the park," and the development comes complete with large parking lots on self-contained super blocks and clean, modest, walk-up brick apartment buildings with modern conveniences like running water and household appliances. The film introduces families moving into their apartments and makes sweeping claims for the salutary effects the new arrangement will have on their lives, including better marital relations and less delinquency—poignantly capturing a naïve faith in the guiding principles of the project. In the end, sadly, the cure was far worse than the disease it proposed to deal with, producing concentrations of poverty, social isolation and violence.

The flaws in the radical modernist prescriptions quickly became evident as projects were built and occupied. Even within CIAM itself, early failures spawned resistance and challenges, but the functionalist blueprint unfortunately developed a stubborn inertia of its own. The "reductive" concepts of CIAM and their derivatives were rapidly adopted by urban planners around the world. Their powerful impacts still reverberate in zoning ordinances and in destructive anticity practices that compromise the ingredients and relationships necessary for successful city building. CIAM's principles shaped the thinking and practices embedded in much of post-war urban renewal and suburban sprawl, which are both deeply antithetical to the health and vitality of cities. Notwithstanding spirited rebuttals and countercurrents, the modernist onslaught on the city has been relentless and all too effective.

CHEAP ENERGY FUELS PERSONAL MOBILITY: THE FLIGHT TO THE SUBURBS

The modernist vision was supported to a great degree by the emergence of the car. A gallon of gas cost just eighteen cents in 1950, and the average cost of a new car was about $1,500, so automobiles were a relatively inexpensive and reliable form of personal transportation. The 1939 New York World's Fair promised to show visitors "the world of tomorrow," and its most memorable exhibit was the General Motors Pavilion. It featured a hugely popular ride called

Futurama, set in distant 1960. Riders passed above a highly realistic miniature landscape featuring extensive roadways to accommodate expanded car ownership. Coming as it did on the heels of the Depression, the voiceover message that riders listened to as they passed through this brave new world would have been exhilarating. Futurama wasn't about the cars GM saw itself building; the ride was selling the virtues and romance of a U.S.-taxpayer-funded highway system.

My own experiences as a kid confirmed just how intoxicating and irresistible this shift in public consciousness was. In those heady days, popular culture was marked by an infatuation with the remarkable possibilities of a sprawling world about to be reshaped by the car, offering unbounded movement and access to country living. This was freedom. Even today, TV advertising for new cars features heart-stopping chases down mountain passes or across wide-open deserts. These potent images still compel us, even if they completely contradict our daily experience of being trapped in stop-and-go traffic.

Before long, the car did become the catalyst for change that General Motors had expected. Having seen the autobahns in Germany, President Dwight Eisenhower introduced the U.S. Interstate Highway System (short for the National System of Interstate and Defense Highways). Authorized by the Federal-Aid Highway Act of 1956, Americans constructed over forty-six thousand miles of highway—which in a few short decades would become the most extensive network in the world. As the name suggests, the system was originally intended to provide interstate linkages for private and commercial transportation, as well as key transportation routes for military supplies and troop deployments in case of an emergency or foreign invasion. But the thoroughfares in this network rapidly evolved into high-capacity conduits that propelled the exodus from cities and made daily commutes to distant suburbs possible. Powerful champions of the program, like New York City's transportation commissioner, Robert Moses, got on board and skilfully used the available federal funding to radically transform their jurisdictions. Other urban centres in America and around the world soon followed suit. Toronto's own version was driven by Fred Gardiner, the first chairman of the metropolitan government created in 1953 (after whom the elevated waterfront Gardiner Expressway is named) and his Metro roads commissioner, Sam Cass. Expressways like the Gardiner in Toronto or the Embarcadero in San Francisco fed huge volumes of traffic into the city and did so with a multitude of accompanying ramps, street widenings and parallel streets changed to one-way pairs. Ultimately, these led to radical re-engineerings of entire networks of city streets, the highest priority being to expedite traffic.

By now the idea—and the ideal—of reassembling cities in a new image was firmly embedded in august professional circles. And the rationale was supported by the means and the desire to make radical change. It was associated with the most progressive thinking, and it was fuelling excitement in popular culture. But there were other, deeper psychological and social motivations behind this escape from the historic city. The move to the suburbs was an opportunity to leave the mess behind, to move on to something new and untarnished. This mythology of striking out into new territory to claim land and "homestead" still resonated powerfully in the North American psyche. In many respects, it was a

34 continuation of the earlier restless migration to the West. The entrenched status markers of city life, with its poor and rich neighbourhoods, were masked among the big yards and ample square footage of the new suburbs. According to historian Frederick Jackson Turner's "frontier thesis," migration had forged the unique American character of rugged individualism at a mobile juncture between established settlement and the wilderness—and this migration was vividly recollected in the mid-century automotive flight.

International precedents for this move to the countryside were already well established. In *Bourgeois Utopias*, Professor of Architecture and Urban Planning at the University of Michigan Robert Fishman chronicles the origins of the pastoral garden suburb and points to a key point in the mid-nineteenth century when affluent Londoners and Parisians, both faced with problems of the chaotic and increasingly inhospitable city core, made radically different choices. Bourgeois Parisians opted to remake the centre to their liking and lined the grand new boulevards controversially carved through the medieval city by Napoleon III's civic planner, Baron Georges-Eugène Haussmann with grand houses featuring protected interior courtyards. Upper-middle-class Londoners took the opposite route and fled the city, entrenching themselves in new garden suburbs that mimicked the country estates of the aristocracy. It was the English response that would have greatest appeal in the New World.

This basic choice touched on one of the great philosophical divides about our nature as social beings. Was the city a place to live harmoniously among our peers or was it Sodom and Gomorrah, a corrupt and corrupting place of suspect cosmopolitanism, miscegenation and loose morals?

To many, the flight from the city was an escape to a bucolic ideal, associated with purity and a healthy and wholesome environment in which to raise a family. It was Jean-Jacques Rousseau and Henry David Thoreau versus Charles Dickens and the horrors of urban life. Finally, the move out to the countryside appealed to the desire of many North American city dwellers to be with "people like us." In the U.S., this had a particular racial overtone and was a reaction to the great migration of African Americans to northern cities during and after World War II. "White flight" was a way to escape from what was different and threatening instead of staying and working through the tensions of living together in close quarters. At some point during the post-war era, the American Dream, for many, had become detached from the notion of the city as a place for self-actualization. The potential to get ahead, to achieve more for the next generation and to re-invent oneself was now attached to the suburbs. Spreading out and separating was the key to success.

35

And it was seemingly effortless. Stepping into a car was like entering a floating space unaffected by gravity; it was almost a form of space travel. And with easy access to automobiles came the removal of social gravity. This sense of weightlessness comes across in contemporary issues of *Popular Science* and *Popular Mechanics*, which feature images of personal jet packs and tiny helicopters parked in driveways. A remarkable exhibit staged by the Smithsonian Institution Traveling Exhibition Service (SITES) with the National Museum of American History in in 1990 called *Yesterday's Tomorrows: Past Visions of the American Future* explored how Americans had imagined the future unfolding in the post-war decades. Images from many sources foretold an unbounded, unfettered world—from furniture that could be hosed down to cars that would convert into airplanes in minutes to flying cities. The irony, of course, was that the actual post-war flight from the city resulted in a relentless, formulaic blandness, but that wouldn't become clear for years to come.

36

A TOXIC CONVERGENCE: DOUBTS SOWN

This complex stew of motivations, fears and desires, added to the quest for personal mobility, quickly led to mass migration. The prowess in large-scale organization learned during the war was applied to rewriting public policy and commercial practices. The results included zoning for separation of land uses and "red lining"—a practice carried out by insurance companies fearful of decline, who accelerated it themselves by making buildings in older neighbourhoods ineligible for coverage. Industrial-scale developers also emerged. Levitt & Sons, Inc., for instance, developed Levittown in Hempstead, Long Island, the first truly mass-produced suburb, which was widely regarded as the archetype for postwar suburbs throughout the country. Massive investment was funnelled into highways and infrastructure to support the exodus and the accompanying sustained anticity propaganda, well documented by Jane Jacobs in *The Death and Life of Great American Cities*.

This toxic combination, enabled by the car, helped city after city divide itself into versions of CIAM's four basic functions: dwelling, work, recreation and transportation. This combination fused with one more enabler: North America's earlier embrace of zoning by use, the practice of creating mapped zones that made it easy to separate one set of land uses from another. First adopted citywide in 1916 by New York City, this system was initially introduced to pro- tect property values by preventing unwanted encroachments of dissimilar uses and neighbours. Together, these practices had profound impacts as they fed the downward spiral of the old city centres.

In its great and increasing numbers, the car isolated and separated CIAM's four "functions," not just by geography but also by sheer virtue of the space cars consumed for parking and driving. Wheels replaced feet and drive-ins replaced walk-ins. Life outside of office hours was sucked from the downtown, and many large U.S. cities began to rapidly lose population: New York City, Boston, Chicago, Minneapolis and Atlanta each lost more than 10 percent of their population by the 1970s.

The narrowly focused and highly specialized discipline of traffic engineering emerged as the dominant force in city building during these post-war decades, and at the same time, the unimpeded movement of vehicles took precedence over all other considerations. Buildings and land use patterns were reconceived and redesigned. Houses now faced the world with multicar garage doors and ever-larger driveways as their defining features. Shopping malls and office parks were surrounded by ever-expanding surface parking lots. Over time, the proportion of space consumed by parking had begun to equal and then overtake the actual floor space used in buildings themselves. The average parking space today occupies over three hundred square feet, and suburban ratios for office and retail use often require four to five parking spaces for each thousand square feet of occupied space.

Suburban ideas and concepts migrated back downtown as interior malls, populated by franchise monopolies, moved into traditional nine-to-five Central Business Districts (CBDs in planning jargon), with food courts that operate only at lunch hour and take away essential business from traditional on-street shops and restaurants. The traditional city was on the ropes.

Not surprisingly, as the suburban vision grew in popularity, a web of entrenched economic interests formed around this new auto-oriented paradigm—from landowners and speculators, developers, contractors, and a veritable army of consultants who became the producers and vendors of these new real-estate products and the specialists in their efficient delivery. Along with petroleum refiners and automobile manufacturers, they formed a powerful lobby that would be extremely difficult to dislodge. General Dwight Eisenhower's admonition about the need to "guard against the acquisition of unwarranted influence" by the military-industrial complex applies equally well to this powerful complex of interests.

As we know from Sir Isaac Newton's Third Law of Motion, ultimately pendulums do swing back. And the more the brave new world of the city-replacement advocates became a reality, the more this massive abandonment of a millennia-old way of life raised doubts. Although it was not so clear to me at the time as it is now, my own early reluctance to accept this change occurred at the beginning of a generational clash with those who had come of age before the war and with their widely shared beliefs in "progress." Seeing the outcomes of the misguided practices that were undoing the cities they called home, communities started to resist. Armed with potent arguments provided by respected observers like authors Jane Jacobs and William H. "Holly" Whyte, and sociologist Herbert Gans, the defence of older neighbourhoods began to shift to offence. *Place*, rather than *function*, was their operative concept: the coming together of people, ideas and synergies, and a feel for the creative interaction that fuels city life.

Although I was very young when I left for good, I have never forgotten the Brooklyn neighbourhood where I was born. With time, this neighbourhood and many like it have proven to be incredibly resilient; the very characteristics that made the generation of my parents, aunts and uncles think about leaving have become the benchmarks of a more sustainable way of living and a newly popular urban lifestyle. Many of my younger New York friends and colleagues now live in these Brooklyn neighbourhoods or similar ones in Queens. Growing up, I had no idea about the big forces shaping my own experience, but through my continuous tasting and losing the pleasures of the city, I developed a kind of inchoate bias for urban life. The independence I enjoyed as a boy playing on the streets of Brooklyn; the relationships with my extended family there (which were made possible by sheer proximity and an individual mobility that had nothing to do with being old enough to drive); the joys of those years in Geneva, where a teenager with a bicycle and some friends could never grow bored: these were the evidence I needed to intuit that there was something terribly wrong with a way of life based entirely on the availability of a car. A German saying from the Middle Ages, *Stadtluft macht frei* ("City air makes you free") came to have particular meaning for me as a challenge to the prevailing narrative of suburbanization.

And I was not alone. Facing commuter fatigue as early as the 1960s and later talk of oil shortages on the horizon, the public began to vote with its feet, repopulating many city centres in renewed appreciation of what cities had to offer. But there was only so much prewar city to go around, which raised a crucial question: How can we make new urban places that recapture the vitality of older city neighbourhoods without reproducing the pitfalls that convinced people to leave cities in the first place?

II

THE CITY REBOUNDING

ACTION-REACTION: THE EMPEROR HAS NO CLOTHES

Jane Jacobs was an activist who became famous in the early 1960s for successfully thwarting plans to push the Lower Manhattan Expressway through the heart of her cherished Greenwich Village. Soon after, she would publish *The Death and Life of Great American Cities*, which tackled conventional wisdom head on by arguing that organically developing cities were in fact highly successful. Contrary to modernist orthodoxy, Jacobs declared that the essence of great cities lay in dense and active neighbourhoods that mixed old and new buildings, many different kinds of users in constantly evolving patterns, and streets that were shared by vehicles and pedestrians. Lacking formal education in city planning or journalism (the latter being her entrée into the cities question), Jane Jacobs came equipped with remarkable powers of observation and a deep curiosity about how things work.

These, combined with passionate advocacy and profound indignation, impelled her to write *Death and Life*, a brilliant response not only to Transportation Commissioner Robert Moses' plans to eviscerate Lower Manhattan but also to the widespread post-war devastation of cities in general, wrought by the planning and design establishments. When *The Death and Life of Great American Cities* appeared in 1961, it sent shock waves through American urban planning and pounded a convincing nail in the coffin of urban renewal. It offered a fresh view from the ground of how cities actually function— as social spaces (streets, blocks, parks and buildings) that facilitate the ordinary functions of daily life. By using in-depth observations of life in these real and enduring spaces to counter damaging practices of planning agencies and politicians who ignored this perspective, *Death and Life* encouraged local communities across North America to rise up in defence of their neighbourhoods and cities.

Jane Jacobs was also one of the first to identify clear parallels between the complex workings of cities and the ecology of natural systems. She developed an appreciation for complex, "self-organizing" survival mechanisms and was frustrated with the kind of institutional wrong-headedness—bureaucratic, political and pseudoscientific—that impedes the creative process of human adaptation. She argued for the fundamental efficiency of cities that used pre-existing resources to provide shelter and sustenance and to produce goods and services. Though couched in different language, her observations presaged the current focus on sustainability.

Jacobs' arguments posed the most fundamental challenge to the still-potent antiurban values and pervasive imagery rooted in Ebenezer Howard's Garden City, Frank

Lloyd Wright's Broadacre City and Le Corbusier's Radiant City. In contrast to these seductive visions of cities in an idealized end state, this determined American activist demonstrated that there were more sophisticated processes at work in real existing cities, which consisted of perpetually unfinished, intensely interactive webs of relationships. She was dislodging the underpinnings of modernist thinking. Borrowing from American scientist and mathematician Dr. Warren Weaver, Jacobs identified three types of problems: problems of *simplicity*, which deal with two variables; problems of *disorganized complexity*, which deal with more variables that are not connected; and problems of *organized complexity*, which deal with more variables that are connected in subtle ways. Her conclusion: cities are not simple mechanical constructs, nor are they randomly chaotic. Instead, as if better understood through the science of living organisms, cities are problems in organized complexity. This deduction came not from nostalgia for a city lost to history but from the intellectual pursuit of hard-headed and practical answers.

Jane Jacobs perceptively saw an order to the city reflected in the productivity of heterogeneous wetlands (to be richly described in works like Rachel Carson's *Silent Spring*, which came out in 1962). The parallel, which was initially ridiculed and took some time to be fully appreciated, is described in the seminal last chapter of *Death and Life* (entitled "The Kind of Problem a City Is"). "While city planning has thus mired itself in deep misunderstandings about the very nature of the problem with which it is dealing," Jacobs wrote, "the life sciences . . . have been providing some of the concepts that city planning needs. . . . And so a growing number of people have begun, gradually, to think of cities as problems in organized complexity—organisms that are replete with unexamined, but obviously intricately interconnected, and surely understandable relationships. . . ."

Other important urban observers were also getting back down to street level. *The Urban Villagers* (1962) by Herbert Gans chronicled Boston's fabled North End and contributed to saving it and its lively street life from the wrecking ball. Bernard Rudofsky's *Architecture without Architects* (1964) illustrated the cultural richness, ingenuity and adaptability of vernacular architecture. It offered provocative glimpses of the kinds of urban places that emerge from methods of construction that use locally available materials and traditions of design that have evolved over time to reflect their environmental, cultural and historical contexts. Such points of view represented the polar opposite of the modernists' universal formula of mass-produced towers in the park. Later, William H. "Holly" Whyte, author of *The Organization Man*, produced a number of seminal works, including *The Social Life of Small Urban Spaces* (1980). In this modest tome, Whyte used techniques like time-lapse photography to illustrate the sterility and relative emptiness of many so-called urban plazas that lacked the qualities that foster active street life. His Street Life Project began in 1969 while he was assisting the New York City Planning Commission in their attempts to understand why some public spaces were consistently well used, while others remained relatively empty throughout the day. Despite being over three decades old, many of Whyte's conclusions and proposed antidotes are still essential ingredients for creating successful public spaces: paying close attention to sitting space; providing sun, wind, trees, and water; taking care of the need for food; and allowing for "triangulation"—the introduction of those things that provide the pretexts for bringing people together.

These works were, collectively, a revelation. Here were more fresh eyes that keenly observed what the modernists had overlooked. Their perspectives offered more compelling arguments for keeping and protecting the traditional city and provided ammunition for the many citizens who intuitively understood that there was something wrong with emptying their cities and hamfistedly rebuilding them in unappealing ways.

As these voices were gathering strength, unintended consequences piled up in the modernist project. Suburbanites were experiencing diminishing returns on the investment in mobility that had lured them outward in the first place: newly built highways quickly jammed up with more cars than they were ever intended to accommodate. In the city, heroically conceived urban renewal projects often went the way of Regent Park in Toronto, producing safety concerns and blighting adjacent areas with boarded-up, unsightly storefronts and loss of property value. While there was no exact moment when the lustre faded, growing dissent appeared simultaneously on several parallel tracks: inside the design and planning professions, among urban thinkers and critics, and as popular resistance within communities. It then gained traction as reform-minded politicians joined these groups in rejecting assertions about "progress" through urban renewal.

In 1953, a group of younger CIAM members formed Team X at the ninth congress and were charged with organizing the tenth. This breakaway group began to criticize the Athens Charter for its lack of flexibility, its sterile and mechanistic models for urban renewal and ex-urban development, and the inhumane outcomes resulting from both. The "Aim of Team X" was debated at a meeting in London and was included as an introduction in the *Team X Primer,* which spoke of a new start, "concerned with inducing, as it were into the bloodstream of the architect, an understanding and feeling for the patterns, the aspirations, the artefacts, the tools, the modes of transportation, and communications of present day society, so that he can as a natural thing build towards that society's realisation of itself."

Struggling to find new stances toward contemporary design and the city, some of the members also looked to the vernacular for inspiration. They searched in the Western world and in places with deeply rooted collective building traditions, such as the settlements of the Dogon of Mali in West Africa, to find examples of people ingeniously adapting their own domestic environments while preserving authentic cultural richness. Team X member Aldo van Eyck from the Netherlands was a leading critic of the old guard who was inspired by such examples. Nearly twenty years after Team X formed, van Eyck and his partner, Theo Bosch, best exemplified this break with modernist orthodoxy when they developed a plan for the historic Nieuwmarkt district of Amsterdam, where subway construction had resulted in the demolition of a large swath of historic buildings and streets. Bosch and Van Eyck artfully showed how it was possible to reconstruct the historic street with contemporary architecture and stitch the celebrated district back together. Their colourful new structures picked up on the scale, rhythm and richness of articulation of the historic street but in a contemporary idiom that made no attempt to copy what had been there before. The profession's *mea culpa* inspired a search for new directions on both sides of the Atlantic. In 1956 Spanish architect José Luis Sert, who had been one of the original pillars of CIAM, organized a seminal conference at Harvard University, where he was now dean of the Graduate School of Design, to launch the new discipline of "Urban Design." Sert invited an impressive group of leading architects and urban thinkers and surprisingly included Jane Jacobs, who had yet to write *The Death and Life of Great American Cities*.

Following Sert's lead, most of the participants at the Harvard encounter sought to reassert the leadership role of designers in addressing the problems of American urban centres, which were then in the throes of being gutted by urban renewal and new highway infrastructure and were already badly hemorrhaging from the middle-class exodus to the suburbs. They focused on the importance of countering sterility by recovering human scale in urban design, but it was from Jane Jacobs, then an editor at *Architectural Forum*, that the most trenchant critique of the damaging anticity ethos emerged. She publicly challenged the limitations of the urban design solutions on display at the conference, in some respects revisionist urban-renewal proposals, and suggested that many of the noted professionals who had created them were still failing to address the inherent dynamism and strengths of existing cities.

THE STREAMS MERGE

In 1966, when I entered the Graduate School of Architecture, Planning and Preservation at Columbia University, many of my teachers were from the generation of these

Team X iconoclasts and their proteges. While I was primed and ready for the idea that the return of humanizing influences to design could actually help undo the damage done to cities, I also read *The Death and Life of Great American Cities* and many of the other accounts that seemed to suggest that the answers actually resided beyond design and within the complex underlying workings of cities themselves. I was eager to see how these parallel but possibly contradictory streams could connect.

My first year began with a design studio led by Professor Peter Prangnell, who had formerly worked in José Luis Sert's office and was a disciple of Aldo van Eyck. Peter Prangnell was assisted by another professor, Ray Lifchez, a remarkable teacher with a strong commitment to design sensitive to the needs of diverse communities. They had developed a unique approach to pedagogy, which pushed students to dig deeply into personal, first-hand observations, provoking a sometimes painful rethinking of conventional wisdom.

This studio took us back to the way we experience the buildings we use and the outdoor spaces those buildings form around themselves, and it did so in ways that echoed the unfiltered observations so integral to Jane Jacobs' critique. The point of departure was the conviction that the design of buildings as places for people to inhabit was not just a matter of manipulating form or aesthetics but a potent way to make things more possible or less possible for the people who lived or worked in them—or who encountered them from the outside.

We were strongly encouraged to dismiss our preconceptions about how a building would be shaped or would look and to become more aware of the actual ways in which

49

people inhabit spaces. I still have materials from a photo stakeout of the neighbourhood where I grew up and a case study of the great New York Public Library at 42nd Street and 5th Avenue. I'd focused not on the library's iconic, neo-classical style but on how its generous volumes and layout accommodated visitors in the library's front-of-house spaces and also on the back-of-house service spaces that enabled this remarkable library to function.

Our first design project was a "summer place" for teen-aged kids. Instead of reverting to a conventional camp layout with bunkhouses and a dining hall, we were to consider with fresh eyes the kids' daily routines of cooking, eating, sleeping and bathing, of being together in groups and being alone. Working for the first time with large-scale models and drawings, I created a plan based on a miniature pedestrian "street" extending out from a wooded area into a clearing, with cooking on an open hearth at the exposed end and water and bathing at the other, more protected end. The edges of this "street" were defined by low walls enclosing a series of sleeping platforms. A large tent structure covered the full length of it and would be ceremonially raised by the kids themselves, working together on their first day in camp.

Architects Herman Hertzberger from the Netherlands and Paco Longoria from Spain were visiting critics at my final review. They provided my first experience of an informed reading of plans that anticipated how the proposed places would actually be used. I was astonished when they told me, "You have created a small city." They saw in the elements of my summer-camp plan stand-ins for the courts, stoops, walls, windows, buildings and streets of a city plan. On the edges of my central spine were the "thresholds" at the heart of all urban situations: places for seeing, for being seen, for interacting and for self-actualization, where the campers could make real choices about how to place themselves in this shared environment. It was about what was public and what was private and what lay in between. I began to grasp that building places where people lived was not a matter of determinism through design but a matter of creating "platforms"—open-ended frameworks that people could build upon as they wished, with the underlying design as an enabler or inhibitor.

This experience got me hooked on the "city" scale, even this tiny one. In a sense, everything I have done since then has been about projecting these relationships between people and the urban environment onto an ever-larger canvas. The crucial difference, of course, was that in a studio my plans were all under my control on paper, whereas effective city building, I would learn, would never be so self-contained. A second provocative design studio made us seriously confront the design potential of a highway rest stop. This turned out to be my first serious reflection on how to deal with the car. What my teachers were implying in this exercise was that it might be possible to challenge the hegemony of car culture and give priority to people on foot. After all, in the end, all drivers do become pedestrians. A third studio took on the ravages of urban renewal in Coney Island, a piece of city that I had known well as a kid and which was now devastated by virulent urban renewal that had demolished large chunks of the neighbourhood.

The values fostered in the Columbia curriculum were focused more on relationships than on eye-catching building elevations or a particular "look," and my own focus had forever shifted from architecture in isolation to the architecture of the city. Meanwhile, outside the walls of the academy, New York City was experiencing a turbulent time. The depredations of urban renewal and incursions into low-income neighbourhoods were being hotly contested, with obvious implications for us as aspiring architects.

The blending and merging of all the issues of the day—civil rights, the women's movement, the environmental movement, growing resistance to the war in Vietnam—formed a highly charged and poignant backdrop to our own questions about the role and relevance of our profession. The deeper we delved into these causes, the more we saw consequences for architecture and city design, and the more out of touch the mainstream practice of architecture seemed to us. In the language of the day, our chosen profession was part of the problem, not the solution, and we felt we needed to challenge that.

My classmates and I joined to produce several editions of a small publication we called *Touchstone*—our own urgent manifesto and attempt to reach out to others in search of a grammar, syntax and vocabulary for responsive and humane architecture and city design. Reflecting our studio lessons, we drew heavily for our precedents on found conditions and vernacular examples of successful places. We championed a strong critique of current professional practice, based on our increasing awareness of the world beyond the drawing board, and called for a rejection of the self-referential (and we believed self-serving) ambitions of architecture evinced in high-profile signature buildings by the "starchitects" of the day. (Among these was the massive World Trade Center by Minoru Yamasaki.) We were uncomfortable with the unbridled ambition of capital "D" design to repress the city's lively dynamics in aid of these empty and heavy-handed plans. And we were also disappointed with the limp rationalizations of architects and urban designers in more corporate and commercial practice who believed they were operating as service providers outside the fray and were unwilling to participate in the self-critique of current practices.

In the place of these "aloof" professional stances, we were advocating an embrace of the messy, imperfect, not necessarily "designed" real city—and an engagement with the overtly political dimensions of all the decisions that shaped its growth. This growing frustration with the profession was in some ways an amplification of tensions that had surfaced at José Luis Sert's 1956 Harvard Urban Design encounter, which had exposed the conflict between architects who wanted to continue designing the city at the formal and symbolic level and those who wanted to engage with real conditions on the street.

But it was no longer 1956. It was 1968, the year the pot boiled over. In May, the student strikes in Paris and throughout France brought that entire country to a virtual halt and nearly toppled the government. Just prior to that, in April, Columbia University exploded when a whole series of inflammatory issues—including Columbia's proposal to build a gym in Morningside Park, encroaching on Harlem; military recruitment on campus; and the university's investments in South Africa—ignited a strike. Most of my classmates and I took over and occupied Avery Hall, the architecture building. While there were common positions that all the strikers supported, each building had a particular set of burning issues. Not surprisingly, ours had to do with the city and the role of

54

the university and our profession as actors in shaping it. The Morningside Heights gym that was being aggressively shoe-horned into a Harlem park, but offered local residents only limited access, was a clear example of the institution's goals trumping those of the community. We pointed to the construction of that gym as an example of the kind of high-handed action our profession was widely guilty of carrying out. Further, it was an example that directly implicated us in its abuse of the neighbourhood in question.

Many of our professors and others who shared our concerns joined us. Among them was Herman Hertzberger, the visiting critic from the Netherlands, whose work and passion for architecture were a great inspiration to me. As the days unfolded, a remarkable set of impromptu seminars took place, delving deeply into what was wrong with our practice and how it could change. Eventually, the police moved in and we were arrested.

Order had been restored to the campus, but the genie would not so easily go back into the bottle. As young architects and planners, we were committed to developing a more ethical practice, in which the real client would not just be the one paying the bills.

LEAVING FOR AMSTERDAM

M any things happened after the strike in that spring of 1968. I got married and, almost immediately, was drafted. I was deeply opposed to the Vietnam War and had to make a decision. I chose to resist by leaving the country. Shortly afterwards, I received an offer to go to Amsterdam to work for Herman Hertzberger and leapt at the opportunity. In Amsterdam, I encountered a very different way of living in a city, in some ways a recall of my youth in Geneva. We rented a small flat in the historic core of the canal rings, joined the city's legion of cyclists and began to discover this remarkable place and its rich traditions.

I also discovered a very different language of contemporary design, a Dutch syntax with its own distinct character and form. Here was the legacy of CIAM and Team X in the European context. At that time, Hertzberger, who was closely associated with Team X and Aldo van Eyck, was pursuing strategies to humanize interior and exterior spaces through an architecture that functioned as a framework. It encouraged users to modify and adapt the spaces it created by applying the concepts of "support and fill," a kind of architectural call and response, to all scales of design—from the room to the dwelling unit, the building, the blocks and up to the scale of city districts. This overt invitation to inhabitants to become active participants in shaping their environments through plans that offered real choices stood in stark contrast to the attitude that architects should design the whole environment down to its smallest details, imposing a consistent order and aesthetic (as is still frequently evidenced in architectural photography, with its insistence on a pristine emptiness, as if the act of inhabiting the space were not the point of designing and building it).

I worked on a number of fascinating projects in Hertzberger's office, including a block of eight experimental "carcass" houses in the southern Dutch city of Delft. These three-storey row houses were designed to give their inhabitants maximum opportunities to personalize them.

56 The buildings were deliberately unfinished, and occupants could decide how to divide the interior space, where to sleep and where to eat. If the composition of the family changed, the house could be adjusted and even, to a certain extent, enlarged.

This project and a number of others developed by the Hertzberger office expanded the ways in which occupants could effectively shape their dwellings themselves through subtle choices in how to use and furnish their spaces, and the same thinking was applied to some larger projects for workplaces. This underlying concept of support and fill, developed by a number of architects (including John Habraken and Herman Hertzberger), and embraced by a number of others on both sides of the Atlantic, was becoming a kind of *leitmotif* for the creation of more responsive living environments.

After a few months, however, it had become unclear whether I could legally stay in the Netherlands or complete my architectural degree. So we decided to come back across the Atlantic to Canada. I did not know it at the time, but my connection with Amsterdam was to be renewed later.

ARRIVING IN TORONTO: A SECOND CHANCE

We arrived in Toronto in October 1968, and fortunately, I was able to resume my studies at the University of Toronto, energized by my discoveries in Amsterdam. In a remarkable first day or two, I had landed a part-time job with John Andrews, the dean of the architecture school. From our attic flat (sharing a kitchen and bath) just off St. Clair Avenue, a bustling neighbourhood "main street," my wife and I began to discover the city, and I had a distinct sense of stepping back in time.

For one thing, Toronto had not experienced the full-bore incursion of expressways and urban renewal that I'd witnessed south of the border. New waves of immigration—economic and political "refugees" from many places, including other young Americans—were already re-energizing many of the older neighbourhoods, reminiscent of the hey-days of earlier immigration in New York. Toronto at that moment was a revelation and a haven for me, but it also appeared as another America, like a sibling who'd chosen a different path. The political backdrop to this comparison was hard to ignore. The U.S. was in turmoil. Martin Luther King, Jr., had been assassinated that April and Robert F. Kennedy, in June. Cities across the country had been consumed by race riots. There were widespread demonstrations against the Vietnam War throughout American university and college campuses. Violent confrontations erupted between police and antiwar protesters at the Democratic Convention in Chicago leading up to the elections of Richard Nixon and Spiro Agnew. Canada seemed a world away, a relatively peaceful kingdom led by Prime Minister Pierre Elliot Trudeau, who in contrast to his American contemporaries, appeared hopeful, urbane and open to new ideas. In Ontario the *Progressive* Conservatives were in the middle of their forty-year reign, succeeding by periodically implementing progressive ideas thrown up by the other parties. To those like me who had crossed the border around this time, the potential here seemed enormous. I shared this sense with another American who came to Toronto that year: Jane Jacobs.

On November 1, 1969, she told a reporter for the *Globe and Mail*: "As a relatively recent transplant from New York, I am frequently asked whether I find Toronto sufficiently exciting. I find it almost too exciting. The suspense is scary. Here is the most hopeful and healthy city in North America, still unmangled, still with options. Few of us profit from the mistakes of others, and perhaps Toronto will prove to share this disability. If so, I am grateful at least to have enjoyed this great city before its destruction."

For me, Toronto became the fertile ground where three sets of insights began to merge: an awareness of larger social and political city-shaping forces; Jane Jacobs' and others' street-level observations of how city neighbourhoods actually work; and open-ended design strategies (like those I'd learned during my stay in Amsterdam) as a way of liberating or empowering inhabitants. With its core neighbourhoods still relatively undamaged, Toronto still had the opportunity to demonstrate that a city can evolve and respond to new pressures and needs without radical surgery.

The question for me was how these streams could be reconciled. At the time, Toronto developers were actively buying up lots in many older neighbourhoods close to the core and the subway lines and planning to tear down large areas of the city fabric for wholesale replacement. In 1970, I was invited as an architecture student to write an op-ed column in the *Globe and Mail* to make "A Case for Saving Toronto's Old Houses." With the passion of a new arrival, I argued that a great deal of harm was being done by neighbourhood clearance and demolition (then under way) and that the existing city fabric was actually a highly adaptable, untapped resource with significant room for incremental growth and change.

THE GLOBE AND MAIL, FRIDAY, MARCH 6, 1970

A case for saving Toronto's old houses

By KENNETH GREENBERG

Mr. Greenberg is a graduate student at the University of Toronto School of Architecture and is working for Toronto architect Carmen Corneil.

ROBERT ANDRAS, federal minister responsible for housing, recently announced he has $200-million available for renovations in the field of low-cost housing. This declaration was followed almost immediately by a decision to drastically cut spending on traditional forms of urban renewal.

In essence, this reshuffling of funds is a recognition of the failure of the urban renewal process. The next step should be to use this federal money to create opportunities for people in deteriorating urban areas to deal pragmatically with their own housing problems, rather than for further experiments in new housing forms by planners, architects, sociologists or builders.

Large-scale construction of low-income housing results directly in the creation of an institutionalized ghetto. No matter how architecturally interesting such projects can be made, their fundamental rationale —to collect the poor in one location—in effect, infringes on dignity and impedes choice. The capacity of a city to generate choice in decent low-cost accommodation depends not on special projects but on the variety, condition and suitability of the available housing stock.

Adaptable to new uses

At present, Toronto is particularly well endowed with a large quantity of low-rise,

Redeveloped houses on Markham Street, an important resource providing accommodation at a price no new construction can match.

I am invited to write a piece for the Globe and Mail *as a student and new arrival; Jane Jacobs and I survey the entries in a design competition (Toronto Main Streets Competition, 1990).*

In 1970, I took up the challenge of demonstrating this unrecognized potential in the city fabric in my thesis project: "Infilling the Toronto Block System." I developed design strategies that would allow a downtown neighbourhood to respond to the pressures for intensification with a viable alternative to the urban renewal model that was being actively pursued by the local development industry. My approach was clearly inspired by Jane Jacobs' thinking, and remarkably, here, hundreds of miles and a nation away from the place we'd both once called home, I was finally able to meet her. She generously gave a "crit" of my thesis and advice about which of my recommendations might work; not surprisingly, she was encouraging while also pushing me hard to consider all the practical implications of my proposals. My thesis began with an analysis of how the Toronto vernacular already provided ways to add density without major demolition. In many areas this modest increase in density was already being achieved more broadly and economically through evolutionary (not cataclysmic) change. The city could go further, I advocated, by harnessing this process of adaptation that was already happening, unnoticed, as people finished basements and attics, added front and rear extensions and converted their dwellings to new uses and purposes, such as accommodating multigenerational households and workspaces. The block pattern in the area of the city I had chosen contained unusually deep lots that backed onto laneways.

I proposed a strategy of low-rise, horizontal, "infill" development, converting these laneways into small streets or mews for added housing to be created by the property owners. I also suggested adding parks, playgrounds and pedestrian walkways that offered shortcuts across the long blocks. The objective was to use the unique generous dimensions and character of the Toronto blocks to add density, financially benefit the existing residents and transform the neighbourhood fabric incrementally without sacrificing its intrinsic qualities. Many isolated examples of subtly intensified mews housing already existed throughout the city from different periods going back to the late nineteenth century, including areas in well-loved areas like Kensington Market and Cabbagetown. Because my thesis included no detailed "building" design, it was almost disqualified by some of my advisors, but in the end, it did win a number of awards. I'd moved away from the conventional thinking in my field (which assumed that urban development meant building new, "perfected" surrogates for the city) to the idea of grafting change at the margins within the existing city, trying to enhance its inherent qualities and capacity with strategic interventions in voids and underutilized spaces. (Interestingly, the City of Vancouver passed a bylaw in 2009 enabling the addition of the kind of lower-scale laneway housing I had proposed. This bylaw change has already allowed for a substantial number of much-needed, affordable rental units throughout the city at little public cost.)

61

This new confidence in the actual city of streets, blocks and lots implied a very different stance and new tools for design. Rather than attempting to heroically call all the shots, the designer would have to become involved in a set of new relationships with many other individuals and parties who have a vested interest in the proposed changes. For starters, streets and public spaces are public infrastructure, and any change even indirectly involving them would require a dialogue with the groups and agencies that managed them. City design would have to become an open process. And it would need to connect not just with governing authorities but also with the people actually living in or using the spaces in question. Often, these people were already making adaptations and modifications to their environments without architects.

All of this led to direct engagement with city politics. I was able to meet and discuss these ideas with future mayor John Sewell, then one of the leading activist voices on city council. He had been a highly successful community organizer in working-class neighbourhoods under threat of impending urban renewal (including the Trefann Court neighbourhood, whose residents had convinced the city not to expropriate their homes as it had in redeveloping Regent Park to the immediate north). Moving from the academy to the street, I became more and more involved with many other civic leaders who were beginning to form a loose coalition, and I found myself joining a growing social and political movement.

Many architects and urbanists had come to Toronto precisely because of the kind of progressive city Toronto was becoming. They were drawn in part by significant competitions like one to design a new city hall (won in 1958 by Finnish architect Viljo Revell). These designers began to play key roles in the defence of the existing city. (On a political level, Canadian cities benefited from a fruitful convergence of otherwise opposed forces: New Left advocacy for communities, imported from south of the border and small "c" conservatives, who through their involvement in local ratepayers' associations, were resistant to the wanton demolition and intrusive disruptions of existing neighbourhoods.)

While still at university, I had moved to the Beach in 1969, a remarkable older neighbourhood in the east end of the city with a three-kilometre boardwalk right on the Lake Ontario shore. There, my kids, Paul and Anna, were born in 1970 and 1972, and grew up. I had begun to get involved with the opening up of the Toronto waterfront, an immense and increasingly obsolescent industrial area, which at that time, was largely off limits to the public. I wrote another *Globe and Mail* piece on the great opportunities the waterfront could offer the city while identifying a potential threat that came from an already-forming "wall of condos" (now a substantial glass-and-steel curtain) that would limit future public access to the waterfront and visually isolate the harbour from downtown neighbourhoods. I worked with my professors, architects Jeff Stinson and Carmen Corneil, on initial plans for the Harbourfront Passage, a simple public walkway with wayfinding, lighting and places to sit along the water's edge, as a first step in opening up public access to ninety-two acres of formerly inaccessible territory on the Central Waterfront that had been purchased by the federal government to create public access to the harbour. Inspired by the work of Richard Saul Wurman, a Philadelphia architect who had been an early pioneer in developing ways to express how we know and navigate the city, I also worked with fellow activist Roy Merrens, a geography professor at York University, on a *People's Guide to the Toronto Waterfront*. This project identified areas of special interest and public access along the entire twenty-kilometre length of the city shoreline, in an attempt to generate foot and bicycle traffic and allow the public to discover, first hand, the remarkable richness and variety of these previously out-of-bounds areas, giving them a stake in the outcomes as redevelopment occurred. Gradually, efforts like these gained traction in the universities and in the profession and moved from "alternative" forms of practice to centre stage as a major readjustment of priorities worked its way through the urban-planning system.

With variations, this infiltration was happening in many other cities too. The successes of community-based efforts like these in Toronto and similar awakenings in Montreal through groups like Héritage Montréal underpinned a competing story to counter the prevailing wisdom. First, recognize and defend existing places and do less harm. Then find the alternatives, the ways to make viable new places as part of the inevitable process of change and evolution. This reconsideration focused heavily on "participatory planning," asking people in affected neighbourhoods what they wanted to see happen in the places where they were living and then working with them in developing plans that respected these goals. This was not just a "recording" or technical support function but the search for a respectful and creative collaboration.

Fresh out of school in 1970, I began Carter Greenberg Architects with one of my former teachers, Phil Carter, rather than going the traditional route of serving an apprenticeship in an established practice. We had won a prize in a housing competition together and, emboldened, set up our small practice with an initial focus on designing co-op housing. This felt like an opportunity to directly apply some of the thinking from my thesis about forging new, community-based solutions in trouble spots in the city. We linked up with a

loose coalition of social housing providers and began searching out opportunities for the Labour Council Development
Foundation and other not-for-profit groups to sponsor community-based housing cooperatives. At that time, only modest
government funding was available for such initiatives, but it
went a long way.

Phil and I worked with others who were pioneering
new ways to get both the federal and provincial governments to expand the range of housing options from just
home ownership and market rental to include cooperatives,
with a sliding scale of monthly rents for mixed-income
populations. One of the consequences of the renewed popularity of older city neighbourhoods was that rising prices
and gentrification were making it difficult for low-income
residents and seniors to remain in them.

Our goal was to create and retain a supply of housing
within these neighbourhoods that would not be vulnerable
to these pressures. Working with local community groups,
we scouted out and assisted in developing a number of sites
for projects to upgrade existing housing stock. A major effort
at Main and Gerrard in Toronto's east end combined reno-
vation, infill and substantial new construction. A small but
extremely valuable federal program, Opportunities for
Youth, allowed us to employ young people to help initiate
these efforts. But Carter Greenberg Architects would soon
lead me away from the big city to Prince Albert, Saskatchewan,
and another important discovery.

JANE JACOBS' IDEAS RESONATE

66   Jane Jacobs passed away in Toronto on April 25, 2006, just one week shy of her ninetieth birthday. Her legacy in her adopted city has been powerful, and at this point I'm going to digress to reflect on the exceptional relationship we developed over four decades. While New Yorkers remember her best as an historic figure from the epic struggles of the 1960s, for Torontonians there was nothing historic about her. While in the late 1960s the city was as yet "unmangled" (to use her term), major demolitions were planned for unique heritage structures and several downtown neighbourhoods. Toronto's streetcars were slated for removal, and more urban express-ways were on deck—not just the infamous Spadina Expressway but also the Crosstown and Scarborough routes, which would form a complete highway network. Jacobs very quickly joined the opponents of those destructive "renewal" projects, and her unique presence deeply influenced this city and continues to do so but in ways that confound easy definition. She never held elected office in Toronto, nor did she occupy any official position. The press sometimes erroneously called her a city planner, but that was not her role. She was sparing in her public appearances: "I'm busy on my next book" was her standard response. She never wanted to be a guru and strenu-ously resisted the temptation to freeze her thinking into cult or dogma. She turned down many honorary degrees and awards and resolutely rejected being "franchised" by groups or individuals purporting to act in her name.

    But for many Torontonians, including me, she was a mentor, friend and neighbour, who would have conversations on her porch on Albany Avenue or in her kitchen while making jam and cookies. She played a unique role as a catalyst, a keen observer and a gadfly. She was irreverent and unafraid and had an uncanny ability to skewer fuzzy thinking and get to the heart of things.

Remarkably, Jane Jacobs' observations almost immediately resonated in Toronto. The timing and conditions were right: back in the United States, she'd seen the results of plans like the ones Torontonians were now making, and she had the intelligence to help stop them. Her ideas quickly came close to being conventional wisdom—in her new home and in many other places. While living in Toronto, Jane continued her life's work as an author and followed *The Death and Life of Great American Cities* with a series of other books about cities and the systems that sustain them. With each iteration, the tapestry of her thinking became stronger and denser. It grew alongside the pro-city movement, each asking and answering the other questions. As time progressed, Jane's combined work felt like a unified theory, a loosely defined but coherent philosophy, with urbanism demonstrating the interconnectedness of seemingly unrelated phenomena. Particularly relevant to my work, in *Systems of Survival*, she put the perceived dichotomies between the public and private spheres in a new perspective, confronting those who wanted to exaggerate the role of either. Advocating for both the strong and reliable guardian framework and the nimble entrepreneurial innovators, Jane was politically unclassifiable on the conventional political spectrum.

Jane's preferred stance in public was as a counterpuncher. She preferred to debate, to react rather than lecture. Socratic dialogue was her modus operandi—a dialectical process of probing and testing the claims and ideas of others. She was famous for debunking nonsense, relentlessly asking hard questions; hardly the sweet little old lady, she could be intimidating and tough. She had an insatiable curiosity and generosity of spirit but an unrelenting gaze and arsenal of challenges when things didn't make sense—and a twinkle in her eye when they did. She always forced us to think harder and see other angles and yet she showed a willingness to reconsider, never seeing her own thinking as infallible. If she was the scientist, then we were the engineers, trying to find new ways to test and apply her concepts. It was one thing to articulate these powerful ideas and quite another to succeed in making real change. Her ideas, after all, deeply challenged enshrined legal, administrative and financial practices, and decades of indoctrination and habit. Jane offered no panacea, no formula for how to pursue her ideas. Her gift was not in prescribing specific solutions but in introducing a way of thinking. Her approach was always based on the interplay of forces acting on the urban environment, not on some reassuring, cozy image of what the city could be. While some detractors have tried to pigeonhole her in this way, there is no "Jane Jacobs world" and no recipe for one. In the end she gave us enough material for a lifetime's work. We have only begun to mine the full riches of her thinking—the power of organized complexity, its endless permutations and possibilities. Almost immediately after she arrived in Toronto, Jane played a leading role in the "Stop Spadina" movement. In 1971, this effort stopped the proposed Spadina Expressway, which would have driven a stake right through the heart of the city (taking out a large swath of prime real estate and, more significantly, turning one of Toronto's great streets into a concrete, dividing barrier). And it ultimately halted the continuation of the entire network of proposed inner-city expressways. Jane also lent her support to similar community-led efforts to prevent further demolitions of viable downtown neighbourhoods to make way for high-rise urban renewal. She was the confidence-building muse behind several bold initiatives in the city.

By the 1970s and 1980s, urban design in Toronto was beginning to reflect a new set of priorities. Mixed-use, infill developments had been built where no one had lived for decades. Affordable housing started to appear in established neighbourhoods. Old industrial structures and office buildings were converted into residential lofts and studios, making downtown itself more of a neighbourhood. And then came the condo boom, which was unfortunately sometimes more about quantity than quality. But still, with a mix of successes and partial successes, Toronto was producing one of the most vibrant, lived-in city centres on the continent.

Jane admonished her city not to be afraid of density but to see how it could be introduced to strengthen the grain and structure of the city by lining existing and new city blocks with increased life and activity. In the early 1970s, she had inspired Mayor David Crombie and a host of others to produce a new, mixed-income city neighbourhood for ten thousand people on the edge of downtown. This was the innovative St. Lawrence Neighbourhood, which revived one of the best traditions of Toronto urbanism: its idiosyncratic pattern of small blocks and laneways, albeit with much higher densities. The success of this ambitious project radically altered perceptions of what was possible.

Influenced by Jane, we were relearning how to make urban buildings and spaces, framing streets with pedestrian-friendly building exteriors that could make the city denser without destroying the neighbourhoods around them. Occasionally, we produced excellent contemporary buildings in an idiom particular to Toronto, such as the downtown YMCA, the additions to the Queen's Quay Terminal and the Galleria (now called the Albert Lambert Galleria in Brookfield Place). Another great testament to Jane's thinking, a development she and I worked on together, was the Kings Regeneration Initiative, a radical experiment carried out under Mayor Barbara Hall in the mid-1990s. For this project, traditional land use controls were set aside, so that four hundred acres in two former industrial districts flanking downtown were allowed to develop organically, with a self-defining mix of uses.

In October 1997, I was proud to be asked to speak about Jane's unique contributions to Toronto at a remarkable event, "Ideas that Matter," held to honour Jane and celebrate her contributions to her adopted city. A wide spectrum of distinguished thinkers from around the world attended, reflecting the breadth of her extraordinary, category-defying life's work in areas like urbanism, the environment and economics.

In that same year, the city initiated the Urban Design Awards, dedicated to Jane Jacobs. In keeping with her focus on the place and not the objects that fill it, these awards recognized valuable, city-building contributions that might otherwise have been missed: a redesign of St. George Street where it passes through the University of Toronto to emphasize pedestrian and bicycle use, the graceful Humber River Bike and Pedestrian Bridge, an attractively designed parking garage with ground-floor shops, pedestrian-oriented lighting for a newly improved Spadina streetcar line, cooperative housing, a school rooftop garden and a reconstructed wetlands in the Don River valley. These projects, large and small, all bore Jane's stamp. Ten years after the Urban Design Awards were initiated a unique program called Jane's Walk began—a coordinated series of free walking tours organized through the Internet and given by locals who care passionately about the places where they live, work and play. These tours combine insights into urban history, planning, design and civic engagement and are undertaken through the simple and very fitting act of walking through and observing a particular neighbourhood. I led two consecutive Jane's Walks in the Lower Don Lands in Toronto and had the opportunity to talk about the evolving plans to transform this part of the former industrial port into a series of new neighbourhoods.

There's keen interest in these walks, shown by participants of all ages and backgrounds exploring unfamiliar parts of town. In May 2009, in twenty-five cities, more than ten thousand people participated. Toronto alone hosted 117 walks, the U.S. was home to about the same number and there were even two as far way as India. The twig-on-the-river theory holds that a twig that falls in the current at the headwaters can alter the river by the time it reaches the river's mouth. In those terms, Jane Jacobs was not a twig but a tree trunk.

A TIPPING POINT

Ultimately, there is a moment when a successful reaction becomes the new mainstream. After six stressful decades of sustained assault, older neighbourhoods came to be valued for their convenience, history and quality of building and also as the means to a more satisfying way of life. Urban pioneers, young singles, empty nesters, young families who had moved there as young singles and businesses seeking to be near a talented pool of employees were repopulating city centres, seeking relief from commuter fatigue, as well as stimulation, a diverse cultural life, tolerance, creativity, openness and sociability. All of this has led to a significant reinvestment in the previously neglected hearts of cities.

The change is dramatic enough that it clearly shows up in census tracts and is being noted by demographers. My own city, Toronto's, unprecedented boom in downtown residential development stands in sharp contrast to earlier periods when North American suburbs were growing more than twice as fast as downtowns. In the U.S., a report titled *A Rise in Downtown Living* by the Brookings Institution and the Fannie Mae Foundation (1998) highlighted this emerging real-estate trend in twenty-four U.S. urban centres. The release of the 2000 U.S. Census data verified the progress in those cities and began to identify a new trend, a corresponding slowdown in suburban development accelerated by the decline of the traditional single-family housing market during the recent recession.

While this phenomenon is still uneven, research is showing that North Americans are now carefully calculating the cost of transportation into their housing choices. Neighbourhoods that allow for walking to shopping and transit are more sought after, and that desirability is reflected in their consistent retention of property value. Moreover, this shift in priorities is not seen as a penance but as an upgrade over exile to far flung auto-dependent suburbs—medicine that is both good and good for you.

In the end, it is the quest for both financial and environ- mental sustainability that is pushing the pro-city offensive to its tipping point. Rising energy costs are impacting every element of post-war housing patterns, including mobility, the size of our personal space, social arrangements, food security and the changing shape of the economy. This confluence of powerful new factors is propelling a profound shift in the way we perceive, use and value the dense and mixed city, both as an ideal and as a practical solution. What we have learned is that it is through our collective actions in cities, that we have the inherent capacity to rest more lightly on the planet. We use less energy if we live in smaller spaces and spend less time on the road. Also, through concentration, cities allow us to draw more efficiently on emerging renewable energy sources—wind, solar, geothermal, heat recovery—and to deal more effectively with our waste through recycling programs. But the move to greater sustainability is not about changing one or two aspects of behaviour or substituting a fuel source. It's about the way that all these elements fuse, how the benefits of each build on the others. To fully realize this potential, a major rebalancing is needed: overcoming entrenched habits, sharing spaces for multiple purposes and creating more opportunities for the kind of mix and overlap that enable people to live closer to where they work.

We are also being forced to move beyond the false dichotomy that has divided our behaviour in the city from our relationship with the natural world. Natural systems perform vital functions in cities; there's no overstating the importance of clean air, water and soil. Global warming is threatening sea levels around many of the world's largest cities, calling into question their long-term viability. The best way to combat the degradation of other, irreplaceable environments that are suffering from the encroachment of human settlements is to increase the density of urban populations. Unless we are fatalistically resigned to spoiling our nest to a point of no return, clearly some big adjustments in our way of life are needed to permit our continued well-being. A synthetic way of thinking about how we live, one that recognizes this fragility and sees human ecology as an extension of the natural world, is infusing our new attitude toward cities.

Sustainability has emerged as the central theme in our efforts to address these challenges. The term was popularized in 1983 by the Brundtland Commission, which had been convened by the UN to address growing concerns about the accelerating deterioration of human and natural environments. Recognizing that environmental problems were global in nature, the commission required all nations to establish policies for "sustainable" development.

Sustainability has continued to evolve as a broad concept, with many dimensions touching on all aspects of city building. It's gaining traction across class, cultural and political lines, especially with younger generations, which are inheriting the mess their forebears have created. Sustainability has evolved from a stand-alone "category" to the overarching concept that describes the whole pattern. Sometimes misused, it is not a technological add-on or buyout. Instead, it forces us to take a completely new view of the entire package of damaging practices we have developed in and around our cities, related to social arrangements, land use, transportation, energy, municipal services, waste, air, land and water. The 75 concept of sustainability offers a fresh vocabulary that is about synthesis and overlap. And conservation—using less in the first place, not consumption and planned obsolescence—is its *sine qua non*.

City regions are now our dominant place of living. Eighty percent of North Americans now live in urban areas (which include suburbs) and we are beginning to understand that they offer us an important edge in the effort to conserve. In their more compact areas, cities stack residences and workplaces vertically instead of spreading them out. They do more things on those smaller footprints with fewer resources and can repurpose those resources as new needs emerge. And our cities have accumulated numerous resources that we have already paid for. Older commercial, residential and industrial buildings, as well as parks, roads, bridges, rail lines, waterways and monumental structures like power stations have significant latent potential to be transformed and reinterpreted for new, sustainable economic purposes as cities are put to new tests.

Cities also offer innovators the room and resources to try out new concepts and find new paths to shared prosperity as they capitalize on the embodied energy in older neighbourhoods, their existing obsolescent structures and the municipal services and transportation networks that service them, their proximity to markets and their educated and creative labour force. We can never predict exactly what form these adaptations will take, and we don't have to. Cities possess an extraordinary wealth of such diverse human and physical resources to draw upon, no matter what changes they face.

We are realizing that there is an invaluable economic and human infrastructure already in place, with concentrations of financial institutions, foundations, advocacy groups, researchers, professional associations, academics and progressive community leaders who can provide resources, support and an abundance of new ideas. By leveraging these advantages, cities give large numbers of people the capacity to act locally on global issues in highly efficient ways. But this really raises the question of how this kind of transformation can happen—because, as I've learned, cities are also places of many conflicting interests. As Columbia University found out when it tried to shoehorn its gymnasium into Harlem, these diverse interests need to be acknowledged. No path to change can be pursued in isolation.

III

THE ELUSIVE ART/SCIENCE
OF CITY BUILDING

A UNIQUE ABILITY TO COMBINE THINGS

If rigid formulas for "functional" cities were missing the point, then what *does* make a city work? Grappling with the challenges of city building requires a better understanding of what the city is in the first place. And such notions eluded Wright, Howard, and Le Corbusier and the original CIAM collective. In broad terms, cities are large and permanent human settlements, usually operating under some status in law or custom and having a degree of political and administrative autonomy. They can be described quantitatively with measures like population, land area, number of establishments for work and commerce, number of buildings, commuter patterns, facilities, services and networks. But while quantifiable, these metrics miss the basic chemistry that makes cities the uniquely dynamic human creations they are. They are, most significantly, by virtue of their large number of inhabitants and the proximity within which these people live and work, places that foster interaction. They provide shared arenas in which goods and services can be traded and economic activity facilitated; they nurture culture and wealth generation through converging discovery, spin-off activities, ripple effects and innovation. They have fluid relationships with their own hinterlands and other urban regions, as well as with provinces, states and nations. Coming to terms with this open-endedness means abandoning any vision of the city as a static entity. A colleague of mine, French architect Antoine Grumbach, has said that "the city is perpetually unfinished," and I find that observation perpetually relevant. As city builders, we must avoid trying to impose any arbitrary and static order on a phenomenon that is continually mutating and morphing with no fixed destination, though it grows and evolves as a result of important relationships that need to be kept in balance.

The real breakthrough in dealing with this fluidity came with Jane Jacobs' concept of "organized complexity." The conceptual shift from an inert mechanical model of the city to an evolving biological one suggests a whole new vocabulary for describing what happens in cities. In environments that are more like gardens than factories, it can be said that ideas, relationships and initiatives are seeded, spawned, fertilized and grown. Grafting and weeding occur and hybrids emerge.

Because of their extraordinary capacity to absorb new populations and new ideas, cities have had a long-standing reputation as places of personal liberation and self-actualization. They have been seen as the places to excel, to develop skills, to compete, to get ahead and as places where people can reinvent themselves. Cities have also been known for their unique ability to accommodate and benefit from differences. Throughout history, they have provided inspiring examples of peaceful coexistence, broad-mindedness and highly productive interchange among diverse populations. Major cities around the world are now grappling with influxes of new arrivals. While far from perfect in this area, Canadian cities have developed a special talent for successfully integrating recent waves of immigration to the point where now half of Toronto's population was born in another country and there is no "majority" population—only varying degrees of minority. A city's belief that its diversity is a positive feature is not just about proximity; it's what happens when there is a genuine opportunity for people to become familiar with each other while at the same time having room to mutually define their relationships.

Kensington Market in the heart of downtown Toronto started out as the "Jewish market" during the Great Depression, when neighbourhood residents, searching for ways to make a living, opened up the fronts of their houses to create small shops and stalls. A modest working-class neighbourhood near the city's garment-manufacturing district, this sprawling, informal street market continued to evolve as each progressive wave of immigrants added its unique foods and goods, providing a vital function as a place of exchange, where local politics and new ideas are still debated daily in lively street-corner repartee. Given the right conditions, similar immigrant reception areas in the hearts of other cities (like the North End in Boston, the Plateau in Montreal and Le Marais in Paris) have historically demonstrated this capacity for cultural fusion. Obvious examples occur in music. A popular Toronto group formed by musicians David Buchbinder and Hilario Durán is called Odessa/Havana, a mashup of Klezmer and Latin Jazz, and the Chicago Blues grew out of a Southern musical tradition transplanted to urban soil in the North. Language also absorbs culture, and cities each develop their own special argot, picking up words and phrases from the groups that settle there. Over the years, New Yorkers have picked up words, inflections and phrases from Dutch, Yiddish, Spanish, Italian and countless other languages, and they continue to add new lingo with each wave of arrivals. With an increase in downtown land values, the first point of arrival in many cities has now shifted from the centre to the near suburbs. In such auto-oriented environments, these kinds of informal exchanges are much more challenging, since there's a greater tendency for immigrant neighbourhoods to form isolated enclaves that no one else visits.

Unfortunately, immigration does not always result in such harmonious exchanges. There are also horrific examples where prejudice, intolerance and persecution have occurred, most often propelled by cultural and ethnic divides that originated elsewhere. Toronto's infamous 1933 Christie Pits riot, in which Jews were provoked by a racist youth gang at a baseball game and fought back side by side with other immigrants, and the recent convulsions among disaffected youth in Montreal and the Paris suburbs are sobering reminders that harmonious exchange takes both opportunity and effort. But it is also true that cities are the places where resistance to these tendencies is organized and expressed in the political arena. Gay pride parades, for example, which began as defiant protests but now draw large, diverse and celebratory audiences, first occurred in the hearts of big cities, the only locations where this could realistically happen. It could also be argued that cities have been the environments where the great gender equality and civil rights movements of our time have played out.

Where cities successfully make room for difference and even eccentricity, they have been magnets for talented and creative individuals and the new economies they create. Through the creative adaption of buildings, skills and resources already present, Spadina Avenue in Toronto became a compelling example of this kind of talent-driven change. In the early twentieth century, a bustling garment district formed in this broad street's robust stock of multistorey industrial buildings. By mid-century, Chinatown migrated over from a nearby cross-street, overlapping the garment district. Then the arts and culture sector arrived, converting nearby warehouses to galleries and studios, and, later still, knowledge-based design, media and technology firms moved in. The intense foot traffic and remarkably heterogeneous population using the popular market stalls, cafés and restaurants in the area reflect this layering and succession. Remarkably, the basic form of Spadina Avenue has barely changed in the past hundred years; almost all of this adaptation has occurred through creative upgrading, with limited new construction.

Examples of these seemingly unrelated overlaps abound in cities. In New York City, if you walk into the AOL Time Warner Center off Columbus Circle at the southwest corner of Central Park, you'll find Jazz at Lincoln Center overhead and a grocery store below. A major hotel, retail, entertainment, restaurants, offices and apartments are all linked into a nexus of subway lines. The old functional categories collapse as our comfort with unconventional mix grows and such unpredictable new permutations continue to surface. In many ways, the city is recapturing the exuberant energy celebrated in Rem Koolhaas's spirited book *Delirious New York*, a retroactive manifesto for Manhattan. It reflects the inventive power of a time when extraordinary new combinations were redefining the intensity of city life in hybrid buildings like Rockefeller Center, with its offices and shops, Radio City Music Hall and its ever-popular skating rink.

With a sensitivity to urban design, architecture, landscape and civic infrastructure can heighten these radical juxtapositions. At the Museum of Modern Art in New York City, passage through the galleries is enhanced by periodic glimpses of life outside the museum on 53rd and 54th Streets. Similarly, the gracefully curved arc of the Galleria Italia at the newly renovated Art Gallery of Ontario in downtown Toronto affords spectacular views of adjacent Dundas Street, Chinatown and the surrounding neighbourhoods. There's a constant interplay between the interior experience of the artifacts and the surprising synergies at play on the streets below. This kind of vantage point occurs not only in the architecture of buildings but also through the creative recycling of infrastructure. Constructed on a nineteenth-century railway viaduct that ceased operation in 1969, the Promenade Plantée is a 4.5-kilometre-long elevated park in the east end of Paris that links the Opéra Bastille to the Boulevard Péripherique and ends a short distance from the Bois de Vincennes. The raised garden walk is used by pedestrians, and cyclists have a route at ground level. The seventy-one arcades beneath the viaduct have been transformed into arts-and-crafts workshops in an area known as the Viaduc des Arts. In places, the walking route passes narrowly between modern buildings and then

opens with expansive views of the surrounding neighbourhoods that are otherwise rarely seen by outsiders.

84   For a time, this elevated linear park was unique in the
world. But, more recently, the High Line in Manhattan, a
2.3-kilometre-long elevated steel structure built in the 1930s
to carry freight trains between 9th and 10th Avenues from
Gansevoort Street in the Meatpacking District to 34th Street
next to the Jacob K. Javits Convention Center, has under-
gone a similar transformation. The result is a stunning new
public space with a whole series of new connections at two
levels. While many adjoining landowners initially objected
to plans for the High Line on the grounds that it might
negatively impact the development potential of their properties, it has dramatically had the opposite effect and has, in
fact, stimulated a wave of exciting new projects across the
country. Currently, there are similar plans to convert the
elevated Bloomingdale Line in Chicago and the old Reading
Viaduct in Philadelphia into greenways.

    A historical example, and perhaps one of the greatest
works of urban design ever produced, is the pedestrian
promenade on the upper level of the Brooklyn Bridge across
the East River, designed by John A. Roebling and opened to
the public in 1883. Exceeding its basic function of conveying
vehicles and pedestrians, and making provision for a future
subway, the bridge has given generations of New Yorkers
and visitors to the city a breathtaking view of the river, the
harbour beyond and the ever-changing skyline, encouraging
passersby to lift their heads up from the pavement to see that
they are sharing something much larger and grander than
their daily routines typically reveal.

WE SHAPE OUR CITIES AND THEY SHAPE US

Fruitful encounters can be enhanced by civic-minded design, but ultimately they are shaped by opportunity and chance in ways that we cannot easily control or force. Winston Churchill captured this notion of interplay through time when he said of the British Houses of Parliament: "We shape our buildings; thereafter they shape us." It's a classic chicken-and-egg situation; the interplay between the conditions we find on the ground and how we respond is the fundamental terrain of city building and urban design. This is not conventional physical determinism à la CIAM; city building means creating a platform—enabling a location's potential. What happens on top of that will all the more accurately reflect the will and desires of the people who live with it.

So how do we intervene in multifaceted "organic" systems in a way that accommodates the will and desires of multiple parties (especially when those parties make their interests known only when the change is on their doorstep)? To start, there has to be humility about dictating outcomes; a city builder's initial designs must aim to create conditions that invite the next moves and encourage a range of possible outcomes to play themselves out. The most important contributions that design can make in cities occur where different activities and land uses overlap.

The members of the CIAM breakaway group, Team X, were absolutely right to lavish so much attention on the phenomenon of "thresholds" in indigenous and vernacular architecture: the porches, porticos, stoops and sidewalks, the in-between spaces that bond the city fabric. When these spaces provide the right supports, they become places where we want to be. They give us opportunities to loiter or sit close to the action with the necessary creature comforts of shade or exposure to sun, shelter, food, drink, public restrooms, a sense of security, interesting things to see and, most importantly, other people. How else to explain the extraordinary and growing popularity of sidewalk cafés and street markets in northern cities where they traditionally did not exist? As some residents of Copenhagen have remarked, we are all becoming Italians. The retail window display is a classic example of a threshold that can enrich the experience of being on a city street. It makes a stroll along the sidewalk more interesting while enticing and informing us about what we can find inside. My stepdaughter, Mika, who has a cookbook and kitchen-accessories store in Kensington Market called the Good Egg, puts tremendous effort and originality into her window displays, but they work only if there are people to appreciate them. Pedestrian flow cannot be generated by one store alone and relies on a combination of reasons for people being on the sidewalk and the quality of the walk itself. In another neighbourhood nearby, a lingerie shop cleverly named Miss Behav'N occasionally features live burlesque dancers in its windows who gyrate to a beat we can't hear and offer friendly waves to passersby—only on a busy city street with a sense of humour. To exploit cumulative effects like this, small, independent shop owners often band together to form BIAs (Business Improvement Areas) and solicit funds from the city to make enhancements to these in-between realms beyond their individual control, including sidewalk lighting, better paving, street furniture and visitor-oriented signage.

Linguistics makes a useful distinction between *langue* (the shared structure of the language) and *parole* (the speech or utterance of an individual). In cities we thrive on enormous variety and variation (*parole*) but still need a certain level of predictability and stability (*langue*) in order to keep the lights on and the buildings standing. That shared language (and its syntax and structure) is supplied by the public realm, which determines where we can safely walk or cycle, the frequency of intersections, what happens at street corners, how we can expect buildings to front onto main or side streets and how we can distinguish private or semiprivate spaces from public ones. Every city has its own subtle variations on this basic syntax—variations rooted in its unique history and form. The public realm not only guides the physical aspects of city life but is also embedded in and informed by cultural norms and expectations. We use the term *civility*, deriving from the Latin *civilis* (meaning "proper to a citizen") to describe how we believe people should behave in relation to others. To demonstrate civility is to express respect and tolerance for others, and this is a precious commodity. As the demographics of cities in rapid flux shift and people from very different cultures are thrown together, the ability to maintain a shared urban culture and common expectations about the sharing of public space become vitally important.

In *House Form and Culture*, anthropologist Amos Rapoport demonstrated the extent to which cultural norms vary from one urban culture to another. Some cultures tolerate and even expect a higher degree of personal closeness, for instance, and there are very different understandings of what constitutes shared space. As cities evolve in a world of increasingly heterogeneous populations, new relationships must be continually renegotiated with respect to these fluctuating differences, and civility effectively underwrites these negotiations.

In some cities, such shared space and the way the city's elements have been put together may at first appear to be based on civility, expressing a rich and urbane culture. But the reality may be different. For instance, from the air, central Caracas and Atlanta bristle with high-rise towers and give the impression of being dense, city-like environments. Yet in Caracas, where political unrest and insecurity (as well as highly subsidized gasoline) have encouraged people to withdraw into guarded compounds and their cars, the streets in many residential areas can be empty of pedestrians, uninviting and dangerous. In Atlanta, suburban habits have been imported into the core. People travel from their high-rise residences to places of employment almost exclusively by car, driving from parking garage to garage or parking lot and leaving the sidewalks almost deserted, except during special events or conventions.

In Mississauga, a suburban municipality west of Toronto with urban ambitions and a population slightly larger than that of Boston or Denver, tens of thousands of people live in very dense high-rises in the city centre surrounding city hall, a library, a "Y," an arts centre and a major shopping mall. But it is currently almost impossible to walk from the residential towers to the facilities, since pedestrians would have to cross one of the city's major arteries and then navigate their way through parking lots to get to their destinations. (Fortunately, though, steps are now being taken to remedy this problem.) By contrast, in the dense heart of Buenos Aires, where walking is a deeply rooted part of local culture and a significant population occupies almost every block in mid-rise buildings, there is a constant flow of animated life on the city sidewalks. As urban designer Jonathan Barnett has quipped, "It is not how dense you make it, but how you make it dense."

Regent Park in downtown Toronto, which I discussed earlier, is one of Canada's oldest and largest public housing projects. I had the opportunity to work with a team commissioned in 2002 to prepare a comprehensive redevelopment plan for it and to make recommendations for its joint public- and private-sector revitalization and its reintegration into the surrounding city. The aim was to create a mixed-income neighbourhood, but Regent Park had already seen a number of failed attempts to do this. A lot of cynicism had resulted, so we knew that, in order to succeed, we would have to engage the Regent Park tenants and the surrounding neighbourhoods in ways that made them truly part of the process of change. To begin, a set of guiding principles was hammered out in numerous meetings and workshops, including feedback from several kitchen-table discussions involving young community "ambassadors" who lived in the project. The most important principle we developed was to respect the residents' aspiration to become a "normal city neighbourhood" instead of being separated from an unwelcoming society. This meant reintroducing a grid of city streets, a change that raised many new issues. Younger kids who had lived in the project were not accustomed to crossing streets. Most people would consider knowing how to cross a street a matter of *langue* and not *parole*, and this shows just how divided Regent Park and its surroundings had become.

Few people who were not tenants in the project had ever ventured into its super blocks, and the reintegration with surrounding city blocks raised concerns about who would be an outsider in the new order and who would be an insider. Issues of sidewalks being visible enough to be safe and of whether walkways and courtyards would be open to everyone or accessible only to the inhabitants of the buildings they served became critical. Equally important was the reassurance that rent-geared-to-income units would be protected in the mix and that tenants who would be relocated during the construction period would be able to return when building was complete. It was only by confronting the fear of change and dealing with these legitimate apprehensions that we were able to forge a new consensus about the future. My colleagues John Gladki and Ronji Borooah and I led highly diverse workshop groups of several hundred people seated at tables of a dozen or so participants each, with translation in up to seven languages. We were able to draw upon the tremendous protective pride of residents and their attachment to "the Park" and to each other. Equally impressive was the popularity of the environmental theme and the across-the-board desire to be "green" in new ways. In the end, this exercise conclusively demonstrated that it was possible to generate broad and enthusiastic support for reintegrating this neighbourhood into the rest of the city by providing mixed-income housing, opportunities for employment, education, culture and community facilities.

The resulting plan, which is currently under construction, is based on a pattern of small urban blocks, where a mix of mid-rise, high-rise and townhouse buildings will be aligned more normally along the new (traffic-calmed) local streets and framing a major, new central park (no actual park had existed before despite the name Regent Park). Interconnected tree-lined "green streets" and pedestrian-only pathways will link a series of smaller neighbourhood squares and parks and schools. Approximately 4,500 new dwelling units (including replacements for the original 2,100 rent-geared-to-income units), space for new businesses and local retail and neighbourhood amenities are being built. I serve on a design review panel (which includes tenants and neighbourhood representatives) that is overseeing the implementation of the plan, the primary focus being the creation of a more welcoming public realm.

As designers invent new forms and relationships in the city, we continually draw from and reinterpret older urban traditions from urban centres around the world. For example, as we try to accommodate family life in the city again, protected play spaces for children become important. The small parks and courtyards found in many European cities were extremely useful precedents for Regent Park with its large number of children.

In *How Buildings Learn*, author Stewart Brand argues that continual feedback from the way buildings are actually used and the modifications made by their occupants enable buildings to "learn." This, he says, is an essential part of a building's capacity to be adapted and to remain useful. The principle is probably even more true of the way that individual buildings come together to form neighbourhoods. For example, as our population ages, in order to make the city safe and convenient and to allow a larger cohort of elderly residents to remain independent, seniors will need new housing options that won't require them to drive. Greater attention will also need to be paid to universal accessibility, eliminating physical barriers like awkward level changes on city sidewalks, in building entrances and on public transit.

Places like Kensington Market, Pike Place Market in Seattle and the street market on Rue Mouffetard in Paris are prime examples of self-organizing, interacting systems that have "learned"—and they are microcosms of what happens in cities in general. With a high level of sensitivity to their customers' preferences, individual stalls in Kensington Market continually alter their offerings; the whole changes with the evolution of its parts. With time, the shops on the Rue Mouffetard have developed a way of expanding their stores by moving their interior display counters out into the pedestrian street space when the market is open.

The emergence of organic food choices and the growing popularity of local growers and producers in these markets illustrate how marginal exceptions become the rule over time. (Meanwhile, supermarkets, which once replaced these heterogeneous street markets with highly structured and centralized distribution of standardized products, are now striving once again to imitate the looser formats of their predecessors, breaking themselves down into semiautonomous sections with fare customized to meet the changing tastes and needs of their local clienteles. Urban Fare in Vancouver went one step further and brought in other traditional market functions, namely a popular café, and new innovations like cooking classes.)

Cities evolve to survive, but as they face new environmental and social challenges, they are being transformed at an accelerated pace. Community input in the redevelopment of Regent Park was an effective means of understanding residents' needs on an intimate scale, but the decreasing availability of cheap energy; security concerns; the need to deal with air, water and soil quality; rising water levels; and the ability to process the waste of huge urban populations are not just local concerns. They make this sort of input-intensive process essential on an enormous scale because cities cannot deal with these challenges exclusively, or even primarily, from the top down. City builders must engage with complex formal and informal politics, and they must maintain an intense and ongoing involvement with independent players pursuing their own agendas.

FALSE TRAILS AND MIRAGES

While rejecting the radical formulations of CIAM, many members of Team X were still not entirely comfortable with streets and blocks as a viable structure for city building. Though this breakaway group from CIAM struggled valiantly to create a more humane version of the modernist paradigm, many of its members still felt the need to reorganize urban life, leading to strategies for "ingesting" the city within their architecture. Pursuing one false trail, they attempted to take on too much and replicate within large buildings the kinds of social spaces that were found on city streets in lively cities. This approach was demonstrated in individual structures like the 1963 prize-winning design for the Free University of Berlin by the French team of Candilis-Josic-Woods and John Andrews' design for Scarborough College at the University of Toronto. These designs were created in the stripped-down, "brutalist" style of the day, with rough "outdoor" materials like unadorned concrete brought into interior spaces.

In some cases, these "megastructures" produced what were called "streets in the air," which separated pedestrians vertically from vehicles below. And Andrews' firm also designed the most ambitious Team X–inspired project in Toronto: Metro Centre, which was intended as a joint venture of Canadian National Railways and Canadian Pacific Railway. It would have extended a web of interconnected, elevated walkways over two hundred acres of obsolete railway lands between downtown and the waterfront. (The project was proposed in 1968 but never built, apart from its iconic centrepiece, the CN Tower.)

I had pored over Andrews' drawings for the Scarborough campus while I was still a student at Columbia and was intrigued. But this approach of moving the public spaces of the city inside buildings or up in the air as a substitute for true public space soon revealed itself to be a troubled and distracting detour from city building. The most infamous example of the failure of this strategy was Pruitt-Igoe, a large public housing project finished in 1955 in St. Louis, Missouri, by architect Minoru Yamaski, who later designed the World Trade Center. Shortly after its completion, the arrangement's flaws became obvious: its "streets in the air" were too isolated from daily pedestrian traffic on the sidewalk. Being largely out of sight, they were vulnerable to crime. Living conditions in Pruitt-Igoe began to decay, and by the late 1960s extreme poverty, crime and segregation had taken their toll. The complex was demolished in stages, starting less than twenty years after construction. It was the beginning of the end for this kind of urban design.

The truth was that the basic structure of the city did not need to be reinvented; the rudimentary city-street grid already had an elegant sophistication and simplicity that worked. Designed to balance the needs of pedestrians and vehicles, the

Recovering from errors: Regent Park demolished as a stand-alone residential housing project and reconceived as a new mixed-use mixed-income neighbourhood in 2010.

city-street grid functioned as the real public framework for a wide variety of uses. There was no need to absorb all those complex interactions into buildings or megastructures. The more realistic and modest challenge was this: how to empower the city's extraordinary capacity for growth and change through more subtle reinterpretation and adaptation.

The failure of the Team X approach was not only a matter of size. There is a difference in kind between designing a building and designing a piece of city because the city is the expression of compound ongoing processes—political, economic and social—and their interactions with their physical world. This complexity defeats the most sophisticated attempts to corral all its variables. It requires a looseness of fit between the parts and the whole, and room to respond to unforeseen circumstances over time. In the 1970s, brilliant planners and designers tried to apply the techniques of "systems analysis," adapted from the military, to planning large-scale city-building efforts. They produced charts (sometimes covering entire walls) with intricate vector diagrams and arrows of varying weights pointing up and down between different manifestations of these processes—but to little avail.

Decades, not years, are the meaningful units for experiencing change in cities—for relationships to form on a street and economic synergies to appear in a cluster of activity. But this essential play of time (and the art of working in this fourth dimension) were ignored or downplayed in the more mechanical constructs for the city. The inevitability of perpetual change and the unpredictable ripple effects of each act by each of thousands of independent actors introduces a different sense of what constitutes order. The aesthetics applicable to a creation that is always "becoming" but never "finished" are vastly different from the appreciation of a finite object, an elegant towering apartment complex or a visually arresting museum or cultural centre. The Internet provides an interesting analogy. Like the city, it ultimately belongs to no one, is not really controllable and is constantly evolving. It is also a world of unexpected connections, triggered by proximity and serendipity. It is not accidental that Internet websites frequently model their architecture on physical cities with "neighbourhoods" and "streets," allowing for constant adaptation of the content while the frame remains.

All of these factors—the overlap of issues, the longer time frames and the great number of actors—suggest the need for a different kind of design, with plans that are not complete in themselves but liberate and facilitate other plans. Not even the most talented individuals can invent an Esperanto to make *tabula rasa* of the apparently "disordered" city that exists, replacing the indigenous languages of urbanism with something new, pure and seemingly "rational."

Even when acknowledging the complexity and heterogeneity of the city, developers and designers frequently head down another false trail by trying to achieve the appearance and feel of "urbanity" without really engaging the dynamic processes that produce the genuine article. Nostalgia is one way to get into this kind of trouble. If things worked well before, why can't we just replicate what we had then? Unfortunately, the older parts of cities we admire grew organically, their scale and pace of growth has been superseded by a world of much larger corporate developers, arm's-length real-estate investment trusts (REITs) and bigger and more complex building programs. (These last need to be completed quickly, with financing from major banks and lending institutions that often have precise formula-based expectations for financial returns.)

"New Urbanism" is a significant movement attempting to work with these new realities while promoting walkable, mixed-use neighbourhood development, sustainable communities and healthier living conditions with reduced dependence on the automobile. While it has made notable contributions to city building, especially in suburban areas, many of its adherents have hitched their wagons to the creation of preconceived development models that employ a combination of traditional town planning and neotraditional architecture. Often applied to new developments in suburban settings, these models focus on the nostalgic "look" of another age. Physically, we can construct something that looks like an idealized small town or village in traditional garb, but there is a downside to forcing new growth into an artificial pastiche. Over time, it will leave little room for the "new" and unpredicted in overly prescribed New Urbanism.

Another temptation is to use bold architecture on a large scale to create a new and dynamic image of "city," substituting an avant-garde visual representation of complexity (the artist's or architect's impression of dynamic visual variety) for the real thing. This approach taps into the allure of engaging "starchitects" for the marketing cachet of their idiosyncratic designs of a whole piece of city, swallowing all its public and private aspects into one bold "architectural" statement. While this approach can produce an exhilarating building or even a building complex, the idea that a single genius can or should conceive an entire urban district (often with a single, large real-estate operation) can only result in monolithic icons mimicking diversity, not the actual substance of urban vitality.

Vast schemes of this type are emerging in rapidly growing Asian and Gulf State markets like Dubai, where the combination of autocratic regimes, exponential growth and the importing of Western prototypes are producing integrated, package-deal developments.

The result is the construction of alluring enclaves that attract an emerging entrepreneurial class because they are consciously separated from their messier, more diversely populated surroundings. But there is a vast difference between real organic growth and developments that only appear to be complex. And the larger the scale, the greater the fall when the market conditions that supported the new construction at the time of its conception inevitably change.

Mirages and false trails can also be produced by overly rigid city planning by numbers and fiats, a condition that frequently occurs when the city-planning pie is too neatly divided into its components. Such rigidity continues to produce the sprawling new subdivisions that replicate old ones (albeit with a somewhat new look) on the suburban fringe. Municipal agencies aren't known for their flexibility, and more often than not, each one remains ensconced in its own silo: the planners handle land use, the engineers the traffic, the parks department the public spaces, the school board the school sites. The components are predetermined and separated, like the foods on a small child's sectional dinner plate. At the other end of the spectrum from the command-and-control model is the laissez-faire model, in which planners just let market forces alone shape development. This impulse may have less credibility in light of the 2008 financial meltdown. While the dynamism and drive of the entrepreneurial sector are critical to making cities function and thrive, there is also a clear need to counterbalance untrammelled market forces. For example, with no requirements for affordable housing, what developer would bother to include such units in their plans? There are significant segments of the population that the private real-estate market just does not reach—despite the recent and ongoing condominium boom in many North American cities. Nor can the private sector alone be relied on to address the needs of new downtown residents for parks, daycare, schools and local shopping.

When cities felt they were losing out to their suburban counterparts, planners faced a great temptation to follow that market trend by emulating their success. Developers whose primary experience had been in the suburbs saw new markets opening up in the city and brought familiar models with them. Re-creations of the suburban mall in downtown areas, with abundant parking, became popular. Unfortunately, by attempting to solve one problem—auto access—the developers of these transplants have created others and have caused their cities to lose the benefits of fine-grained block patterns favouring pedestrian activity and independent merchants—the very qualities that would ultimately allow cities to compete and thrive.

By detaching themselves and internalizing their focus, some of these malls have led to deterioration in their urban neighbourhoods. Meanwhile, even in suburbia itself, numerous dying malls offer a sobering lesson. *The Wall Street Journal* has chronicled their closings and abandonment by the hundreds across North America, and Deadmalls.com, an independent, not-for-profit website, lists nearly three hundred malls in the U.S and Canada that have failed or are in the process of failing. Along with suburban-style malls, housing and office enclaves, car-oriented standards have been applied to downtown areas: zoning regulations that demand extra-wide lane widths and turning radii to accommodate fire-fighting equipment, as well as large garbage trucks that fit poorly in the more compact spaces of urban neighbourhoods.

Politicians and planners are also lured into difficulties through the perennial attraction of quick fixes. If only we had a (fill in the blank with the latest and greatest silver-bullet facility), we would be a world-class city, and that would bring back tourists and provide jobs. Casinos are a common version of this familiar litany. After working in downtown Detroit for a number of years, I had a public falling-out with the mayor when, under enormous pressure from casino interests, he publicly shifted from his stance against casinos on the river to expropriating sixty acres of prime waterfront land exclusively for this purpose.

Casino Nova Scotia in Halifax perfectly illustrates how these quick fixes can do more harm than good. No doubt intended to help open up the waterfront, the building presents a bleak and lifeless presence on the harbour's edge, with blank walls and dark glass windows facing the water and a large access ramp for tour buses facing the city. Its design understandably focuses attention exclusively on the gambling that happens inside. With absolutely no reason to occupy the valuable waterfront site on which it's located, a site that clearly called for an extroverted and publicly minded presence, the casino has probably retarded the redevelopment of what is potentially some of the most valuable real estate in Maritime Canada.

The silver bullet has also appeared in the form of a convention centre or a stadium or arena for professional sports or a bid for the Olympics, a world's fair, the Pan American Games or some spectacular megadevelopment that, by virtue of its sheer size and originality, promises to turn things around in tough economic circumstances. Some of these facilities, handled in the right way and skilfully harnessed to broader city-building initiatives (such as Barcelona's use of its Olympic facilities to spur the creation of impressive new neighbourhoods), can make very positive contributions. But none has the power to alter the fortunes of a city on its own, and these "campaigns" can divert attention from broader city-building efforts that would ultimately make a greater difference. New York, for instance, wisely rejected plans for a new football stadium to house the New York Jets in the West Side Yard in Midtown Manhattan. The stadium would have hosted too few home games per year to justify its huge footprint on the limited land available in the city. New York opted instead to develop an area of new, intensive, mixed-use city fabric that would contribute much more vitality on an ongoing basis.

A subset of the silver bullet is the packaged development formula. In this case a design concept that has worked well once is then copied elsewhere because its success seems assured, despite the limited evidence. A prime example is the "festival marketplace," which was pioneered by the Rouse Corporation in Boston for Quincy Market Faneuil Hall and was then widely exported to American cities as a downtown revitalization tool during the 1970s and 1980s. The festival marketplace had been conceived to overcome negative perceptions of a deteriorating city centre and attract suburban residents and out-of-town visitors to the downtown area. It provided the downtown with a combination of chain restaurants; specialty retail shops with tourist-related, non-essential offerings; an international food court; entertainment; and secure parking.

It worked in Boston (although, according to pedestrian surveys, visitors still rarely venture into the surrounding areas of downtown). But efforts to transplant Boston's success to other cities have been problematic. When a replica festival market appeared in the South Street Seaport in Lower Manhattan, New Yorkers stayed away in droves. Locals and tourists alike had many more interesting options in the real city neighbourhoods around it and did not respond well to its shallow, ersatz feel; it is currently being redeveloped as a mixed-use neighbourhood. Similar ventures are reported to be struggling in Tampa, New Orleans, Norfolk and Toledo.

Unfortunately, in a world of quick fixes, these "franchised" package deals are too often an easy sell to local governments who are under the gun to turn around the fortunes of their depleted cities. (The reckless and desperate attempt of Flint, Michigan, to revive its fortunes by building such a tourist-oriented downtown mall is poignantly documented in the Michael Moore film *Roger and Me*.) These developments come as fully fledged templates, bearing little or no relationship to the *genius loci* of the places where they land. And the festival marketplace is just one type of package deal. Some Asian cities, for example, have become fascinated with replicating the look of an entire North American suburb, a form North Americans themselves are now struggling with. Meanwhile, North Americans create clusters of miniature, European-inspired, monster-home "châteaux" on suburban cul-de-sacs.

The fundamental shortcoming of all these seductive surrogates and short cuts is that they pre-empt and block a city's evolution. As prepackaged products, they are inert—financially and physically frozen. Their parts are not easily interchangeable, and they cannot evolve. They are, too often, stillborn urban corpses that need to be repurposed and replaced. This is not a purist argument for authenticity, nor is it snobbery about mass culture. The problem with these developments is that they are not legally or physically flexible enough to allow the ongoing processes of organic growth and adjustment to occur—and that is a high price to pay.

What might be gained in instant appeal or illusory predictability is lost over time to the economic zero-sum game played by these transplants. They serve only a known quantity of users, companies, purchasers, tenants or consumers, thereby preventing cities from generating further wealth and expanding a fixed pie. For example, there are "no competition" lease agreements in most malls. By contrast, in markets and urban shopping streets, heated competition between a number of vendors offering similar goods can create a specialty focus that draws shoppers from a larger catchment area. We've seen this in the concentration of galleries in Chelsea in Manhattan, for example, or in the string of furniture design establishments on King Street East in Toronto or among the wholesale jewellers on the Rue du Temple in Paris.

Ultimately, such restrictions are tied up in power and who wields it. It is not by accident that in medieval cities, it was frequently the "burghers" (the middle-class merchants who were residents of "burghs"—that is, cities) who challenged the attempts of the aristocracy to control and limit trade. The people who made cities work in the first place often have a good sense of what makes them work best.

A REVIVAL OF CITY BUILDING

The collective unlearning of old ways and learning of new ones is never a smooth process. An immense and powerful machine produced the post-war paradigm that has so deeply undermined cities. We have erected an impressive array of standards, norms and practices that would make many aspects of the world's most cherished urban places illegal if we wished to replicate them. The streets in many obviously successful districts are too narrow. In Toronto's Kensington Market, the facing distances between buildings are too tight; in Boston's Fort Point Channel District and Montreal's Plateau, the loading bays are undoubtedly inadequate by current standards. Behind these rules and others governing the creation of new places, however, are powerful interests, so it is extremely challenging to reproduce these grandfathered infractions.

Even when there is a new vision at the leadership level, recognition that the old regulatory infrastructure has outlived its usefulness, digging down into the administrative level to dislodge its wiring, is a formidable challenge. In the Regent Park example, to ensure vibrant life on the neighbourhood's streets, the architects included street-level, townhouse-style units in the two lower storeys of multistorey buildings. Each unit has its own front door and porch on the public sidewalk.

But several unexpected issues have arisen. For one, Canada Post has indicated that it will not deliver mail to these municipal addresses even though it will deliver to all the neighbouring townhouses on the same streets. Since Canada Post insists on treating these townhouse units as apartment dwellings, their occupants will be forced to use the building's interior mail room.

Secondly, the city's Public Works Department is resisting picking up garbage at the curb for residents of these units. In addition, the developer is concerned that the townhouse owners will prefer to access their cars in the building's underground garage without having to go outside, so the developer is providing an interior corridor to access these units. If that happens, the front porches on the sidewalk could very well become superfluous and possibly just areas for outdoor storage, defeating the whole purpose of the townhouse-style design.

Meanwhile, the primary pedestrian route in the neighbourhood, which goes between a school, a new community centre, a new cultural centre and the major central park and public swimming pool crosses a large street. The crossing occurs far enough from the surrounding traffic signals to allow for a new pedestrian crossing, but the city's Transportation Department initially resisted on the grounds that the proposed crossing would slow traffic. Fortunately, it eventually relented.

These kinds of "rulings" and judgments are not intentionally destructive. They are the unintended consequences of a system that was designed to produce a different kind of world with different priorities and values. And that system is still on automatic pilot.

There is cause for optimism, however. In contrast to these layered Catch-22s in Regent Park, a new way of thinking about cities is starting to form, along with our appreciation for the value of open-ended plans that invite creativity back into city building. A greater sense of urgency in making these kinds of changes may be propelled by larger forces, such as the escalating cost of energy and a better understanding of an environment in crisis. And while changes in the way we build cities are occurring on many fronts through a combination of leading-edge projects and systemic policy reforms, it is the momentum of persistent and forceful change at the margin—how we shape and encourage evolution that is already happening—that matters most. We need a new modus operandi, new teams and new tools to find a better way.

In 1977, the pragmatic process of discovery, through which we're finding these tools, had taken a significant step forward for me, and my work in a small city, well outside the mainstream, that was facing all these pressures and temptations: Prince Albert, Saskatchewan.

IV

NEW TOOLS AND TEAMS

In 1977, the Province of Saskatchewan issued a public request for proposals. It was seeking a master planning study for downtown Prince Albert, a modest Prairie city of thirty thousand people. Carter Greenberg Architects got the job. On April 1, I stepped off a train in Prince Albert after midnight in a snowstorm and, despite the rough beginning, spent the better part of the next three months learning something about city building I could not have predicted. With assistance from Leo Linn, a city planner from Taiwan who was employed by the city and was living in PA (as this Saskatchewan city is known), I set up shop in the impressive 1892 opera house, which had been converted into the Prince Albert Arts Centre on Central Avenue. We then began preparing a conceptual plan for the downtown. We focused particularly on four city blocks that had been identified for early action. Physically, Prince Albert had a lot going for it. It was a small city with a highly walkable street grid in a compact, historic downtown that had many unique assets and strengths: significant frontage along a dramatic stretch of the North Saskatchewan River; several fine late-nineteenth- and early-twentieth-century buildings made by highly skilled Scottish stone masons, including the opera house; and the remnants of an historic town square.

But the downtown was forlorn and dusty: the streets were listless, the shops marginal, and the energy that had once driven life in the core had clearly dissipated. Virtually all the usual destructive post-war forces were in play, including proposals for the obligatory downtown shopping mall (which was built after I left). The city was also preparing to make the usual concessions for cars: demolishing more buildings for parking lots and introducing more one-way streets to speed up traffic. Instead of playing to the city's strengths, these were exactly the moves that would further drain the life from this small downtown.

Prince Albert gave me my first opportunity to apply the techniques I'd been refining to a whole (albeit small) city. To counter the negative momentum of destructive practices that we identified in the downtown, Leo and I proposed a mixed-use strategy for new infill housing on vacant lots in the form of mid-rise courtyard buildings that lined the sidewalk edges, with parking tucked underground to avoid surface lots. By locating planned new government buildings, including a new city hall and provincial and federal offices, right on the main street spine along Central Avenue, we tried to encourage daytime foot traffic and other pedestrian activity.

This, in turn, supported our recommendation for the revival of the historic town square as a central gathering space. More frequent bus service, improved sidewalk width and convenient angled parking to take advantage of the wide Prairie streets were all included to strengthen the retail presence on Central Avenue. A shopping mall was being planned, too, so to counter its inevitable impact on the surrounding storefront retailers, we proposed weather-protected arcades connected to the existing stores as an alternative to the mall's introversion. These arcades led to a block-long covered public street, which would run perpendicular to Central Avenue.

It soon became clear that my study was destined for the proverbial shelf. The gears in government that I'd hoped it would set in motion were not engaging. First of all, I realized how very difficult it was for a small city like Prince Albert to buck the prevailing push for the continued "suburbanization" of its downtown. While talking with merchants who ran local outlets of national retail chains, I experienced first-hand the phenomenon of "western alienation," as the merchants were continually frustrated with the decisions being made in distant financial centres, based on little knowledge of, or interest in, the needs of Prince Albert. Similarly, citizens of PA had little capacity for influencing decisions made in Ottawa or even in the provincial capital, Regina.

This sense of disregard from a distant capital or financial centre wasn't specific to the Canadian West, of course; there are parallels in just about any smaller city in any country I've ever worked in. Another very difficult issue was the isolation of the large and largely poor Cree population, which had a significant presence downtown and which clearly needed attention beyond the scope of this planning effort. But most importantly, it was extremely difficult to succeed in promoting or implementing ideas that challenged the prevailing template for progress without a strong and informed local constituency. Jane Jacobs had no local equivalent in Prince Albert, Saskatchewan.

During my time in Prince Albert, I developed a close relationship with the city planner and the city engineer, and I was particularly struck by how directly their daily decisions about the city's basic infrastructure were shaping the city's future. Matters like the positioning and treatment of the streets, sidewalks, street trees, sewers, water pipes and other services were viewed as unglamorous "technical" decisions. They were the bread-and-butter work of the annual capital budget cycle and the stuff of ongoing maintenance and operating budgets, but they were not viewed as "planning" or "urban design." It struck me that, notwithstanding some of the large forces in play, my city hall colleagues were continuously shaping the public realm and in a profound way directing development and influencing the way people thought about and used the city. If Prince Albert had adopted different strategic goals in making these investments, they could have paved the road into their downtown, rather than the road out.

Who, then, were the real city builders? Planners and urban designers obviously had a role to play, but so did city engineers, politicians, mall owners, business people and local communities acting individually and together in implementing changes. Formal plans aside, the real outcomes at street level arose from the cumulative effect of many seemingly unrelated actions by many parties. And many of the key decisions were made by unseen hands both distant and local, which were not necessarily conscious that they were reshaping the city. Could these disparate forces be effectively orchestrated in other ways, in order to deliberately guide city-positive changes like the ones my study had recommended? I left Prince Albert with the kernel of an idea stored for future reference about how this might be done.

TESTING A METHOD IN TORONTO

Several months after returning to Toronto, both chastened by my Prince Albert experience and energized by my observations, I received an invitation to join the staff of Toronto's Department of Planning and Development to initiate an urban design program. The opportunity to start a design-oriented group inside city government was too tempting to turn down. I was thirty-three years old and a partner in a small architectural practice. Not seeing the logic of my decision to enter the civil service, many friends and colleagues offered their condolences, but I had become totally intrigued by the potential to work at the city scale from within.

In 1977, Toronto was in the throes of a minor revolution. The "reform council" led by Mayor David Crombie had been trying to reverse the destructive pattern of postwar development entrenched in the city's 1969 Official Plan. The plan was supported by a network of old-guard councillors, development industry lobbyists, a civic bureaucracy trained and inclined to implement the plan's practices and a legal structure that enshrined them.

The reform council had committed itself to protecting the city's existing neighbourhoods and architectural heritage, halting the expansion of urban expressways, promoting public transit and pedestrian environments and establishing a new direction for city development, including the virtual reinvention of the activity of city planning itself. After the reform faction gained control in 1972, one of the first tasks council gave itself was to review the 1969 plan for the downtown core. The rapidly expanding business district was becoming a virtual monoculture of high-rise office towers surrounded by parking lots.

Under the mayor's leadership and through his ability to develop consensus, council enacted a forty-five-foot-height holding bylaw in the early 1970s as a moratorium on high-rise development. They made the move to buy themselves time, and it worked. In 1974, they brought forward the resulting Central Area Plan to supersede the initial holding bylaw and curtail expansive downtown office growth by aggressively exporting future office development to emerging suburban centres and bringing residents downtown. The new plan aimed to limit office growth to fit the capacity of the city's public transportation system while at the same time introducing provisions for mixed-use development. As a result, developers could optimize their land value only by including residential units, which would draw a substantial new population into the core. These ideas were fiercely contested by a development industry accustomed to having its own way.

This resulting struggle was the backdrop for my invitation to the city's team. I was to join a select group of ambitious, idealistic young professionals recruited by the mayor and the councillors to effect this major shift in policy direction. Like the councillors themselves, this unusual brain trust came from many countries and diverse backgrounds. We were a mix of planners, architects, landscape architects, economists and transportation experts, but some had no professional background in any of these fields. Many of us had cut our teeth as community activists or academics or had experience in the professional and business world.

In the city, new enterprises often start their lives by being grafted onto others that already exist, and ours would be no different. Though we worked primarily in the Department of Planning and Development, my own role was combined with a recently minted function, initially called "civic design," which had been assigned to the city's chief planner, Dennis Barker, who was preparing to step down. When I began to work with Dennis and a skeleton staff, I started with, literally, a chair and an open-ended assignment.

I was well aware of the Urban Design Group created in New York by Mayor John Lindsay (1966–1974). Committed to "bustling, diverse and dynamic neighbourhoods," Lindsay was convinced that market forces alone could not be relied upon to achieve these goals in areas undergoing change. So he had been seeking ways to infuse the thinking of both urban design professionals and local communities into the development process.

With his strong support, the Urban Design Group was formed and began to conceive plans for Midtown and Lower Manhattan that included incentives for developers of new buildings, allowing increases in density and height for designs that provided useable and attractive spaces at sidewalk level. Two of my former professors at Columbia, Jaquelin Robertson and Richard Weinstein, and other well-known practitioners like Jonathan Barnett were among the first leaders of this group. They were an inspiration for me when I set up what we later renamed the Urban Design Group in Toronto.

The primary focus of my mandate at the planning department was to guide developers in their implementation of the new Central Area Plan and the accompanying zoning bylaws. The city wanted to ensure that the industry produced well-designed buildings that actually delivered the mixed-use activity and enhanced public spaces the plan called for. The unspoken assumption was that tough architectural guidelines were needed—with solid criteria for improving relationships between new buildings and adjacent streets and sidewalks and for including animated retail frontages in new plans. This represented a radical departure, since the bulk of the building proposals coming forward at that time were still largely for single uses (either residential or commercial). They were set back from the street and were designed as withdrawn and unresponsive "towers in the park" and "towers in the plaza."

Not surprisingly, I strongly supported this emphasis on using public policy and strengthened design review to shape and influence private development. But the discipline of urban design was still being defined and legitimized, and I wanted to take it beyond just influencing architecture. I wanted to make urban design more proactive by placing an equal focus on the city's civic infrastructure. I wanted to tap into the process of perpetual transformation by multiple actors that I had become so conscious of in Prince Albert, and to influence ongoing cyclical spending on the entire network of streets, lanes, squares and parks that typically occupy half the land area of any city. If I could do that, I could leverage better designs in new private (and public) developments.

To play this dual role successfully—steward of the city's guidelines for physical development and a sort of community "convener" who would corral both public and private interests to maximize a development's contribution to the life on city streets—I'd need some help. I immediately began assembling a small and very enthusiastic staff of people with design skills, some of whom were already working in the planning department. Incrementally, that staff expanded to over thirty people.

We got our feet wet with two high-profile projects. The first took us to an area that became known as the St. Lawrence Historic District. The second took us to Yonge Street—Toronto's main thoroughfare. At the time, city planners called the St. Lawrence Historic District simply "East Downtown." This was the site of the original Town of York, the most significant heritage district in the city. With the bustling St. Lawrence Market as its focal point, many businesses had been drawn to set up shop in the area in its nineteenth-century heyday. Among these were lawyers' chambers, hotels, restaurants and stables, which surrounded the courthouse and municipal offices. King Street East, between Yonge Street and the Don River, was the district's commercial spine, with dry goods stores and boot- and shoemakers and a surprising number of photographers' studios. By the late 1970s most of this was ancient history. The original building stock had been largely demolished for urban renewal projects and anticipated large-scale redevelopment by the private sector, very little of which had happened yet. Only isolated remnants of the original fabric were still standing, including some fine warehouse structures with cast-iron facades. However, the lonely survivors that did remain were surrounded by large expanses of parking lots serving downtown office buildings and wide streets. Combined, these gave the area a forsaken, gap-toothed appearance, with very little pedestrian life.

However, two noteworthy public structures of great historic significance had survived. One was the magnificent St. Lawrence Hall, which had been built in 1850 after the Great Fire of 1849 had destroyed Toronto's first city hall. Though St. Lawrence Hall didn't take over the function of city hall, it did serve as the city's public meeting place, hosting, among many memorable events, the 1851 North American Convention of Colored Freemen, which had brought prominent abolitionists like Frederick Douglas and Samuel Ringgold Ward to town, and musicians like the world-renowned Swedish soprano Jenny Lind (also in 1851). Even P.T. Barnum's diminutive star, Tom Thumb, had made an appearance there. Then, in 1967, St. Lawrence Hall was restored to celebrate Canada's centennial year, and that really marked the beginning of the district's twentieth-century turnaround.

The second great survivor was the St. Lawrence Market, an enormous, barn-like building with a voluminous interior covered by vaulted trusses. Built in 1845 in response to the city's dramatic population growth, it had been a true multi-functional building. In addition to being home to a wide variety of food and produce vendors, it had housed a police station and jail cells, and it had served as city hall from the time of the 1849 fire until 1899. St. Lawrence Market had suffered a near-death experience in 1971, when it was slated for demolition, but in response to a huge public outcry, it was renovated in 1978.

These few enduring elements became the initial building blocks for regeneration of the district. Developers and owners with vision, who valued the history of their properties, had already started to respond to the city's overtures with sensitive renovations and restorations of the few other remaining structures in the area. Among these was the Gooderham Flatiron Building.

The Central Area Plan had set the stage for an important next step in revitalizing this eastern flank of the downtown. It called for the insertion of new, mixed-use development on vacant parcels but encouraged new development to be compatible with the district's historic shape and feel. The Urban Design Group began to demonstrate the two-pronged approach I wanted to develop (that is, not only attempting to influence the architecture of the district but also tapping into its transformation by many actors and influencing ongoing investment in the public realm). And we saw this valuable "shoulder location" on the edge of downtown as an ideal testing ground. One of our first moves was to establish contact with local business people, both individually and through an association they had formed. The relationships we built developed into a planning alliance with key allies in the private sector that included entrepreneurs and landowners, as well as heritage interests and city council members who were supportive of the vision.

Working with this loose St. Lawrence Historic District coalition, we developed new tools for cooperatively planning how the neighbourhood could develop in the coming years. Among these was a crucial tool that we created: the "getting it all on the same drawing" plan. These were layered, visual/pictorial, easy-to-read plans for the entire area that comprehensively illustrated what had been there historically, what was there now, what construction was planned and in the works, and ideas that could yet be realized. These unofficial plans (as opposed to the highly technical Official Plans and Zoning Maps mandated by the Provincial Planning Act) had no formal status and were not governed by any statutory process. However, they quickly became indispensible.

Through them, we were able to explore future development opportunities, see physical and land use relationships between groupings of buildings and public spaces, and identify synergies that had been obscured when individual interests in the area were still working in isolation. These integrated plans demonstrated how a combination of public and private investments could add up to more than the sum of their parts in revitalizing the neighbourhood. Just by creating the plans, we had added monetary value to the real estate by helping to restore confidence in its future. Soon, nearly every vacant space and property was being used or redeveloped.

An equally important goal of our work with the St. Lawrence Historic District coalition was to build on the growing interest in the city's history and raise the profile of this unique area, where Toronto had been founded. The city's archivist, Scott James, and his team, along with architect Bill Greer of the Toronto Historical Board, helped compile an extensive inventory of the existing structures, including early photos and drawings and accounts of key events from the district's rich past. The images were highlights at exhibits about the neighbourhood's history at the newly created Market Gallery in an upper floor overlooking the interior of the St. Lawrence Market.

While these historical connections were vitally important, we did not aspire to freeze the district at a particular point in time. Instead, we strived to make the next generation of uses part of a continuum, one that capitalized on the value of the district's history in perpetuity and thereby raised both property values in the area and quality of life for all who lived and worked there.

From these initial steps, we developed a two-part strategy for advancing the common goals of public and private interests. On the public side, we invented a method for the city, developers and individual benefactors to make phased annual capital investments in public spaces. Directed by an area-wide Public Improvement Plan, we assembled an enhancement kit from a common family of materials, including pavers, light standards, street furniture, crosswalks and tree planting. These phased public improvements were meant to make the sidewalks more comfortable and the walk more interesting. Dead spaces would also be eliminated by adding new public spaces, including small parks, courtyards and pedestrian lanes. The program was supported by modest federal, provincial and municipal grants. And we hoped to generate further desirable new development, creating movement by example. The program did gain momentum, and we searched continually for special opportunities—and there were many. In order to follow a curve in the city's original shoreline, Front Street (one of the key streets in the district) shifts alignment at one point, forming an acute angle whose apex had produced a small gem, Toronto's own wedge-shaped Flatiron Building. Behind it was a parking lot that was converted into Berczy Park (named after an early settler). At the initiative of our Urban Design Team, the space was also made larger by removing one lane of traffic on Front Street. Surrounding sidewalks were expanded, street trees were planted and a fine-grained network of pedestrian walkways were added to break up the block. A lane of traffic was also removed from a neighbouring section of Front Street to create a landscaped median for easier crossing and widened sidewalks for café patios. One block north, the historic St. James Anglican Cathedral on King Street had been rebuilt three times on its site but had never faced a break in the buildings across the street. So its 305-foot spire could never be properly viewed and appreciated from that vantage point. However, since a site on the opposite side of King Street had already been cleared for urban renewal, this was now possible. The fact that we had now created a "district plan" also helped us attract private sector donations. One of these was a donation from Louis Odette, the head of a large construction company who had a keen interest in contemporary sculpture, and in 1981 our team designed and created the Toronto Sculpture Garden across from the cathedral using these funds. Other private donations were added to public resources to create more distinctive places. A Victorian garden was built in St. James Park next to the cathedral with the participation of the Garden Club of Toronto.

Public art also played a key role, including the well-known theatrical mural by artist Derek Besant. The result of a privately funded competition, the mural forms a dramatic backdrop to Berczy Park on the rear wall of the Flatiron Building.

In the second part of our strategy, we worked intensively with the private sector, investors, developers and designers in shaping each new development proposal as it came forward. We would take often introverted schemes for individual towers (relatively square high-rises) or slabs (much wider ones) with little relationship to their surroundings and reshape them to make more generous gestures to the neighbourhood—active retail ground floors, colonnades, public mid-block passages and accessible courtyards. The public improvement program provided a significant incentive for developers to cooperate (since the public investment would enhance their properties), and greatly increased the city's leverage in putting these design-oriented issues on the table when it reviewed development proposals and sought improvements that went beyond the narrow provisions of the zoning bylaw.

A prime example of our success with this program, which became an influential prototype in the city, was a full-block development called Market Square at Front and Church Streets. Our guidelines had called for opening up a four-metre-wide walkway from behind the Sculpture Garden on King Street right down to Front Street, with St. James Cathedral always in view. The architect, Jerome Markson, responded to the challenge by skilfully designing a mid-rise residential development that filled out the block around an interior courtyard (providing the requested walkway and extended visual opening to St. James Cathedral), with roof-top gardens and active ground-floor retail, which currently includes a popular grocery store.

As this wave of infill development progressed, it filled in almost all the gaps and forged the missing link west to the downtown core and east to the new St. Lawrence Neighbourhood, a ground-breaking, mixed-income neighbourhood which came to be known as one of the key initiatives of Mayor David Crombie and the reform council of the 1970s. Through a chain reaction, this pattern of mixed-use redevelopment now extends into a series of new precincts, including the Distillery District, East Bayfront, the

West Don Lands site of the Athletes' Village for the 2015 Pan Am Games and the Lower Don Lands. All will contribute to a major repopulating of these once-barren lands on the edge of downtown.

The St. Lawrence Historic District became a priority project because of the great opportunities its location and history presented. The second key project assigned to the fledgling Urban Design Group came about in response to a crisis. Yonge Street is often cited as the longest street in the world, extending almost 1,900 kilometres north from Lake Ontario. Historically, it was home to Toronto's bustling downtown shopping district. More recently Canada's first subway line, which opened in 1954, ran under Yonge. Unfortunately, the construction of that line was traumatic. From 1949 to 1953 open trench excavation limited access to local stores, putting some out of business. When the subway was finally completed, development did appear at the stops, but the once-continuous retail in between, nurtured by the previous streetcar line, did not fully return. A second trauma hit Yonge Street two decades later: the introduction of the Eaton Centre, a massive, enclosed shopping mall, the first phase of which opened in 1977. It ran parallel to the street for three blocks, connecting to two subway stops. Once more, the long period of construction combined with an introverted mall left this once busy commercial area to atrophy.

By the mid-1970s downtown portions of Yonge Street were out of control. The popular clothing stores and other retailers that had once lined the thoroughfare had given way to a drug scene and a proliferation of body rub parlors and trinket shops. At first, a series of temporary pedestrian malls, which closed portions of the street to traffic for several weeks at a time in the summer months, had mixed success in bringing visitors back, but in the end, they only amplified the problems of prostitution, panhandling and drugs and created an uneasy atmosphere. Yonge Street's deteriorating condition came to a head with a tragic event in 1977 that galvanized the attention of the public. A twelve-year-old shoeshine boy named Emanuel Jacques, the son of Portuguese immigrants, was lured into an apartment above a body rub parlor with the promise of work. He was brutally assaulted and murdered. A crime of this nature was considered unthinkable at the time in Toronto. Numerous protests and marches demanded that the city clean up "the strip" and provided the catalyst for shutting down the numerous "adult" stores and body rub parlors.

Our new Urban Design Group was called in by city council to coordinate with a specially assigned task force and the business community to find ways to change the image and use of the street and spur its renewal. It was felt that if Yonge Street could be made more attractive to a greater variety of people and to better-quality businesses, this would deter further physical and social decay. A strategy emerged combining physical changes to the street with local business initiatives, intensive policing, bylaw enforcement and social action; this was urban design under fire.

The city considered turning Yonge Street into either a permanent pedestrian mall or a "transit mall," open only to pedestrians and small buses. In the end, however, the solution that best balanced the needs of all users seemed to be to simply widen the sidewalks and enhance them with new trees, street furniture and pedestrian-scale street lighting.

We also proposed transit shelters and canopies for vendors at the intersections. Council approved the plan, committed itself to fund the improvements over five years and asked the Urban Design Group to coordinate the physical changes. Work would begin in 1978.

At this point the project went off the rails. While the city was ready to proceed, Metropolitan Toronto, the regional government body created in 1953 that had jurisdiction over Yonge Street as an arterial road, was not. The regional body considered the street to be first and foremost a traffic carrier. Despite an expensive and extensive traffic engineering study that proved it was technically feasible to widen the sidewalks, Metro steadfastly refused to bend. This was extraordinarily frustrating. It was one more example of what I'd seen in Prince Albert: a city that was not in control of its destiny and therefore unable to innovate its way out of critical problems. City council still felt it had to act, so it shifted its attention to a number of streets perpendicular to Yonge, over which it had sole jurisdiction. Along those routes there were sidewalks it could widen, along with a few limited sections of Yonge Street itself where changes were possible.

As in the case of the St. Lawrence Historic District, this undertaking became a multiyear, staged-capital program, which, in tandem with increased policing efforts and the initiatives of business owners, did produce some degree of positive change. Over time, Yonge Street has gradually become a more people-oriented corridor. New developments such as the introduction of Dundas Square in 2002 and the continued expansion of Ryerson University, with plans for a new library and Student Learning Centre to be built right on Yonge, have significantly helped to stabilize the area, eliminating some of the seediness, reintroducing successful businesses and making the street more appealing to a diverse population. And now that a political reorganization has given the city full control of Yonge Street, the time may even have come to revisit our original proposal to widen the sidewalks.

The fledgling Urban Design Group was inventing its theory, policy and practice all at once. Notably, we were faced with the challenge of introducing and expanding this new group and its new modus operandi within the city's established bureaucracy. Powerful people had worked hard to claim important turf inside city hall, and it wouldn't be easy to convince them that an ambitious young group like ours deserved a new place within it. So we worked hard, to demonstrate that we could add value to their work. In an environment of specialists, our ticket for admission often came from the growing reputation of our studio as a place where disciplines and departments came together. Getting a project "all on the same page" was our key urban design tool, and the models we created allowed others to see the whole picture and their own part within it.

We built a three-dimensional model of the downtown area in our storefront workspace, into which new proposals were inserted and tested. We also pioneered the use of CADD (Computer-Assisted Drafting and Design) models for entire city districts (in those days, these were produced by a single operator using a gigantic Intergraph computer, which, as we used to say, was like piloting a 747). We made those models available to others both in and outside of city hall—including architects, developers and community groups. Not only did this openness and transparency make the process less threatening; it also helped to make the work of others more effective. Because they could come to us to plot and model their own initiatives in three dimensions, they could better understand the impacts those projects would have on their surroundings.

In seeking opportunities for our work, we watched for initiatives in the public sphere (improvements to streets and parks and the creation of new public spaces) and in the private sphere (planning for new, primarily residential downtown development) and successfully sought donations for public art and improved public spaces. We also educated ourselves about the city's ongoing cycle of capital renewal and improvement. To help our understanding of this cycle, we developed strong relationships with key people in various city departments, including Public Works, City Property, the Toronto Transit Commission (TTC) and Toronto Hydro.

We were looking for opportunities to piggyback our incremental qualitative improvement of public spaces onto the annual processes already in place for infrastructure renewal—another inspiration from observations I'd made in Saskatchewan. At that time the Department of Public Works had an annual tracking system for its one-, two-, five- and ten-year cycles of renewal and upgrading for all elements of the city's infrastructure. Matching our efforts to these helped us avoid randomly tearing up areas of the public right-of-way that still had a useful life. It also saved money. To build on the practices we had developed in the St. Lawrence Historic District and the Yonge Street Corridor, we sat down together each spring with the other departments when the annual budget was being prepared. With this advance warning, the Urban Design Group could prepare conceptual design plans or have them prepared. This potential for coordination of budgets across municipal departments was a crucial discovery for us. Even minimal resources harnessed to a common set of objectives and larger projects can buy a lot more over time than multiple, small, independent budgets, each paying for projects that begin from scratch.

Gradually, the Urban Design Group came to be seen not just as a provider of aesthetic finishing touches but as an in-house team playing a valuable early role in shaping the underlying physical structure of the city. By marrying broad policy initiatives for physical design to changes in the regulatory framework and annual capital budget cycles, we were discovering our full potential for creating incremental change that could transform neighbourhoods. For example, in concert with Public Works, we developed a set of new design details for sidewalks and crosswalks that were friendlier to pedestrians and which became the new citywide standards. Instead of being just painted lines crossing the street, crosswalks became literal extensions of the sidewalk with paving material laid right across the intersection. Sidewalks were widened; street trees became an essential "utility" with their own reserved space in the right-of-way; lighting scaled to pedestrians was introduced on sidewalks. The look and feel of the street space was modified block by block to make it more comfortable and inviting to people travelling on foot.

As development began to spread from downtown into the obsolescent industrial, port and railway lands at the southern edge of downtown, the Urban Design Group was called upon more and more as a key collaborator in dealing with large-scale infrastructure. In the early 1980s, we took a lead role within the wider team of engineers and planners assigned to lay out the new streets, blocks and park spaces that would establish the underlying structure of a new set of city neigh- bourhoods (including the spaces to be dedicated to the city for public ownership). As our range of responsibilities grew, the Urban Design Group, eventually renamed the Division of Architecture and Urban Design, grew larger and more diverse. We became involved in many new issues and challenges, from public art and heritage preservation to environmental protection. The essential idea of urban design as having a critical integrating role in city building had taken hold.

Most significant to the city's investment in our work, however, urban design was winning recognition as a key economic development tool, stimulating investment in areas where we improved the quality of life and ultimately resulting in increased tax revenues. Thanks to this benefit, we had developed strong supporters at city hall, as well as among both local community groups and the business community. As it turned out, my career would place my efforts almost equally on both sides of this public-private dialectic.

TAKING IT ON THE ROAD TO SAINT PAUL

After ten years I felt I'd accomplished almost everything I could from within city government. So, in 1987, I joined two colleagues from the city, Joe Berridge and Frank Lewinberg, to form a partnership called Berridge Lewinberg Greenberg (BLG), which we later renamed Urban Strategies. BLG was a consulting practice in city planning and urban design that would draw upon the practices and techniques we'd developed over the previous decade. While I had considered returning to an architectural practice, I discovered that the market in urban design was varied and interesting enough to sustain a professional practice.

As I became involved in American projects, I was discovering a whole new kind of energy and determination born of crisis conditions. Cities in the U.S. had been more severely tested by the forces of suburbanization and urban renewal, and new coalitions for their defence and revitalization had formed. These initiatives linked city government with community-based and philanthropic groups, important foundations and the private sector, all sharing a genuine interest in salvaging and reassembling the places in cities that were seriously damaged. These groups felt that the experience I had to offer from my time in Toronto would be useful to their efforts. But the benefit would prove to work both ways.

One of BLG's early opportunities came in Saint Paul, Minnesota. In the midst of working on a master plan for the University of Minnesota, I was approached by the newly elected mayor of Saint Paul, Norm Coleman, and three of his key advisors, Dick Broeker, Patrick Seeb and Jack Hoeschler. This was 1995, a critical time in the state capital's history. Saint Paul had been founded at the most northerly navigable point on the Mississippi River. The city was hemorrhaging—losing population, jobs and confidence in its future. There were a few notable exceptions, like Lowertown, a re-emerging warehouse district, whose renewal had been spearheaded by well-known planner Weiming Lu. But for the most part, the downtown was in decline, its adjacent neighbourhoods were struggling and hemmed in by the highway network that surrounded them, and its commercial office sector was weak and failing. It was also feeling vulner-able in relation to its twin city upriver on the Mississippi, Minneapolis, which seemed to be capturing any positive momentum in the area.

Numerous high-profile projects, federal programs and targeted subsidies to the development industry had been launched to stimulate a rebirth in Saint Paul, but none had seemed to make a major difference. A year before, Ben Thompson, native son of Saint Paul and well-known Boston architect, had been summoned to help. Instead of a plan-ning document, he produced a single watercolour image entitled "The Great River Park." This remarkable and pro-vocative illustration took enormous liberties by imagining a verdant river valley running through the heart of Saint Paul. It turned people's eyes back to the Mississippi, then a degraded and neglected "back" of the city, and Thompson's vision set the stage for the next round of creative thinking. This came in the form of a study by the husband-and-wife team of Bill Morrish and Catherine Brown, of the University of Minnesota's Design Center for the American Landscape, and it demonstrated that the Mississippi's watershed actually touched every one of the city's neighbourhoods. Feeling strongly that Thompson's imagined return to the river was the right way to correct his city's course, Mayor Coleman and his team asked me to help develop strategies to revitalize downtown Saint Paul and reconnect it to the Mississippi. The effort would draw on many influential forces from the city—the Saint Paul Riverfront Corporation, a newly formed private, not-for-profit umbrella group with broad represen-tation from all sectors of Saint Paul's community (business

and institutional leaders, neighbourhood activists and environmental leaders), the downtown, business-led Capital City
Partnership and, of course, the city itself.

The scope of this challenge was extremely broad. It
extended over an area of several square miles and clearly
involved the full gamut of physical, social, economic and
environmental issues. We would also need to show some
early results to keep the momentum going while not losing
focus on the long-term challenges. Members of the BLG
staff and I assembled a diverse team of interdisciplinary
collaborators, including local landscape architect Bob Close,
transportation engineer Walter Kulash from Florida, and
environmentalist Steve Apfelbaum from Wisconsin. We began
searching for common ground through a series of planning
and design workshops involving hundreds of stakeholders:
members of city departments and agencies, environmental
and neighbourhood groups and business leaders. Building
on Saint Paul's strong tradition of community involvement
(a critical condition for a successful effort), a method emerged
of working through the issues together in collaborative
design sessions called "charrettes." To help everyone better
understand the condition the city was in and how it got to
be that way, we scanned the areas's evolving history. What
we saw was a narrative that began with Saint Paul evolving
in a unique natural setting on the Mississippi River, which
had been formed by the distinctive limestone bluffs and the
natural upper and lower "landings" on the river. Next came
the arrival of the barge fleets and the hardening of the river
banks with industrial dockwalls and the rail lines that spurred
industrial growth. And then the familiar post-war noose of
highways isolating a downtown area of approximately one

square mile, which included some fine buildings now surrounded by parking lots. That brought us to the present:
the nine-to-five Central Business District, which was losing
occupants and value; the institutions; the hospitals; and the
small residential population of rich and poor and assorted
committed urbanites. While the imposing state capitol
building stood just across the highway, it seemed remote
and inaccessible, and the current downtown had little foot
traffic or retail activity. Many of the wide streets had been
converted to a one-way system designed to rapidly empty
the city at 5 p.m. Above these ran an extensive network of
pedestrian "skyways" suspended over the street grid, com-
pounding the problem of lifeless sidewalks. And the
Mississippi River itself was extremely difficult to access,
even though the city paid lip service to its value as a communal touchstone and a source of great natural beauty.
Within our team and the many people we spoke to, there
was already an implicit shared vision that had to do with
returning to the city's river origins. People began to understand the magnitude of the vast river valley and its potential
to be improved and reinhabited as a new "green" face of
the city, even though its banks had been hardened by industry and virtually all traces of nature had been removed. Our
efforts turned to Ben Thompson's watercolour image and
to figuring out how to translate its aspiration into real
spaces and opportunities.

What was soon called the *Saint Paul on the Mississippi
Development Framework* grew out of our community-wide
discussions and initially focused on four key areas: environment, urban structure, movement networks and the public
realm. This was a tailored version of the "unofficial plans"

Taking a method on the road to Saint Paul—the Saint Paul on the Mississippi Development Framework; *a drive-in bank and parking lot transformed into a new park.*

that the Urban Design Group had developed for specific districts in Toronto. In Saint Paul, we worked simultaneously on two scales: broad concepts for the whole and individual precinct plans for key subareas of the downtown and the river corridor. Within these, the framework identified development opportunities block by block that could promote the vitality of these mixed-use neighbourhoods. From there, residents and community members called our attention to the particular ingredients in the mix that we could exploit: the individual buildings, popular family businesses (like the Original Coney Island Tavern or Mickey's Diner), places where people gathered. In conjunction with these, the framework identified major improvements and additions to the public infrastructure, including vertical connections up the bluff faces to neighbourhoods overlooking the river basin. These would be implemented through the creation of a multiyear capital "Renaissance Project," drawing, through the combined efforts of the city and the Riverfront Corporation, on public, philanthropic and private funds.

Extremely valuable in this effort was the preparation of overlays on tracing paper (similar to the multilayered drawings developed in Toronto), which allowed us to get everything on the same page. On these composite drawings, all current initiatives appeared, even if they existed only in early conceptual stages: development proposals, transportation and infrastructure and public realm improvements in all stages. Through this opportunistic lens, the remarkable difference that a shared vision could make began to come into focus: the potential, within relatively short time frames, to orchestrate linked sequences of street, park and trail improvements; trail connections; and active ground-floor uses, all tied in some way to the river, to make the down-town, once again, a place where people would want to be.

138   The framework plan began to take shape as a shared nar-rative, not just a plan and not just a set of projects, but a belief in the power of a collective vision, one that posed some clear challenges to existing practices. Downtown Saint Paul had developed such a serious attachment to its network of skyways that it was entirely possible to use the downtown without ever touching the ground. While this network undoubtedly offered convenience and weather protection in a northern climate, it was also making it extremely difficult to develop successful downtown retail and a lively street environment that would encourage visitors and locals to spend time in the city. The need to break the circular logic of Saint Paul's love affair with these skyways in newly developing downtown locations became the subject of many heated debates. In the end, their continued use of skyways in new areas was to be extremely limited, and efforts were launched to better connect the already-established skyway network back down to street level with animated two-storey frontages, more stairs and escala-tors, and elevators tying the levels together.

The preparation of the framework also forced a strategic reassessment of some projects already in the pipeline, includ-ing the proposed Science Museum of Minnesota. There were plans to have the museum sit on the bluff line overlooking the river, but on one side, its own parking ramp, an independ-ent structure, pushed the museum back from its frontage on Kellogg Boulevard, and on the other side, it had no access to the valley more than fifty feet below. Once our group pointed out the potential rewards of a river-centric perspective for the museum, the mayor insisted that the plans be adjusted. As a result, a better relationship with Kellogg Boulevard was created, as was an elevator and grand public stairway down to the Upper Landing on the river. Since then, a new neighbourhood has emerged on the site of a former scrapyard at the foot of the bluffs between the river on the one side and a now-relocated highway and the rail corridor on the other.

Simultaneously, we were fleshing out, in a series of diagrams and descriptions, how the city centre could be repopulated as a web of interconnected, pedestrian-oriented "urban villages." Our mix of living, working, shopping and local park space was set within a lushly reforested Mississippi River Valley (faithful to Ben Thompson's vision) alongside a more vibrant and increasingly mixed-use downtown. When we released it, the broadly endorsed *Saint Paul on the Mississippi Development Framework* consolidated all these ideas in a call to the community to redefine Saint Paul's relationship with the river (and in doing so to reassert the city's future role in the Twin Cities region). By bringing new attention to the city's inherent strengths, the framework vision has fostered investor confidence in adaptive reuse of heritage structures, new retail and new housing, all in the downtown area, and it has provided broad direction for mutually supportive and integrated private, public and community projects. It has been nationally acclaimed and has won a number of awards.

The framework remains a living instrument and a set of practical tools. Like the city, the document designed to guide its resuscitation is perpetually unfinished. But as new challenges come forward, the framework provides a vocabulary and syntax for planning discussion and has spawned a whole range of charrettes, workshops, seminars, publications and lecture series. Now, after more than a decade, the framework's concepts and vision have proven resilient enough to remain relevant as the locus of change in Saint Paul has migrated outside the originally targeted downtown precincts. And so, new chapters have been produced in this living document.

In the end, however, the framework is only as good as the people who use it. Needing a clearing house for vetting proposals from developers and public sector actors, we recommended that the Saint Paul on the Mississippi Design Center be set up under the umbrella of the Riverfront Corporation. With its own director and a small staff, the Design Center was created to have a core membership of individuals who already worked within city hall as "city designers" in various capacities. Among these would be city planners and architects in Planning and Economic Development, landscape architects in the Parks Department, Building Department officials, and transportation and civil engineers in Public Works. The city would donate a portion of these staff members' paid time, though it took some effort to get the reporting structure worked out. Ultimately, the mayor's participation smoothed over the wrinkles in formalizing the arrangement. Building on what we'd learned in Toronto, the Saint Paul office would also include a larger ancillary group, with staff from the county and other agencies, and participation from the design faculty and students at the University of Minnesota. I served as the centre's interim director for the first year of operations. The Design Center occupies a renovated storefront within the Riverfront Corporation offices near city hall. As we initially hoped, it has provided a forum where design and city-building issues can be discussed and where lateral thinking is encouraged. Often, in these conversations, it is discovered that the "solution" in one area resides in another. For example, it was there that we conceived and coordinated the initiative that moved Shepard Road, previously a river's-edge highway to Minneapolis and the Minneapolis–Saint Paul International Airport, away from the riverbanks to simultaneously improve traffic circulation, increase flood protection and free up the lands of a contaminated scrapyard for the new Upper Landing Neighbourhood.

It was also in the Design Center that the plans for the North Quadrant Neighbourhood (later known as Wacouta Commons) was developed. In an area dominated by parking lots, a new park was created; the local street network was revised; and a mix of new housing, converted warehouses and new businesses was introduced. The Design Center established its credibility through such efforts. To pursue long-term goals seriously, a city must, among other things, be able to pass the baton from one political administration to another by turning these goals into enduring civic aspirations. Since many senior appointments inside city hall are typically purged with each change in political administration, the ongoing role played by civil society is critical. Longevity requires actors outside electoral politics—civil society "stewards" who ensure that city-building efforts that can take decades are sustained. In the case of Saint Paul, that steward has been the Riverfront Corporation. With the full support of three successive mayors, this arm's-length, not-for-profit corporation occupies a place at the city cabinet table and has made a formal commitment to work with city government, the Saint Paul Port Authority and the business-led Capital City Partnership, in order to help realize the long-term vision for a renewed Saint Paul. The continued financial support of the foundations in this community (including the Saint Paul Foundation and the McKnight Foundation) has been another critical component, and funding from corporate supporters like 3M and the Saint Paul Companies has also been essential to the revitalization of the city. Their stewardship of the framework vision opened my eyes to something that I hadn't really seen outside the U.S.—especially in Canadian cities where there was greater faith that government would fulfill this role on its own (an assumption that would soon be put to the test). The framework has provided the consistent vision needed to attract and keep investors in the community and benefited the private sector.

Over the years since the framework was created, many new initiatives have been implemented: new downtown housing was built, and parks, trails and new public spaces were created—all by different actors. One of the most significant early efforts related to the framework was the "Great River Park" initiative, taking its name directly from Ben Thompson's drawing. This was an early community endeavour to plant thirty-five thousand new trees in the Mississippi River Valley. School kids were involved, and companies gave employees time off, provided the saplings and helped transport volunteers into the valley to plant them. The sense of ownership this produced mattered because it gave the community a vital stake in all subsequent outcomes.

There have also been an increasing number of special seasonal events like the annual Millard Fillmore Dinners, which celebrate the city's reuniting with its river. (The dinners are named for the U.S. president who organized the 1854 "Grand Excursion" by steamboat up the Mississippi River to Saint

Paul.) There have also been periodic quantitative and qualitative assessments of the progress made in fulfilling the framework vision—including a 2004 study which revealed that over $2 billion in public and private funding had been invested in riverfront initiatives over the previous ten years. At present, the National Great River Park is in the making. It will cover 3,500 acres along the entire length of the Mississippi as its passes through Saint Paul and links to Minneapolis. Conceptualized as "The City in a Park/A Park in the City," it will integrate the Mississippi River Valley's unique natural systems and recreational resources with community and economic development in the adjacent neighbourhoods. The creation of this new National Park has become the subject of a new chapter in the framework.

THERE IS A TIME TO SAY NO

On September 5, 2007, in front of a packed council chamber, Saint Paul's city council dealt a fatal blow to a proposed $1 billion retail and housing development project on the city's riverfront. With the framework as a guide, the city had seen years of slow and steady progress—and not just in matters of urban redevelopment. A reduction in industrial effluents had also greatly improved the water quality of this stretch of the Mississippi. Sensing the terrain's fresh appeal, a major developer had come forward with a huge project that he contended would lift the community to a whole new level of prosperity. He had spent years, and millions of dollars, trying to convince residents and city officials to support his thirty-two-acre "European-style" development called "The Bridges of Saint Paul." The request for approval from city council was his last shot, and the decision was not an easy one for council to make.

Though the Bridges project had been made possible by the revitalization of the downtown market, the proposed development was a repudiation of the very method that had produced it. The plan was to build the Bridges development on the West Side Flats, on riverfront lands owned by the developer directly across from downtown Saint Paul. It would have included more than 1,000 housing units, a 250-room hotel, nearly 400,000 square feet of destination retail space (a mall, in fact), a movie theatre, two glass-enclosed botanical gardens and 2,000 public parking spaces. Convinced that his proposal would produce a boon for the city, the developer was asking for $125 million in tax breaks. The enormous proposed infusion of private investment was tempting for a city that was still trying to grow its economy. The Saint Paul Riverfront Corporation had asked me to prepare an analysis of the Bridges proposal in terms of its fit with the framework. I did, and I reported back that it was highly problematic. The challenges it raised reflected in microcosm the larger debate about how to create new places in cities: the "big bang" theory of development versus the theory of "incremental growth." Exemplifying the big bang, the Bridges put as many components as possible into one super-sized integrated package with consistent branding across its breadth.

What was wrong with this vision for Saint Paul's West Side Flats? It was clearly an improvement over the traditional mall and it did achieve density; it was more mixed than what was already there; and it had a finer-grained pedestrian network of outdoor spaces with sidewalk life, which represented an attempt to simulate the experience of being on a city street. But while the Bridges "lifestyle centre" appropriated the image and language of the city—parks, streets, squares, neighbourhoods, urban village—it was ultimately a carefully regulated commercial realm, centrally managed, just like a shopping centre, and insulated from the real messiness of urban life.

Like some of the "mirages" described above, it lacked a city's diversity, vitality and ability to grow, modify and adapt over time. It located ramps to underground parking at the ends of existing streets, but it was intentionally introverted, designed to concentrate commercial activity within itself. In this respect, it was profoundly different from a genuine piece of city. And so it was not the right or best answer for a site on the Mississippi River in the heart of Saint Paul. It would always be nothing more than what it had started out to be, and the upland areas around it would remain isolated and cut off from the river by the unclear pedestrian circulation within its enormous girth, and the traffic volumes it generated.

Because the Bridges was a complete vision for redeveloping the West Side Flats, it was presented as a stark "take it or leave it" proposition. In a fragile market such as the one in Saint Paul, where growth is slow and incremental, that could have profound consequences. And the consequences would be heightened because of the size of this new development in relation to the downtown right across the river. Conceived as an extension of downtown, the development was intended, in many ways, to supplant downtown functions, particularly through its retail and restaurant roles.

The sheer size of the Bridges was also disproportionate to the city's ability to absorb such a large number of new residential units and retail outlets. If the proposal had been successful, the Bridges would have sucked up all the growth in town and pre-empted progress elsewhere. And with its reliance on auto access, it would have required costly and disruptive enlargements of the road network to handle expected traffic volumes. Such likely outcomes reflected a very different intention from the framework's vision for a relatively dense but moderately scaled mixed-use urban neighbourhood on the West Side Flats that would complement and support, not compete with, downtown functions. For all these reasons, I recommended against this very high-risk strategy. While the Bridges concept was tempting to some, in the long run an expanded West Side Flats neighbourhood with attractive public spaces and functions and a public water's edge would more effectively extend the benefits of a waterfront location deeply into the surrounding fabric. It also made sense to maintain the primary focus on downtown on the other side of the river, in order to support and sustain the major commitments to incremental growth that were already paying off (through significant infill investment on the Upper Landing and within downtown itself). At the conclusion of the council meeting, Mayor Coleman agreed with the council's rejection of the Bridges proposal. It's sobering to consider what would have happened when the economic downturn struck in 2008 if this project had actually started and Saint Paul had committed its limited resources to it.

This intense debate in Saint Paul was typical of many that have been occurring in North America and elsewhere about urban waterfront redevelopment. Most urban centres are now rejecting the "big bang" option in favour of an incremental growth model. There are many variations, but the fundamental benefits of, and reasons for, adopting such an evolutionary approach are both highly practical, given how cities work.

Among other things, this approach reduces risk. Development can be broken down into achievable phases and can evolve in response to changing market conditions—and to changes in demographics and the types of real-estate product that are popular or suited to a particular time and place. The evolutionary approach also permits incremental decisions, which allow individual market segments to proceed relatively autonomously. It does not require a municipality to make huge upfront investments in infrastructure and allows for phasing of public investment to correspond to actual market-driven construction activity. Most important, the evolutionary approach results in authentic diversity based on the efforts of multiple actors over time—and this produces real city character. Slow but steady wins the race.

OPTIMIZING THE WHOLE, NOT THE PARTS

In Saint Paul, the cleanup and restoration of a degraded Mississippi River (obviously desirable in its own terms) was also instrumental in reviving a moribund economy and attracting new residents. Win-win-win outcomes like this are a benefit of lateral solutions that address multiple problems using the same resources: one fix can lead to others.

Specialization, which solves one problem at a time in what might appear to be the most efficient way, ultimately invites waste. Parking lots built to serve only one specific building or user sit empty much of the week. Transit lines with one-way rush hour travel that send empty cars back the other way and power plants that serve only one set of users at peak times are all inherently wasteful because their intended purpose is too narrowly defined. Whether it's energy, water supplies, schools, pipes or streetcars, the principle is the same for all. By filling their schedule with complementary, off-peak, "mixed" uses, we can take advantage of their full capacity. The Campo dei Fiori in Rome is a classic spatial example—a popular morning market, at midday it shifts to tables and chairs for outdoor eating, and in the evening it becomes a popular gathering spot. Even elements that seem completely benign can become detrimental if they're designed without their full context in mind. The perfect environment for planting street trees may require making sidewalks so wide that buildings are pushed too far apart and the street loses its "containing" feel. Bicycle path networks pursued in isolation may dominate and overrun pedestrians. Transit lines rammed through neighbourhoods with continuous elevated platforms or curbs designed to keep pedestrians from crossing rights-of-way may introduce barriers almost as damaging as an expressway.

Overkill in use can have a similar deleterious effect. When an area is specifically designed for tourism, it can overspecialize in a way that will inevitably drive the locals away. A too-great concentration of nightclubs in a small area brings noise, after-hours commotion and drug-related crime. This has happened in the Kings, an area in downtown Toronto, and has recently become a source of conflict for residents and other businesses. Even too much green space resulting in too little development or activity in critical areas can make an area less popular. Finding the right balance between facilitating the objectives of the individual components and optimizing the effectiveness of the whole is a critical skill in sustainable city building.

The most memorable city streets may not be perfectly designed for any of the individual purposes served—traffic, walking, retail frontage, social space, services or utilities— but as these parts come together, we appreciate the street as a whole. This is why streets like Hanover and Salem in Boston's celebrated North End are so appealing. The traffic lanes and curb radii are tight, so drivers and pedestrians are forced to make eye contact. The placement of trees, street furniture, signage, café tables and shopfronts are all constrained by each other, but they create a dynamic that makes the North End popular with both locals and visitors.

Underlying this concept of suboptimizing the parts to optimize the whole is the public and private dialectic, which needs two strong sides kept in reasonable balance, as Jane Jacobs argued in *Systems of Survival*. The city needs to create and maintain the public realm and set the ground rules. Equally important is a strong and agile private sector that can respond to opportunities for redevelopment, creating jobs and expanding on the fabric of the city. Civil society and major institutions like universities, colleges and museums also have important roles to play as city builders. But public-private partnerships need to be carefully structured to make sure roles are clear. City building requires working simultaneously at different scales on both sides of this dialectic, with the big picture (usually public) and the individual project (typically private) creating room for plans within plans. While I was working on a plan for a privately owned twenty-acre site on Boston Harbour, for instance, colleagues were working on the publicly commissioned thousand-acre South Boston Seaport Plan. These parallel exercises enriched each other as the seaport plan gave my team key information about the larger context, while we provided their team with a fine-grained understanding of specific opportunities in our neighbourhood.

In my work, I am constantly coming up against the tensions between narrowly defined tasks I have been assigned and my long-term goal of city building. For example, federal stimulus funds were secured for a new regional sports complex containing a four-pad hockey arena in the Toronto Port Lands. The location will make this facility the critical first step in launching a new, mixed-use, waterfront neighbourhood. However, the development's fit with its eventual neighbours and the surrounding public realm would need to be carefully tended in order to integrate this complex into its surroundings and make it a catalyst for further regeneration. Welcoming this challenge I joined an architectural team that competed for and won the bid to build this facility.

Unfortunately, none of the several public agencies involved were given clear responsibility for managing these larger issues of context and fit. Halfway through the process the department tasked by the city to act as developer for the sports complex decided that it could only afford to build a sprawling suburban version of the facility. This key project of a plan that is supposed to demonstrate sustainability would be surrounded by surface parking. Paradoxically, the opportunity cost to using this land so inefficiently far exceeded the cost differential between the two plans. I resigned at that point, expressing my reasons. Then the entire Waterfront Design Review Panel created by Waterfront Toronto (the tri-government funded corporation with a long-term mandate to transform the brownfield lands on Toronto's waterfront into beautiful, accessible, sustainable mixed-use communities and dynamic public spaces) also threatened to resign. Ultimately, the decision was reversed (although it is unclear whether the project will proceed).

In another Toronto case, a new subway line was being introduced with a stop that fell on a municipal boundary. While the transit authority's budget had been allocated for the line and the station (and the whole intent was to create the conditions for new, transit-oriented development at the stop), no one in this picture was responsible for reworking the major arterial road that ran right through the middle so that pedestrian crossings to the station would be safe and attractive. The "public" was making a huge investment in transit, but no mechanisms were in place to guide the positive changes the new transit line could stimulate. In cases like this, the agencies involved often recognize the need and the gap, but they don't feel they can step outside their jurisdictional frames of reference to deal with these issues. By whatever name we give them, cross-disciplinary, interagency design centres like the ones we set up in Saint Paul and Toronto (and like a number of others throughout North America, including the original Urban Design Group in New York City) have become indispensable new places of convergence for city building. They create the forum for a crucial, unbounded and unprejudiced conversation about integrated solutions that use scarce public resources as an investment in the future. Like the argument for "full-cost accounting" in public finance, which starts from the premise that there is one taxpayer, these overseers are able to work from the premise that there is one physical "place" into which all the pieces fit, so it's essential to make sure that all affected parties are brought to the table.

NEW KINDS OF COLLABORATION

Building on early exploratory steps, a whole new way of working on cities is materializing, and all the old arguments about who leads are becoming moot. The hierarchy has flattened as leadership migrates to the team builders and those who can facilitate interactions among groups and people with different kinds of knowledge.

These new teams bring together urban designers, city planners, architects, landscape architects, engineering specialists (civil, municipal, transportation, marine); economists and market specialists in different sectors, including community development; environmental scientists, ecologists, hydrologists; sociologists, community service providers; artists and arts organizations along with local community representatives and municipal leaders. Breakthroughs can and often do emerge from any member of the team. Credit for city-scale design must now be spread broadly, and while this may frustrate the media's desire to fixate on individual "star designers," it's usually misleading to single out one team member. The teams, including clients (the public and private actors who commission the planners and designers), are the ones who should share the credit or the blame. Human nature being what it is, the need for collaboration does create challenges, as egos duel and turf struggles crop up, but driven by necessity, city builders are getting better at managing this.

A clear demonstration of this fusion occurred in the mid-1990s in a project I took on with a consultant team for Lyme Properties, a prominent developer of life science laboratories, in the heart of Cambridge, Massachusetts. The owners wanted to turn a ten-acre brownfield site off Kendall Square (surrounded by the MIT campus, the Charles River and the historic East Cambridge neighbourhood) into a mixed-use community consisting of biotech labs, a four-star hotel, housing and a range of street-related amenities and retail uses. We and Lyme Properties organized a design competition for each of the four blocks within the development plan. As the evolving designs for individual buildings and open spaces bounced off the master plan and each other—colliding, taking cues, influencing and being influenced—the plan took on unexpected layers of richness. Skylit atriums enhanced the interiors of the large floorplate research buildings and flowed seamlessly into streets designed to favour pedestrians with generous sidewalks surrounding public squares that were treated like intimate, outdoor living rooms.

This small city plan was realized not only through the work of many talented designers but also because of an inspired developer-client and the addition of critical city and community inputs. All invested parties came away with something. The enlightened self-interest of the developer ultimately produced a more marketable project: the community received needed amenities (such as useable public space) in return for allowing the developer greater flexibility with its plans.

Teamwork like this demands ongoing and effective dialogue. And this kind of interaction has become easier because of new communications technologies, including "sharing" software that links far-flung teams and allows them to work

154

together in real time. While sitting at my desk in Toronto, I can comfortably work on designs for the Boston University campus with my clients and other members of the project team in Massachusetts and New York. Thanks to this technology, we can each draw our designs on top of the same underlying plans. And new software like Sketchup means we can easily create accurate, three-dimensional digital (and physical) models of streetscapes as they exist and as they would look at eye level once a project was finished.

But sometimes the right parties are not at the table. This happened during an "eleventh-hour" study I did for the Ontario provincial cabinet about the fate of a large, abandoned industrial site on the Toronto waterfront. The Ontario government had expropriated the lands at the urging of the city. The objective was to create a new community of fourteen thousand residents called Ataratiri, in order to alleviate Toronto's pressing subsidized housing crisis. After a huge investment in purchasing and clearing the site, the project failed in large part because the site was flood prone and the contaminated soil needed expensive cleanup. While both of these conditions were known, they had been treated as technical problems that would be solved later. When the costs of dealing with them finally surfaced, it became obvious that they would be prohibitive, though by that time the city and province had altogether already invested more than a billion dollars. My assignment was part of a last-ditch effort to see if the project could be salvaged. I worked with Jim Dobbin (a Canadian environmentalist based in Washington), and we rapidly developed a revised plan shaped by a better understanding of what was happening underground and dealing with the most serious hotspots, including removal of heavy metals and PCBs. Unfortunately, our plan came too late politically; the project was cancelled in 1992 and the land was mothballed for over a decade. The undertaking has now been revived under a new name, the West Don Lands, and it will be the site of the Athletes' Village for the 2015 Pan Am Games. This time, integrated solutions for flood proofing and soil remediation were not left to the end but were critical starting points.

As my own work progressed, I found that I was always working simultaneously in a number of places with different groups of colleagues. It dawned on me that I could be more effective and spend more time working creatively by setting up business on my own but continuing to work in collaborative groups whose personnel varied with each location. So, in 2000, I hung up my shingle as Greenberg Consultants Inc. I was flying solo but in the company of many others who had joined me in forming pickup teams tailored to handle the complex variables inherent in each specific challenging situation.

As I saw in Saint Paul, linear thinking does not match well with organized complexity. Despite this, many professional Requests for Proposals (RFPs) still require consultants to stick to a laborious process that moves sequentially from data gathering to analysis to formulation of options to winnowing of those options and then to the selection of a plan. Far more agile and intuitive, the "iterative" method allows for early hunches and full-blown hypotheses about solving a problem, and these first instincts often have great validity. This method also allows participants to examine issues from many points of view to see how and where plans and revisions fall short. Then they can regroup and reformulate the problem and try again.

This process of kicking the tires repeatedly by pitching ideas and getting all voices in the room to react at once expands the collective "brain" of the team and, in a sense, simulates the complexity of real-world conditions.

Lateral thinking like this can also expose dangers. For instance, in downtown Toronto, a situation has arisen where innovative land use policies in former warehouse districts on both sides of downtown have successfully cultivated a real mix of uses, including many successful small businesses operating in older buildings. In the wake of this success, completely out of left field to those involved in city planning, the city's Finance Department and the Province of Ontario saw an opportunity to increase property tax revenues. Ignoring the value of the actual buildings, they assessed the theoretical value of new condominium towers on the sites of these buildings. (This was an outcome no one wanted and which was imaginable only because of the improvements that these buildings and their tenant businesses had brought to the neighbourhood.) As a result of the tax hike, many of the small businesses are no longer a viable part of the mix—Catch-22. This is the kind of unintended consequence that can be avoided when there's communication between the silos.

I encountered another form of the iterative method in Ottawa. I was working there with a multidisciplinary "Innovation Team" including architects Bruce Kuwabara and Barry Padolsky, landscape architect Greg Smallenberg and representatives of a number of other disciplines to prepare a community design plan for the redevelopment of the 310-acre former Canadian Forces Base (CFB) Rockcliffe on the Ottawa River. With the goal of making this site a showcase sustainable community, our team fell into a working method whereby all

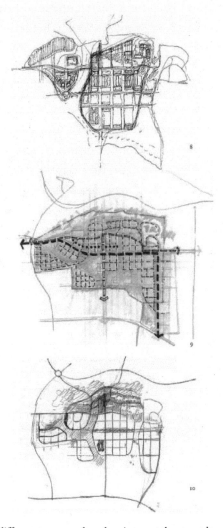

Iterations: different team members drawing over the same plan to shape a new community on the former Rockcliffe Military Base in Ottawa.

team members would take their turns redrawing the same basic neighbourhood plan from their individual professional vantage points: urban form, transportation, habitat corridors, hydrology, economics and so on. Each time the plan was redrawn, it evolved to reflect a particular set of priorities or imperatives. By allowing it to morph continuously (and awkwardly) through these iterations, we arrived at a point of balance that could not otherwise have been foreseen and which no one team member could have drawn alone, even with inputs from the others. Through this nonlinear and nonhierarchical progression, the best ideas often emerge.

In sketches by different members of the team, there emerged the notion of a "hilltown" at the north end of the site as the rectilinear grid of streets began to defer to the folds and flats of the topography. An east-west "high street" came into focus as a retail spine, centred on a new market square. More fluid lines shaped the greenways, creating public promenades that lassoed the emerging neighbourhoods. In a sense, this iterative method simulates the longer, slower process of organic growth that shaped our cities when the variety of influences on the process were fewer and material limitations ensured greater coherence. When I was in Saint Paul, one of the mayor's then advisors, Dick Broeker, said to me, "Beauty is born ugly" (or, I might paraphrase, awkwardly). More often than not, it's true.

A NEW TOOL KIT

Even as we experience a major move back toward the city, we still face a critical disconnect between the quality of life we say we want and the means we have to achieve it. Stuck with some combination of zoning codes originally designed to do exactly the opposite of what we now intend, we find our desires and our means to be at cross-purposes. It's like trying to use a hammer to turn a screw. An early-twentieth-century concept, zoning is by nature defensive. It does not describe desirable activities, but generally defines what is allowed in a particular "zone" by identifying everything that is prohibited or forbidden using impenetrable language like this:

> "the following uses shall be permitted within a CR district
> . . . .those residential uses permitted within a CR district
> in section 8(1)(f)(a), and subject to the qualifications in
> section 8(2), provided that those non-residential uses
> permitted within a CR district in section 8(1)(f)(b), and
> subject to the qualifications in section 8(2) where appli-
> cable, except for an automobile service and repair shop,
> cold storage locker plant or commercial parking lot."

This verbal torture is a little like a quiz show on which the panellists have to guess the identity of the mystery guest through a process of elimination. Unfortunately, it's almost impossible to arrive at a good place for cities by just preventing bad things from happening. Further, it's obvious that this kind of obscure and pedantic language is written by lawyers for lawyers, not mere mortals. (In writing the zoning bylaw for the Lower Don Lands in Toronto, when we were forced to use this language, we also prepared an "annotated version" complete with a running commentary in simple English to explain what these inscrutable interdictions actually meant.)

Likewise, post-war transportation manuals were designed specifically to facilitate the rapid and unencumbered movement of vehicles between zones, not necessarily to promote accessibility or enhance the quality of the travel experience. And our building codes and fire safety standards were premised largely on new construction, not the adaptive reuse of older building stock. Taken together, these tools and the practices that surrounded them were a recipe for the step-by-step demolition and replacement of the historic city.

Another unstated assumption behind these guidelines and documents was that at some point the plan (or the urban district) would be finished. By creating a hard-and-fast set of rules, we bought into an illusion that we could make planning into an objective administrative function: new developments would either comply or they would not. Of course, the rigid analytical categories and the static nature of the formulas do not hold up well when idiosyncratic circumstances, dynamic market forces, changing programs and new needs come into play. When the public interest is clearly not being served by the old rules of separation, which are in many cases at the core of these ordinances, we should apply "sunset provisions" to them and get rid of those rules that are no longer useful.

In the 1970s, as I noted earlier, I had worked on the detailed regulatory framework for the two hundred acres of former railway lands between the waterfront and downtown Toronto. The land use provisions for this bold and ambitious plan for future development (a successor to the 1960s project that resulted only in the construction of the CN Tower) were based on the unquestioned assumption of the

landowners—the real-estate arms of Canadian National
Railways and Canadian Pacific Railway—that development
in the area would be driven by the office sector. Two decades
later, when development really got underway, the office
market had virtually collapsed and the actual driver for
new construction had become a strong demand for downtown housing. Ultimately, those land use provisions in
the regulatory framework had to be dramatically revised.
Years later, working with CBT Architects in Cambridge,
Massachusetts, on a plan for an area known as NorthPoint,
I saw first-hand how a more flexible approach could benefit
the city-building process. The goal of this project was to
create an attractive, mixed-use neighbourhood on another
former rail yard, drawing a significant number of jobs and
residents. Employers in the "knowledge" economy actually
prefer to locate in lived-in neighbourhoods that offer their
employees places to live and to have lunch—and things to
do after hours—rather setting up business in protected
"employment districts."

Working with the Cambridge Planning Board, our
planning and design team created a radically simplified and
illustrated one-page statement of design objectives for each
city block within our new master plan. Seeking to create
room for desirable flexibility in both form and use, the plan
specified the amount of floorspace permitted within a
three-dimensional building envelope, as well as footprints,
heights, places where buildings needed to be set back from
the property line and places where buildings needed to
come to the sidewalk. It also detailed a range of desired
uses that could mix and overlap based on evolving needs
and outlined how a particular block should relate to its

surroundings (including where entrances would be located). And it described the quality of life at street level, as well as identifying important views and vistas. Local conditions like microclimate and anticipated relationships to adjoining buildings had been studied, and the implications for form and function were carefully considered. But for all these guidelines, the plan left a great deal of latitude for their interpretation and for responding to changing market conditions within the loosely defined *envelopes*, or *volumes*, rather than within prescriptive zoning regulations. Such flexible envelopes give developers greater latitude in the ways they propose to meet their own goals—as well as addressing public objectives for the neighbourhood such as the animation of new public space—but they require regulators to use more discretion than they would if they were following the cut-and-dried formulas of conventional zoning. In one area of our NorthPoint plan, four architectural teams were selected to compete on a very challenging site requiring a vertical pedestrian connection from a viaduct that once traversed an adjacent rail yard, to the redeveloped land below, now becoming a new neighbourhood. Taking full advantage of the greater flexibility in the envelope and guidelines for shaping the building, each team came up with a very different, highly creative solution.

Not making all the decisions at once about a new development can be deeply disconcerting to planners and neighbourhood groups who seek protection from change and secure property values. We also have a legal system with litigious reflexes directly connected to these rules and practices tending to overspecify permitted uses, and the precise size and shape of buildings. Even when it seems intuitively right, any change can be threatening. Within administrative silos there is also typically a reluctance to surrender predictability and control. The individual actors, each for their own reasons, often hold on strenuously to the notion of planning by recipe but each in isolation. They may see themselves as having little choice, a feeling exacerbated by a deeper malfunction in the way cities allocate authority and resources in mutually exclusive compartments: city planners whose charge is land use may rely too much on zoning that allocates exactly what mix of uses will occur and where; urban designers wishing to influence outcomes come up with physical-design guidelines that are so detailed that little is left for architects to do but fill in the blanks on the facades; and engineers trying to size the pipes most efficiently make unrealistic demands for determining in advance exactly what uses and densities will go in which blocks so the number of toilets flushing at peak times can be calculated.

While these quantifiable relationships are important (for example, planning for a transit network requires that it be supported by a reasonable level of users and trips), there are limitations to the reliability of these calculations. Obviously, too great a level of precision quickly becomes illusory. Life takes over and trumps the expectations on which the overly rigid plan was based, and planners—or the city trying to live with the results of their plans—have little to fall back on.

When Barbara Hall became mayor of Toronto in 1994, she did what many newly elected politicians do and reached out for innovative ideas. I contributed some thoughts about how to use some of Toronto's unique assets to greater advantage— our talent pool in emerging creative industries, our legacy as a relatively safe and open city, and in particular the tremendous stock of underutilized industrial and warehouse buildings in the downtown core. I ended up working with a small group convened by the mayor that included Jane Jacobs, economist Gary Stamm, developer Bob Eisenberg and the city's then chief planner, Paul Bedford. The idea was to put one of Jane Jacob's seminal concepts into practice—to let change of use occur freely and organically without all the stifling constraints of traditional land use zoning.

We zeroed in on four hundred acres of formerly industrial areas on the east and west shoulders of downtown—The King-Spadina and King-Parliament Districts—dubbed "the Kings." These once-thriving manufacturing zones had declined in the 1970s, a process that accelerated in the 1980s and early 1990s as manufacturing migrated offshore or to the suburbs. Zoning permitted only industrial uses, but vacancies were increasing and property owners began to demolish buildings of irreplaceable heritage value to lower their property taxes. Parking lots by the dozen had appeared in their place.

Based on our recommendations, the city decided to strip away the long-standing zoning prohibitions that were blocking conversion of properties in the Kings to new uses. Big ideas don't always require significant outlays of money, and this act of deregulation was a case of simply giving free rein to pent-up forces for change. By abandoning the area's inflexible industrial planning policies, the city sparked mixed-use reinvestment that retained much of the heritage character of the areas' architecture, added new construction on vacant sites, enhanced public spaces (including a set of neglected nineteenth-century public squares), created jobs and encouraged a synergy between employment and residential uses by allowing people to live much closer to their workplaces. The new simplified planning approach included these principles: as-of-right (that is, without requiring any zoning changes) development, with maximum flexibility in land use for new buildings and conversions to almost any use; the removal of density restrictions in favour of envelopes specifying building height and some pushing back of the upper floors to protect privacy and access to sunlight and view; and the relaxation of parking and loading requirements for new buildings, with exemptions for existing and heritage buildings. Consultations with landowners, who saw impediments to their business needs removed, and with the surrounding communities both produced broad support. The radical change was received as common sense. The only initial resistance came from some city planning staff; however, planning and zoning amendments to implement the new approach were put in place barely eight months later, in 1996. On balance, this experiment in deregulation has been an extraordinary success and a stunning demonstration of how market-driven recycling of valuable building stock can produce a rich blend of old and new housing and commercial properties, combined with some entertainment enterprises and some residual design and manufacturing (in the fashion industry).

For more than a decade now, adaptive reuse and new construction have been turning these two areas that had been virtually uninhabited for over a century into vibrant neighbourhoods with tens of thousands of new residents. Employment activity in both areas has increased at a rate that has dramatically outpaced citywide growth, and many new jobs have been generated in media, business services and computer services. The fact that job creation has been so effective in this mixed-use setting casts doubts on attempts to preserve exclusive "employment lands," a designation that is still applied to vast acres of vacant sites and unoccupied buildings. Total taxable assessment had already jumped by over 28 percent (approximately $400 million) between 1998 and 2002 and has continued to climb rapidly. Among the many collateral benefits is the fact that the Kings, with their proximity to downtown, have the highest ratios of walking and cycling to work of any neigbourhood in the city, as is evident in the heavy morning and evening pedestrian traffic on local sidewalks.

My wife, Eti, and I were among the first to move into a beautiful new building on Niagara Street in the redeveloping King-Spadina District. We were married on our new rooftop. When we first arrived, the streets were deserted and we were surrounded by parking lots. But it has been incredibly satisfying to see this former industrial area come back to life so brilliantly as the pulse of daily activity grows stronger year by year. New buildings, new neighbours and new businesses are filling in all the voids around us.

Deregulation, of course, dealt with only the private side of development. Recognizing that improvements were needed to prepare these former industrial districts for new businesses and residents, city council also adopted Community Improvement Plans for both areas. These plans focused on enhancing heritage character, parks and sidewalks, and in particular on finding ways to break down the extra-large superblocks in the Kings (which had served the needs of industry) with a finer-grained, pedestrian-oriented network of streets. Prepared by city staff with community input, the plans provided a basis for negotiations with developers to make needed improvements to the public realm incrementally (including street lighting, pedestrian crossings, sidewalks, boulevards, parks and open spaces). And to make this plan truly successful, as the population expands, the city will need to make upgrades to the "soft" infrastructure of community services, such as daycares, playgrounds and schools.

The Kings experience has been an overwhelming success, but it has also provided some important lessons. While the level of private sector activity has been remarkable, the public side of the effort, including work on public spaces, has been under-funded, giving rise to considerable frustration. Architectural success has also been mixed. Through a combination of active community and political involvement and enlightened developers, excellent new residential buildings have been created in some areas. But because of restrictive provincial planning legislation, the city itself is still hamstrung in its ability to consistently demand quality of design and contextual fit.

Not all mix is good and not in all proportions. One major land use challenge has arisen, for instance, because of conflicting policies in the King-Spadina area. Although the new policies encouraged residential use, old policies of segregated land use designated the area an "entertainment district." This inadvertently encouraged the rowdy, industrial-strength, late-night club scene mentioned earlier. More than fifty thousand young people, many coming in from the suburbs, have ended up congregating for several nights a week inside a few city blocks, with outbreaks of violence at closing time and widespread drug use. The problem stemmed from the hyper-concentration of this use in a relatively confined zone, and the ill-conceived and toxic mix has new residents struggling

168

to protect their fledgling neighbourhood. The built-in conflict has proven very difficult to defuse, but over time, due to increased redevelopment activity and their own changing economics, a number of the larger clubs have closed or changed their formats to other forms of entertainment aimed more at local residents, including a sophisticated new bowling alley. In the interim, residents and the local councillor are applying pressure to refuse licence renewals as redevelopment continues. In hindsight, this particular use should have been limited through strategic zoning provisions to reduce the number of licences in a given area, and it should have been dispersed to more manageably serve the nightclubs' tens of thousand of patrons.

We learned another lesson from the Kings redevelopment. In order to allow room for maximum design creativity, we prescribed no density (specific amount of floor area) for each building envelope. But we didn't predict that in a highly speculative land market, developers would exploit this flexibility in a way that was completely at odds with the spirit of the planning approach. They chose to fill the entire "flexible" envelope with floor space, without setbacks or courtyards, occupying every square inch of their sites to the borders and to the maximum square footage allowed, as if doing so were an entitlement. They then applied for additional zoning changes because their buildings were unworkable. This, too, could have been remedied with some limits on the amount of development that would be allowed within the envelopes.

Although limits need to be clear, it is also still important to supplement these with descriptive and sometimes non-quantifiable design guidelines to be interpreted by qualified staff or peer-review panels and to reduce the elements in a plan that are dealt with through hard-and-fast statutory zoning. This gives developers the right mix of clarity and latitude. In fact, part of the exercise of reform has been to change the very rulebooks that dictate planning policies and standards (and the funding formulas based on them), rather than fighting the zoning battles case by case.

169

"Performance zoning" is another way to set targets that may be mandatory but do allow for different approaches. This approach to zoning can be used to define a desirable microclimate in public spaces by specifying hours of sunlight and desirable wind levels for pedestrian comfort for different kinds of activities—sitting, walking, eating at a café—based not only on wind velocities but also on frequency and persistence. Performance zoning can also be employed to identify and establish a range of required public amenities, locations for retail street frontage or the need for a reasonable mix of housing options and a percentage of affordable housing. Some of these performance criteria may be more measurable and precise and some more qualitative, requiring interpretation.

In a parallel effort, enlightened members of the engineering profession have devoted considerable effort to modifying basic traffic engineering manuals in North America to make them more responsive to the presence of pedestrians, cyclists and transit vehicles.

SERIAL CREATIONS

Great plans create an open-ended invitation to which other things can gravitate. In some ways the city resembles jazz: its overall plan is the rhythm section, which provides the context and springboard for improvised solos. Unlike classical music scores with fully worked out orchestration, jazz and open-ended plans elicit and invite unforeseen responses. There is always a place for both the pervasive rhythm of high-quality "background" buildings, which provide the majority of the city's themes, and the solo spots, the exclamation points—the special buildings whose sites and programs merit a unique treatment. The common starting point has to be the shared culture of the city, an awareness of the adjacent properties and neighbourhoods, a generous extroversion toward public spaces and a commitment to including expressive edges, not blank or sterile enclosures.

Cities with well-established structures like Barcelona, Paris, London, Berlin, New York, Chicago and Copenhagen share an appetite for opening up new opportunities within those structures through bold and innovative design. Thanks to signature efforts like Paris's *grands projets*, Copenhagen's return to its harbour, Berlin's rebuilding of the Potsdamer Platz and New York's High Line, these cities have become known for their capacity to attract city-building talent to build on the rich urban layers created by previous generations. And when one talented designer or group of designers leaves, it's critical to pass the baton on to others who celebrate the city by heightening its qualities, not erasing them. That level of inspiration doesn't just flow automatically out of city-planning diagrams.

Recently, there has been a revived interest in design competitions as a way of attracting the talent that can keep the creative momentum going. They range from "ideas" competitions held at an early stage to more definitive design competitions for actual projects after the basic parameters and program have been set. It is important to be clear about what competitions can and cannot do. They are not a panacea and should not be seen as a way to circumvent or pre-empt the need for meaningful community engagement and dialogue; in fact, they can enrich that process. Fortunately, many cities are using competitions rooted in solid urban design and planning as a way of finding the most imaginative solutions for infill and revitalization, engaging the public, calling attention to important opportunities for change and reinvention, and promoting city design as a vital part of the larger urban culture.

V

CITIES PERPETUALLY RE-INVENT THEMSELVES

In the nineteenth century, the big city-shaping forces tended to be centripetal—pulling life into the centre of major urban areas as commerce and industry expanded. A wave of canal construction joined industrial port cities to inland cities; later, with the advent of rail, great central railway stations became national and international hubs. Their marshalling yards were often located in low-lying areas near water and their construction expanded port districts while becoming magnets for new commercial activity. By contrast, the big drivers of the twentieth century were centrifugal, made up of a combination of flight and dispersal, and after World War II, the spread of interstate highways in the U.S. and similar highway-building programs in other countries propelled the suburban explosion. The push outward swallowed up large areas of rural farmland and left gaping holes in its wake, diluting the vitality of cities. Today's big, city-shaping forces are again consolidating ones, but they are operating in response to very different and accelerated pressures. These interrelated phenomena create serious challenges but also offer important opportunities for resetting the urban agenda. Rising energy costs are one reshaping force. Pressure from this economic driver is still being felt unevenly as oil prices fluctuate, and cities like Copenhagen or Portland are responding through city-building efforts faster than others. But on the whole, urban centres are finding ways to house more people in less space, with more mixed uses. We are finding ways to shorten our commutes and live in smaller spaces in more compact, transit-oriented and walkable communities. Convenience is trumping size. This shift will allow us to own fewer and smaller vehicles, to make use of alternatives to ownership like car sharing and also to rely on walking, transit and cycling to a much greater degree. Many older neighbourhoods and downtowns are becoming denser, and many of the former port lands and rail yards are being transformed into new neighbourhoods as developers respond to the demand. And access to public transit has become a major factor in the price of real estate.

Meanwhile, turmoil and major shifts in the world economy are being experienced directly in cities with the rise and fall of individual sectors. As the manufacturing base shrank in North America, there has been growth in the knowledge-based and service sectors, and arts and culture have taken on an expanded role. This "creative economy" has reinforced the centripetal pull, as it has increased the need for face-to-face contact and location decisions based on quality of life. And contributing to that quality of life, cultural venues and institutions like Millennium Park in Chicago, Fort Mason Center in San Francisco, and Harbourfront Centre and the Distillery District in Toronto, along with cultural entrepreneurs and not-for-profit "cultural" development organizations, have emerged not only as major attractions but as significant economic catalysts and contributors to job creation in downtown areas.

Market forces are dynamic and evolving. According to analysts like Jeff Rubin (author of *Why Your World Is About to Get a Whole Lot Smaller*), rising transportation costs (driven by rising energy costs) will outpace labour costs and as a result local manufacturing will re-emerge. If this happens, the drivers of the centripetal shift could expand well beyond the creative and service sectors, and cities would need to hitch their economic development strategies to new economic sectors and to the sustainability agenda as they cultivate new jobs. To grow these new "green" sectors means providing the spaces and relationships for them to prosper, including connections between where people live and work. This type of initiative has already been launched in Boston and Cambridge, in collaboration with the Massachusetts state government. The major universities, health-care institutions and life-science research clusters that circle the downtown core will eventually be joined by an "Urban Ring" for transportation, evolving from buses to fixed rail with underground segments intersecting with all the historical radial lines of the "T" (Boston's subway network).

Current forces for change also have powerful demographic dimensions. In many parts of the developed industrialized world these are taking the forms of a low birth rate and an aging population, along with global migration and the absorption of immigrants and refugees. This migration has provided a needed labour force and re-balancing of the population, but it has also presented a major challenge in providing the necessary social services and support networks. During the decades when city centres were devalued, they were often home to concentrations of new immigrants and people on low incomes. In the early stages of the return to the city, these areas also provided opportunities for new renters and young, first-time buyers to find reasonably priced accommodation. But as the competition for these older neighbourhoods has increased, many lower-income residents have been pushed out. Such are the strains of gentrification. In 2007, David Hulchanski of the Cities Centre at the University of Toronto produced a study entitled *The Three Cities within Toronto: Income Polarization among Toronto Neighbourhoods, 1970–2000.* His research painted a disturbing picture. It revealed demographic patterns that reflected Toronto's accelerating division into three separate cities: a growing area of poverty (housing a large population of recent immigrants) in the post-war suburbs, a growing high-income enclave in the city centre and a shrinking middle class in between that is being forced out to the farthest suburban fringe. These findings point to a major social equity issue. As populations increase in the downtown core, a mix of housing options needs to be provided through a combination of publicly funded programs and techniques like inclusive zoning, which require the development industry to provide a mix of units for different income levels through access to government programs or internal cross subsidies.

Better choices also need to be provided for young families. In the prevailing pattern, young households have often been choosing, or have been compelled by economics, to live in the suburbs or in much smaller centres. This raises the question of how we can make affordable new urban places where families can live while still preserving essential housing stock for lower-income groups.

In many respects, earlier incarnations of the city had the very qualities that we're seeking for urban centres today. They were constructed in a pre–World War II, pre-automobile era and were of necessity more mixed and dense and less energy consumptive. Recycling these districts and structures makes it economically possible to create new developments because the infrastructure is already partly paid for. The former warehouse districts in many North American cities fall into this category—including LoDo (Lower Downtown Historic District) in Denver, the Fort Point Channel District in Boston, Chelsea, Soho and DUMBO (short for Down Under the Manhattan Bridge Overpass) in New York City and Lowertown in Saint Paul. As Jane Jacobs has observed, these older buildings are ideal places for innovation, experimentation and the incubation of new enterprises in old structures.

But anything can be grist for the mill. Even some of the harsh, modernist interventions of urban renewal that were threatening and awkward when introduced have gradually been absorbed now that they are not being replicated. Take the cluster of office towers in the heart of the financial district in Toronto, for example. These buildings displaced some fine historic structures, creating empty, wind-swept plazas and relegating retail uses to basement level. However, now that this area is an isolated exception and no longer a template for further erosion of the surrounding urban fabric, so the individual towers and their plazas, designed by renowned architects like Mies Van der Rohe and I.M. Pei, can be appreciated as elegant exceptions in a heterogeneous fabric. They have also become a platform for city-building interventions as they are surgically altered to contribute to a more lively downtown. Other famous icons of the urban renewal era like Constitution Plaza in Hartford and the Prudential Center complex in Boston have been significantly modified with street-level additions, such as new retail flanking the adjacent sidewalks. They've been reintegrated with their surroundings with varying degrees of economic and planning success depending on the strength of the local economy and what is happening around them.

It's not just the significant individual structures that have value; it's also their arrangements and the in-between places those arrangements form. The original land surveys, the underlying patterns of streets and blocks, along with the urban fabric that has grown up on them provide the long-lived "bones" on which the city continually rebuilds. New places materialize from existing ones as new elements are added and hybridization occurs. In the heart of New York's Financial District, for example, there's an intricate colonial street network (the legacy of Dutch "New Amsterdam") with a large number of older office buildings that had become less desirable for contemporary office use. But they had high ceilings and interesting architecture and made great apartments—and a new residential neighbourhood has emerged there over the past few decades. A similar phenomenon has occurred in Boston's historic Financial District within its fine-grained, pre-gridiron street pattern. And when Tokyo was rebuilt after World War II, the city retained much of its prewar small land ownership and narrow streets, producing new neighbourhoods of remarkable intimacy and human scale within the world's largest city.

The city is replete with these traces and palimpsests that can be exploited to preserve important cultural memories. And each city has such a distinctive set of physical traces and patterns that contribute to its particular *genius loci*.

180

It's now clearly North America's turn. As its much younger cities grow more dense, a broad range of city-building responses is required to make sure that intensification makes the best possible use of pre-existing resources. These come in many forms—from infilling one underused property at a time to the surgical retrofitting of entire neighbourhoods and districts that have inherent cultural, social and economic value; from finding systematically underdeveloped soft spots where density could be increased without disrupting a neighbourhood dynamic that already works to wholesale recycling of large obsolescent tracts of former industrial lands. Toronto, for instance, has many traditional one- and two-storey main streets—portions of King, Queen, Dundas and Bloor Streets—that could easily handle more substantial street walls of six to eight storeys. San Francisco's Mission Bay is a prime example of inserting an entire new neighbourhood into an underutilized portion of the city fabric on the edge of downtown. Or, at a finer grain, Vancouver has approved both rental laneway housing and "suites within suites" (that is, the ability to add new units by subdividing larger existing dwellings) throughout the city.

In tackling the transforming forces of our era, we need to identify the momentum that is already in play—the projects and plans, the aspirations, the big moves and small. As in the martial arts, where the objective is to capitalize on an opponent's momentum rather than confronting his or her energy head on, in city building we employ a kind of "urban judo" to marshal the latent or misdirected forces. We often see a foreshadowing of impending changes in the *version sauvage* of a new phenomenon. Fresh ideas or tentative first steps appear in unclaimed or relatively cheap and adaptable spaces, where people can improvise and test them before programs, policies or official sanction are put in place. Long before the ideas of mixed use and converting unused space in older buildings gained credence, there were widespread illegal loft conversions in warehouse districts. In many cities, cyclists forced a reallocation of the road surface on city streets by making motorists acknowledge their presence long before bicycle lanes were painted or built. In the postwar suburban areas of many cities, start-up businesses serving newly arrived immigrant communities surface not in the more formal and controlled shopping malls but in the run-down strip plazas or industrial buildings. These creative adaptations of the old point the way to the new. As uses serving a particular market or need appear on the horizon, they often point the way to desirable changes that can be supported and nurtured.

As these indicators for change present themselves, so does the opportunity to expand or reconsider the use and purpose of existing urban assets. The need to replace aging transportation infrastructure, for instance, provides the perfect opportunity to change the role of streets from just accommodating cars to building in more room for pedestrians and cyclists. New regulations like those limiting energy consumption or managing waste create major opportunities for innovation if they are treated as a chance to move from minimum compliance to aspirational change.

The spontaneous incubation of businesses for new immigrant communities that used to occur in the old market districts now happens in the suburban strip mall.

By adopting the toughest environmental standards, Germany and the Scandinavian countries encouraged the creation of domestic industries and consulting firms in recycling and alternative energy sources like solar and wind power, and these enterprises have been able to export their experience and talents worldwide. Flood proofing can provide the occasion to create new parks and naturalized areas, piggybacking city-building efforts on the functional need to reserve undeveloped areas to absorb spring runoff and heavy rainfall. Soil cleanup of contaminated lands results in salvaging many useful by-products, including minerals and clean soil that can be reused. Crisis or a sense of urgency can be the crucible that enables change that would otherwise be impossible.

Different kinds of change follow different time frames. For dynamic uses like retailing, adjustments to consumer preferences have to occur very quickly. Shifting patterns in residential and employment have a slower rhythm and greater inertia, since the choice of a dwelling or an office involves a greater commitment. Needless to say, when planning for the long term, it is important to get the foundation right. The width of streets, the depth of blocks, the floor-to-ceiling height and available space of ground floors—these parameters set the basic constraints and opportunities. Having spaces that are more generous and adaptable, not built to minimum standards and dimensions, is essential for a building's longevity. When we look for the places that absorb change best, warehouse districts and older neighbourhoods score well. Their buildings tend to have robust, open structures with simple floor plans that can be easily retrofitted to serve other purposes. Their components—stairs and elevator shafts, the layout of internal walls and corridors, heating, cooling, power, room sizes and configurations—are malleable, unlike "solid state," disposable buildings, custom designed to serve only the businesses that built them. The structures built for fast-food chains and big box outlets fall into this category, as they have little to salvage or reuse.

184

Accepting the inevitability of change, a city builder's challenge is to deliberately build this flexibility into the contemporary city, creating new buildings (and neighbourhoods) with the capacity to adapt and evolve. Our home is in a building designed by architectsAlliance, which sought inspiration, in part, from the structural simplicity and more generous dimensions of these older, adaptively reused structures. In the twelve years since it was built, many adaptations have already occurred, including units combined and divided and the rooftop addition where I have my office. In some cases there are identifiable patterns of succession, such as the rediscovery of neglected older neighbourhoods by "pioneers" (often artists seeking cheaper living and studio space). The districts then become popular, causing rents and prices to rise and putting pressure on lower-income residents and the sorts of pioneers who initiated the revival in the first place. Anticipating and recognizing this kind of pattern, we need to build in ways to protect portions of the existing housing stock from this disruptive escalation, which pushes low-income residents out of the city. For instance, a pool of protected units can be created by removing them from the private market and turning them into co-ops or designated affordable housing.

Similarly, it is critical to build new neighbourhoods for a full life cycle so that residents can age in place. A new subdivision made up entirely of identical units of a similar size and layout that is targeted only at young families who all move in at once produces an inevitable problem of schools that are too small, requiring portables to accommodate the bulge in student population. Then the schools become too big as the bulge begins to graduate, and then they stand empty when the school district becomes a neighbourhood of empty nesters. The antidote is found in areas like the St. Lawrence Neighbourhood in Toronto, which is designed to self-renew, with a mix of unit types and living options serving a broad demographic.

But the direction that succession like this will take in cities is not always obvious. So it's important to have many horses in the race at any given time. In cities, as in business or science, experimentation by trial and error is a critical part of innovation. It is important that there be some spaces, sources of financing and technical support that allow for the incubation of new ideas. Because of their general aversion to risk taking, financial institutions and lenders are often not amenable to such arrangements. They usually prefer to replicate past patterns and successes than to open up future possibilities.

This is the kind of short-term thinking that often causes the development industry to exhibit herd behaviour and focus only on one "product type" at a time, like commercial over residential in one decade and the opposite in the next, or an exclusive focus on small residential units for first-time purchasers or renters followed by a run on large units for empty nesters. Eventually, each of these swings produces a saturated market and a glut, so there are times when the city has to step in.

In the 1970s, the development industry in many North American cities wanted to build offices only in downtown locations. That's when Toronto's countercyclical Central Area

Plan I discussed in Chapter IV was introduced. It promoted an increase in the downtown residential presence by allowing developers to make full use of their allotted density only if residential units were part of the mix. Today, in the midst of a residential condo boom, the opposite is true and many North American cities need to ensure that employment is added to the mix.

DOING MORE WITH LESS

Because land in cities is limited—and valuable—there is a built-in incentive to seek city-building solutions that overlap in time and space, doing multiple things with great economy of means—the very essence of sustainability and urbanity.

In many cities, streets and rooftops are being transformed to expand "urban forests." By substantially increasing the tree cover and vegetative canopy in this way, CO_2 emissions are reduced, climate is tempered and air quality is improved, quite apart from the obvious aesthetic pleasure that people derive from the additional trees and greenery. In May 2009, the City of Toronto adopted a mandatory green roof bylaw, requiring green roofs on all new commercial, multi-family and industrial development above certain sizes. With a single bylaw change, the very footprints that buildings occupy will help enlarge the city's lungs.

Buildings account for almost half all CO_2 emissions, and it's easier for cities to reduce the energy consumption in these structures than in low, sprawling developments. By virtue of sheer proximity and numbers, living in mid-rise and high-rise buildings that share walls, floors and ceilings with neighbours, we consume less energy; we heat less and cool less, as David Owen argues in his book *Green Metropolis* (2009). He shows that New York City residents have a per capita environmental footprint that by almost all measures is a fraction of the national average. New York's many tall buildings help. By extension, it becomes economical to share locally generated energy within city districts, and, increasingly, this energy can be supplied by emerging technologies like geothermal and co-generation (which captures heat as a useful byproduct of electricity production).

We also tend to live in less space in denser downtowns because so much is at our fingertips just outside our homes. We don't need bowling-alley-sized rooms or home entertainment centres when we can share recreation and entertainment spaces and meet friends in numerous theatres, convenient and attractive public spaces or neighbourhood pubs and cafés. All of this contributes without special effort to a lower carbon footprint (the commonly used measure of the greenhouse gas emissions we cause directly and indirectly).

While the first attempts to measure sustainability focused on the performance of individual buildings, it quickly became apparent that context mattered. The greatest reductions in carbon output could be realized by lower-impact lifestyles made possible in city neighbourhoods and urban districts. The now widely used LEED (Leadership in Energy and Environmental Design) standards, a rating system for environmentally sustainable construction first formulated by the U.S. Green Building Council, took this into account in 2009. These LEED standards were then expanded to include LEED for Neighbourhood Development standards, which recognize

188 the greater mix and proximity of day-to-day activities measured by walkability, cycling friendliness, transit availability and reduced auto dependency. These LEED-ND standards also take into account technological advances like combined district energy services, greater use of alternative energy sources, improved waste management and treatment, and new approaches to stormwater and wastewater management.

Reduction and recycling of waste are also inherently more feasible in dense cities, where the combination of volume and proximity boosts the ability to separate streams and recapture valuable components closer to home. While previously relying on exporting to landfills, most cities facing the enormous pressure to deal with their waste locally are changing their practices by developing integrated strategies to cut down on volume through more effective sorting, recycling and disposal. In Australia, for instance, of the total waste produced in 2002/03, a good percentage was recycled: 30 percent of municipal waste, 45 percent of commercial and industrial waste and 57 percent of construction and demolition waste. The water cycle is another area where compactness gives cities an edge. Wasteful water-use practices have now come under fire—including using potable water for all purposes, creating large quantities of impervious surface in the form of roads and parking lots, and directing all surface runoff into storm sewers. New urban neighbourhoods are employing techniques for the management of stormwater—retaining and slowly releasing it, creating more pervious surfaces to get more water back into the water table, and collecting and using rainwater for nonpotable uses. Treated water is a scarce and valuable resource, and various cities are demonstrating their ability to reduce consumption by recycling and capturing "grey water" (non-sewage household waste water) for second uses like irrigation. Many of these practices are most practical in dense cites where economies of scale can be realized.

Perhaps one of the most surprising changes we are witnessing is the growing capacity of dense cities and their hinterlands to become their own partial sources of food. With rising costs of transportation, importing agricultural products from long distances becomes less and less feasible. Cities are adapting, putting local producers in touch with innovative and reasonably priced distribution networks. In Toronto, for instance, companies like Front Door Organics provide a key link between regional producers and city residents. Seasonal farmers' markets are rapidly springing up again in neighbourhoods and city centres throughout North America and on other continents. Urban agriculture—from small urban farms on vacant and underutilized lots to allotment gardens to rooftops and apartment balconies—demonstrates yet again the innate ability of cities to adapt. Detroit, taking advantage of its vast areas of underutilized vacant sites has become a leader in producing food on urban farm plots within city limits. What is new here is the increase in intensity and the way all of these practices are emerging or reappearing as integrated efforts in urban neighbourhoods.

The sense of crisis and urgency is helping to liberate us from old strictures, and cities are actively learning from each other as they specialize and leapfrog ahead. Examples abound, but here are just a few: the Vauban District in Freiburg, Germany, where a derelict military zone has become a Sustainable Model City District; Viikki, a model sustainable neighbourhood a few kilometres from downtown Helsinki, Finland; a former docklands "Boo1" site in Malmö, Sweden, which has been designated as an ecological quarter with strict environmental codes for developers; and Dockside Green in Victoria, British Columbia, where residents have moved into a new community in a former industrial wasteland now built around a generous central greenway that processes stormwater. The greatest value of leading-edge projects like these is their ability to reshape norms and expectations, providing an important roadmap to broader systemic changes.

Another significant step has been taken in Vancouver, British Columbia, on the site of the Olympic Village in Southeast False Creek. A model sustainable community has been built there on the last remaining large tract of undeveloped waterfront land near downtown. When Vancouver was awarded the 2010 Olympic and Paralympic Winter Games, this prime development site of eighty acres was chosen as the location of the Olympic Village. It was seen as an opportunity to showcase the integration of the core principles of sustainability with a focus on mixed use and housing for families. In the resulting community of up to sixteen thousand people, goods and services are within walking distance and housing is linked to local jobs by transit. The streets are extremely tight (twelve to thirteen metres wide—much less than the norm, which is almost double that). They are also pedestrian oriented and some are curbless (like a new generation of streets in the Netherlands, where, ironically, better eye contact is made between vehicles and pedestrians because there are no sidewalks, so pedestrians must look at drivers and vice versa to ensure safety). And contrary to Vancouver's traditional reliance on high-rise towers, the community will feature a midrise fabric with courtyards and high-ceilinged ground floors that will help integrate retail at street level. Fifty percent of the building tops across the entire village are covered by green roofs. The village is also a LEED-ND pilot project that has achieved Platinum status.

These advances in sustainable design have gone hand in hand with provisions for on-site agriculture and requirements for social housing and affordability. Twenty percent of the units have been targeted for nonmarket social housing, with another 11 percent being rental in the modest market afford-ability range. There is also a new sea wall, and a community centre and public square that opens directly on the water, incorporating significant public art. The village and the larger area surrounding it is heated and cooled through a neighbour-hood energy utility that uses heat recovery from sewage. This is Vancouver's first significant foray into district energy, and similar facilities (also using complementary technologies like biomass) are already being replicated in planning for other large sites across the city.

Many of the village's other design innovations are caus-ing changes to the regulatory system in order to allow for features like exterior hallways and stairs, thru-units with opening windows front and back to permit natural ventila-tion, passive solar shading, walls insulated to a higher stand-ard and height exemptions to allow for solar or green roofs. And these regulatory changes are resulting in an innovation model for influencing changes to the zoning system city-wide. The Olympics-driven timing created the opportunity to force a much more integrated approach to approvals. And as a result, the important legacy of the village is a new way of doing business for the rest of the city.

Promising changes are occurring in other countries, too—and not just in advanced economies. Curitiba, the capital city of Paraná, one of Brazil's southernmost states, has distinguished itself internationally because of its range of progressive strategies in transportation, social services and environmental practices. Curitiba faced all the same problems of overcrowding, poverty and pollution as other large metropolitan areas, but it had extremely limited public funds. However, led by its inspired mayor, Jaime Lerner, Curitiba developed some unique, low-tech solutions. For example, multiple vehicles were combined to create bus-trains with raised boarding platforms and pre-paid fares, and this created a network that operates for less than a tenth of the costs of running a subway.

While extremely important, all of these targeted innovations still represent only a small advance in addressing the accumulated weight of post-war planning and sprawl. And this raises a fundamental question: how quickly can the lessons learned from these examples help reverse the momentum of the status quo? Another huge, unanswered question is also looming, and it has extraordinary consequences for the planet. As we search for a more sustainable balance in cities and attempt to curb our environmentally harmful addictions, the question becomes this: will emerging economic powers like China and India follow our unsustainable twentieth-century path or will they skip over our mistakes in favour of sustainable city-building practices? Achieving real sustainability in cities requires more than a single epiphany. It occurs in bursts created by special opportunities like hosting an international event or the accelerated development of best practices in a city or region, and from these the trend can quickly gain momentum. Some changes do happen relatively quickly. For instance, seeing films from just a couple of decades ago reminds us how ubiquitous social smoking was. Redefining "normal"—people's expectations—can actually happen quickly. A short time ago, we North Americans were all taking our groceries home in plastic bags provided at the supermarket. Now we take our own bags or, in some cities, pay a small premium. In small ways we're adjusting to different priorities and expectations and to a more modest and sustainable "normal."

GETTING OUT OF OUR CARS

As we prepare to hit the wall of peak oil, with "peak car" following closely on its heels (at least in the West), we'll have to change how we get from place to place. Beyond the limit of oil supply, there simply is no more room for cars. We have saturated our urban centres with roads and road widenings. If we want the benefits of dense, active and competitive cities, something has to give. And then there are basic public health issues. Even low-emission vehicles contribute heavily to the pollution that afflicts city dwellers. And the unhealthy consequences of a sedentary, car-dependent lifestyle are clear. Driving to the gym or health club is no substitute for walking as part of a daily routine, nor is it a solution for serious obesity challenges and the skyrocketing rates of diabetes among North Americans (close to one in seventeen in the U.S.). We're also facing a critical population bubble as baby boomers who have grown up with the car as a way of life are approaching an age at which many can no longer safely drive. In a few years, without walkable neighbourhoods or good transit options, they'll be stranded. There is no silver bullet for making this fundamental shift from car dependency. But land use—affecting where people live and work—is one important place to start. As density and mix of land uses increase, amenities become more accessible and it becomes more practical and economical to live without a car, or at least to make very limited use of one.

Paradoxically, with greater density, we can rely less on public transit. It becomes feasible to walk and cycle to pick something up for dinner or take the kids to daycare if the facilities are close to where we work or live. In the dense residential and mixed-use neighbourhoods of Paris and Buenos Aires or the intricate, village-like neighbourhoods of Tokyo, nearly every city block has stores catering to almost all the basic needs of local residents—from food to hardware to financial services—as well as specialty shops catering to a broader surrounding market.

But even an ideal self-sufficient urban village can't have everything. To shrink our roads, get out of our individually owned private cars and redistribute the space they presently occupy, city builders have to give people better ways to get around. And to accomplish this, cities can offer both carrots and sticks. A vastly expanded public transit network is essential, along with intercity rail. Here again, a greater number of people living and working in an area increases the financial viability of high-performance public transit through efficiencies of scale. With its great concentration of people, Hong Kong can operate subways at one-minute intervals with immaculately kept trains, well-designed stations accessed with electronic card readers, clearly audible announcements and helpful videos. On major routes, these are broadcast in three languages: Mandarin, Cantonese and English.

Urban transit is not just about subways, light rail and

other large projects. With density come innovations to fill more specific needs, such as bus routes that stop on request and jitneys (also known as "share taxis"), a form of transit often seen in the developing world that falls between private transport and the conventional bus. These taxis often have a fixed or semifixed route but are willing to stop anywhere on their flexible schedules.

Clearly even the combination of all of these measures is not going to entirely replace the car as we know it; there is still a need to come up with transitional systems and solutions that can cope with the highly dispersed polycentric pattern of living that we have inherited in many North American cities. But the way in which we will access cars (when and if we do need them) is also changing. In the developed world, rental car share services and car pooling are rapidly becoming ubiquitous alternatives to individual car ownership. We purchase access to a service rather than owning and storing vehicles as personal possessions. This service has the potential for integrated fare cards that provide access to these vehicles-on-demand along with many other modes of mobility. Much investigation is already being done to expand the use of distributed transportation systems, utilizing existing infrastructure (highways and roads) and emerging safety innovations, like P2P (Peer to Peer) communications. Major automakers and transit authorities are considering options like fleets of self-guided vehicles that we call up as needed, combining hand-held technology with a new generation of smaller more efficient vehicles.

As the range of non conventional–auto options expand, a number of cities from Singapore to London, Stockholm and Milan have introduced congestion pricing, charging tolls on routes leading into the city. This has been most successful when combined with readily available information about different available modes of transportation, including car-pooling programs. A comprehensive package of these and other inducements, including the advantage of not spending hours stuck in traffic or paying for expensive parking, can encourage people and businesses to choose more sustainable ways of getting around and to opt for housing closer to work (or offices closer to residential centres). While most observers acknowledge that congestion pricing in more cities is inevitable, the great challenge for politicians is to communicate its benefits to reluctant electorates. Market pricing for parking is another powerful inducement for people to adapt; in the private sector, adaptation is a function of supply and demand. Interestingly, one of the most difficult nuts to crack in this regard consists of public sector agencies who have built unrealistic expectations for free or highly subsidized parking into union contracts. But even now, after several generations in which people's sense of self has been tied to the kind of car they drove, many young people are choosing not to drive at all and they are taking particular pride in the fact that they don't need to. For them, preferred neighbourhoods are measured not by how big or grand the houses are but by how far they have walk to the grocery store, the transit stop and the playground.

The cities that are making this shift most gracefully and rapidly are emerging as the big winners in terms of quality of life and economic competitiveness. When I was working in Amsterdam in the mid-1990s, that city was at a crossroads. While Amsterdam had never lost its reliance on cycling, cars were choking the city centre. Historic canal edges were cluttered with parked vehicles, and pedestrian-vehicle conflicts were happening everywhere. So the city adopted a phased policy of year-by-year auto reduction, incrementally removing parking spaces while adding bicycle lanes and decreasing wait times between trams. People were soon amazed to discover that they could actually hear their footfalls in the city again.

New York City has discovered that Broadway, the great diagonal slicing through Manhattan, is not really needed for traffic, given the extensive grid of avenues and streets that surround it. So from 23rd Street through Columbus Circle, Broadway has been transformed into a high-amenity pedestrian space paralleled by bicycle lanes on 8th and 9th Avenues. And an additional hundred miles of identified bicycle lanes have been introduced throughout the city.

Paris has developed the Vélib network of ubiquitous bike rental stations and hundreds of kilometres of new reserved lanes. Montreal's BIXI system has built on this success. Copenhagen, a northern city which has distinguished itself in many ways by its sustainability innovations and a very high quality of life has returned much of its street network to pedestrians and cyclists and is aiming for a 50 percent share of commuting trips to work by cycling. Similar efforts are underway in Portland, Bogotá, San Francisco, Berlin and Barcelona, among others; over a hundred cities around the world now have bike-sharing programs.

RETROFITTING INFRASTRUCTURE

As we get out of our cars more and more, we need to renew, replace or remove our aging mid-twentieth-century transportation and highway infrastructure, which is

Experiencing New York in a whole new way—the city turns Broadway over to pedestrians from 23rd Street to Columbus Circle at 59th Street.

now reaching the end of its life cycle. To some extent, the damage done by these systems can be undone by playing the tape in reverse. That is, the old infrastructure can be replaced or upgraded to become infrastructure that favours a more environmentally sound means of getting around and that harmonizes with a more human-scale urban fabric. The most dramatic examples of this aging infrastructure are the deteriorating concrete and steel elevated expressways, ramps and approaches that have been exposed to intensive use and, in northern cities, to road salting for about fifty years. At a certain point, the cost of maintaining or rebuilding these structures raises the question of whether it makes sense to keep them. A further disadvantage of hanging on to these old systems of transportation is that while they do perform important functions for the transport of goods, they're designed primarily for private automobiles, and, as such, they discourage urban density.

Decisions like this are never easy to make. They involve major costs, dislocations of traffic and population, and logistical challenges, to say nothing of having to rally the necessary political will. But they are decisions worth making. The cost of replacing these aging structures, when added to the opportunity to gain access to all the lands they occupy or sterilize by their presence, will often (but not always) out-weigh the costs of making the change.

Numerous cities have reached this conclusion, and they've engaged in elevated highway takedowns. Most famous, per-haps, is the extraordinary Big Dig, in which Boston moved its elevated Central Artery underground. But there are other examples: the Embarcadero Freeway in San Francisco and West Side Highway in New York both literally collapsed, one due to an earthquake and the latter due to its deteriorating structure. Neither was replaced. To these we can add the Central Freeway, San Francisco; Fort Washington Way in Cincinnati; a portion of the Gardiner Expressway in Toronto; the Alaskan Way Viaduct in Seattle; Harbor Drive in Portland, Oregon; and the Cheonggyecheon Highway in Seoul, South Korea. With over a hundred examples of such highway removal or downsizing on record, transportation researchers have generally found not only that the affected areas improved and prospered but also that the redistribution of traffic onto other facilities and transit has worked when the alternatives have been well planned in advance and well managed.

Many European and Asian cities have already made great advances in integrating high-speed intercity rail, commuter rail, expanded subway networks, light rail and the innovative use of bus technology to give urban dwellers and commuters a range of effective transit options. But because of our massive investment in highway building and our lower energy costs, North American cities have dragged their heels on this front. However, there is lower-hanging fruit that North American cities could easily reach: modifying streets throughout the city fabric.

Street locations remain largely fixed, and their surfaces occupy about 30 percent of most cities' land area. Every aspect of their surfaces and subgrade components (the parts below the surface) has a limited shelf life and needs to be periodically renewed. This creates an opportunity for incremental change, as pedestrians and cyclists stake their claims for a greater place in these public rights-of-way. Roads, which were remodelled in the post-war decades as the almost exclusive domain of traffic engineering, are being reconsidered as "complete streets" serving all modes of travel.

It is sometimes possible to make what is old new again in unexpected ways. Husband-and-wife team of Allan Jacobs, the former director of the San Francisco Department of City Planning, and Elizabeth Macdonald, both professors at the University of California at Berkeley, unearthed an earlier, almost-forgotten paradigm for great urban boulevards. The classic divided boulevard had fallen victim to street design that catered to unencumbered traffic flow. But Jacobs and Macdonald conclusively demonstrated that the traditional, tree-lined boulevard with slower lanes for local access separated from faster-paced through lanes by landscaped medians still had great efficacy and potential as a modern street type. And their conclusions proved to be even more valid after their redesign of Octavia Boulevard in San Francisco was implemented. Their valuable studies are now widely used as references by students and practitioners in planning and traffic engineering.

Numerous cities, notably Amsterdam and Copenhagen, have developed outstanding multimodal street design. And some North American cities are trying it, too. Often, the transformation begins with high-profile streets that have or will likely have heavy pedestrian use. They serve as important pilot projects to change public expectations about the purpose of city roadways. There's the pedestrianization of Broadway in New York, the retrofit of Commonwealth Avenue through the Boston University campus and the refurbishing of St. George Street through the University of Toronto. As the examples multiply, the exceptions become the new rule. New pedestrian-minded standards can have a

A new hierarchy of "complete streets," no longer just for cars, but designed to share the right-of-way, in the future Lower Don Lands, Toronto; already in evidence in Copenhagen.

profound cumulative effect as redevelopment proceeds and new projects are required to rebuild the sidewalks and street spaces on their frontages.

Included in an exciting new lexicon of twenty-first-century city streets are mews dedicated to pedestrians only, streets opening out into intimate squares and plazas, Dutch-inspired *woonerfs* (curbless streets combining slow-moving traffic and pedestrians on a single surface) and larger streets and multimodal boulevards with more room for cyclists and transit. These streets and squares are often lined with terraces for eating outdoors during warm seasons, and their use can be extended into fall and spring by windbreaks, canopies and heaters. Contemporary public spaces extend seamlessly into the interiors of buildings with high-ceilinged ground floors and great transparency (the ability to see activity inside a shop or restaurant from the sidewalk), so life flows easily from outdoors to indoors. Interior extensions of streetlife can be seen also in the adaptations of the historic *traboules* in Lyon (hidden passages through the ground floors of buildings once used by silk manufacturers and other merchants to transport their products under cover) and a network of new mid-block routes in Midtown Manhattan linking public lobbies and courtyards.

As in architecture, it can be tempting to overdesign or excessively clutter these pedestrian-oriented public spaces with objects or with an overabundance of fixed street furnishings. But this would inhibit flexible use of the space. The first generation of treatments of the public water's edge in Toronto in the 1980s, for instance, had many complex level changes, retaining walls and enclosures, but by the early 2000s it had become clear that these elements were impeding use and enjoyment of the space. The walls were removed, simple walking surfaces were enlarged with an expanded boardwalk and a continuous wide stone bench facing the boardwalk and paved promenade at different seating heights, and visual access to the water was increased. A tired and unpopulated area became busy with locals and visitors once again. Less is often more.

We can learn this, too, from the developing world. In India, for instance, the nonstop flow of the streets works only because of constant eye contact among the drivers of cars, trucks, buses, rickshaws (motorized and pedalled), bicycles, motorcycles and mopeds, along with pedestrians and a variety of horses, oxen and free-ranging sacred cows. This phenomenon relies on human interaction as a complement to a minimum of signage and has been taken up in the latest and most sophisticated European engineering in what are sometimes called "naked streets." By reducing the number of traffic signs, this approach encourages eye contact and increases pedestrian safety. After two years, a scheme that cleared London's Kensington High Street of markings, signage and pedestrian barriers has yielded significant and sustained reductions in injuries to pedestrians. Citizens often lead the way in these innovations. When it comes to walking and cycling, Torontonians are far ahead of their municipal government. Despite the lack of safe and comfortable spaces to ride, there has been a remarkable uptake in cycling in Toronto in recent years. A 1999 Decima poll estimated that 48 percent of Torontonians were cyclists, making some 3 million trips per week. Twenty percent were "utilitarian" cyclists using bicycles for work, shopping and errands, although only 2 percent were regular commuters.

While this number is increasing, it is nonetheless small and demonstrates a lack of comfort with the current state of the city's cycling network. Land use changes are helping, and there are now thousands more people living downtown and closer to where they work than even a decade ago, making alternatives to auto dependence practical. But the city is struggling to keep pace with its citizens' demands for a more equitable apportionment of space in public rights-of-way.

These initiatives and bottom-up pressures are all part of the fundamental rebalancing as we reverse-engineer the intrusive "cars first" post-war interventions. In learning low-tech solutions from our own past, other cultures and new discoveries, we are revisiting Robert Frost's "Road Not Taken," which he famously "marked . . . for another day." That day has now arrived.

GREATER MIX AND OVERLAP

Cities may contribute most to greater sustainability through their intricate mix and overlap of uses. As cities densify, uses that previously occupied their own discrete and sometimes isolated spaces begin to overlap and intertwine to mutual advantage, and new relationships emerge. A useful concept from ecology is the "ecotone"— a transitional zone between two adjacent biological communities, containing species characteristic of both as well as other species. My developer client in Kendall Square in Cambridge, David Clem, once described his desire to create a "train wreck" of development programs at the edge of a neighbourhood where his life-science labs were located. These facilities would mix with housing, offices, hotels, shopping, restaurants, cafés and

entertainment to create a work environment that would help him attract and retain top scientific talent. In a sense, that was an urban "ecotone," and every major city seems to have places with such characteristics.

In November 2004, Project for Public Spaces based in New York posted an admittedly subjective list on its website of what its staff considered to be some of the world's best and most interesting urban neighbourhoods. While chosen for a range of qualities, these neighbourhoods clearly had much greater appeal than the more homogeneous areas that surrounded them: Granville Island, Vancouver; the East Village, New York; North Beach, San Francisco; the Plateau, Montreal; Kensington Market, Toronto; Le Marais, Paris; Neal's Yard, London; Old Delhi, India; Habana Vieja, Cuba; and the Pedestrian Center of Copenhagen. One of the greatest challenges in city building is to make sure that life in these valuable neighbourhoods is not siphoned away by overdevelopment around them, while planting the seeds that will allow new neighbourhoods to take on some of their highly desirable characteristics. Failures or partial successes are instructive. For example, the celebrated Eastern Harbour redevelopment in Amsterdam—Borneo Sporenburg and Java Islands—broke much new ground with award-winning master plans and exemplary architecture, but it failed to re-create the active and vibrant neighbourhoods of the nearby historic canal rings. With large amounts of quality housing but little employment or shopping, a new kind of dormitory suburb emerged; it was left largely empty during the day when its legions of bicycle commuters departed.

Whereas urban renewal inflicted total clearance to make way for the new, fitting today's higher-density buildings into an established urban fabric raises much more subtle considerations: what kinds of buildings are appropriate? what role can high-rise towers play? how can new construction complement and strengthen the existing fabric without overwhelming it? It is not just a matter of shoehorning in new buildings and filling them with whatever mix of commercial and residential use the city is asking for. For instance, residential buildings must be thinner than commercial buildings, and they require greater access to light, view and privacy. Active retail streets, on the other hand, need deep ground floors and high visibility. Suburban developers sometimes import their familiar formula of towers and townhouses from the suburbs to the city core. Mid-rise structures are actually the most useful at framing the public realm because they provide a satisfying sense of enclosure—the "walls" of the street—without overwhelming it. But every case of infill is unique and requires its own solution. Toronto's Distillery District, the former Gooderham and Worts whiskey distillery, is a remarkable ensemble of low-scale original stone and brick buildings, and it's an excellent demonstration of the value of strategically deployed density. By absorbing new residents in a limited number of slender high-rises, the development has actually protected the overall lower scale of the neighbourhood.

There is great richness in preserving the continuum while making room for the new. Not far from where I live in Toronto's King-Spadina District, there's a richly layered spot: a nearly forgotten eighteenth-century European burial ground with over four hundred unmarked graves, among them the resting place of a daughter of Ontario's first lieutenant-governor, John Graves Simcoe. In the 1830s, Victoria Memorial Square was laid out on top of the cemetery as one of two squares linked by a grand boulevard forming the ensemble called Wellington Place, which was intended to be the green spine of a new, upscale neighbourhood. Then the railways arrived nearby, attracting instead a generation of solidly built manufacturing and warehouse buildings. A century and a half later, a mixed-use neighbourhood is colonizing those obsolescent structures and adding new ones. Traces of the old plan remain, but change is the only constant. Victoria Memorial Square carries memories that go back to the city's origins, and its story will finally be told through interpretative plaques and a renewed landscape design that surrounds the historic burial ground with a granite border. The French student slogan in the 1968 nationwide demonstrations *"Sous les pavés la plage"* (under the paving stones there is a beach) has meaning here, but in a new sense. At the same time as it embraces its history, the city needs room to evolve. This sometimes leads to very difficult decisions about which structures or locales to consider sacrosanct. There is no ready, foolproof formula for striking that delicate balance. The thousand-year-old cities of Europe and other parts of the world have had to contend with this issue periodically, finding the interstitial spaces and means to insert new technologies, upgrade their infrastructure, renew their public spaces and introduce new uses and populations.

A neighbourhood that seeks to integrate structures of different periods can be difficult to achieve where the zoning regime treats every site in a zone the same way. Innovative tools like heritage easements (agreements between the property owner and the city that identify which elements of a building must be retained in perpetuity and which may be altered or developed) and varied building envelopes, like those applied in the Distillery District, are needed to balance the protection of existing building stock with the need for diversity as neighbourhoods grow more dense. But creating viable downtown neighbourhoods requires more than just striking a balance between housing and offices. The public realm must also be nurtured.

In Central Business Districts, public sidewalks and minimal green spaces are often bleak and inhospitable, with heavy traffic arteries that are difficult for pedestrians to cross. Adding new buildings that juxtapose new uses and introduce new populations is not enough to make these areas become true neighbourhoods. They require some appealing common ground shared by the people who live, work and shop in and visit the area. And that requires resources. So cities need to make sure that a share of tax revenues are directed toward upgrading public spaces. This can be done, for instance, by designating some areas as special financing districts (where impact fees are levied on new developments).

The City Parent Network is a group of young Toronto parents who formed to challenge the myth that living downtown in multifamily apartment dwellings is not a good option for raising children. This group is communicating its needs to both urban developers and city government to promote better designed and more affordable housing options for families. They are strong advocates for improved neighbourhood services—the parks, playgrounds, good schools and daycare that make it possible to raise a family in the city core. Designing for true social diversity in new and repopulating downtown neighbourhoods also means providing a range of tenure options—rental, condominium and co-ops—and offering a full spectrum of smartly designed dwelling units in high-, medium- and low-rise structures for everyone from young singles to multigenerational families. This mix of unit types and sizes is a cornerstone of social sustainability.

The Toronto Community Housing Corporation, with a portfolio of sixty thousand affordable rental units, has been working for over a decade with local residents and private sector partners to successfully convert some of its low-income residential "projects" into denser, mixed-income, mixed-use neighbourhoods. I've already discussed Regent Park in Toronto, and other areas in downtown Toronto, like Alexandra Park, are on deck. Similar impulses are noticeable in the private market, as developers advertise their projects on the basis of neighbourhood, not just the qualities of units and views. They stress access to transit, shopping and schools as key selling points. One such mixed and active neighbourhood is taking shape in Liberty Village in Toronto, on the site of the former Massey Harris farm machinery factory and other departed industry. The private sector has been successfully attracting a mixed population to this area, including young families.

One of the single most important ways of making downtowns more liveable for the entire spectrum of the population is significant reinvestment in public education. With the withdrawal of the middle class from city centres and the corresponding withdrawal of funding from inner-city schools, young, middle-income families who cannot afford private schools often feel that they have to relocate to the suburbs to make sure their kids get a good education. This is especially true in the United States, where there is great disparity in local school board funding.

As populations grow and overlap, many new relationships and tensions appear, and these have to be negotiated and resolved. Neighbourhood parks that are also regional draws need to be protected for local use, passive and active recreation places need to be combined (for example, the same park may need places to sit and stroll and playgrounds with ball fields and courts) and conflicting needs may require negotiation (for instance, the needs of dog walkers and young families). Balancing these social dynamics requires skilful design solutions for limited space.

CITIES IN NATURE

In the words of Betsy Barlow Rogers, the former executive director of New York's Central Park Conservancy, "As the city becomes more park-like, the park becomes more city-like." And in places, cities are becoming more like parks, with green rooftop gardens that collect rainwater; green walls; green courtyards, lanes, streets and squares; and parks that follow natural water courses through the city. These green fissures and breaches are erasing the sharp distinctions between city and nature. New urban places are being created that are deeply rooted in their geographic contexts, and the underlying layers of the local natural setting are being revealed. In many cities, buried watercourses that were drained or placed in pipes are now being "daylighted" (made visible again)—both to improve environmental health through habitat renewal and to reveal and celebrate a location's natural history.

This way of handling the public realm was better appreciated by visionaries of the nineteenth century like Frederick

Law Olmsted and Horace Cleveland, who advocated for city-scale developments that were often integrated with natural systems. Their seminal projects include the Emerald Necklace in Boston and the Chain of Lakes and Grand Rounds Scenic Byway in Minneapolis–Saint Paul. The latter was conceived as an interconnected series of parkways and parks, centred on the Mississippi River. It was never completed but today serves as the inspiration for the ongoing expansion of one of the best urban park systems in the world.

Today's renewal of this consciousness was anticipated and fostered by writers and practitioners like Ian McHarg in *Design with Nature* (1971), Ann Spirn in *The Granite Garden* (1984) and Michael Hough in *City Form and Natural Process* (1984). Their ideas suggested cities work with natural processes, rather than just mitigating the impacts of urban life upon them. Greater density paradoxically goes hand in hand with the preservation of nature, giving urban dwellers easier access to the natural world than is the case for their suburban counterparts. Great urban parks like Central Park and Prospect Park in New York, the Bois de Boulogne in Paris, Chapultepec Park in Mexico City and the Toronto Islands have historically been possible because of the larger populations nearby that have built and maintained them. And there are also newer generations of spaces: the extensive ravine network in Toronto (preserved for flood protection in the aftermath of Hurricane Hazel), the five-kilometre-long Leslie Street Spit extending out into Lake Ontario (the overgrown result of a failed attempt to create a new industrial harbour), the extensive greenway network in Bogotá (which has been integrated with regional drainage) and a similar plan in Hartford. All follow new (and very old) logics for integrating landscapes within the city fabric. They are appreciated and preserved as living systems integral to the urban whole, contributing to air quality, temperature moderation and water filtration, and they provide habitat for diverse flora and fauna.

Some of the most vexing and complex issues for city builders are where and how to build, and whether or not to build, as cities expand into vulnerable geographical settings. In many cases, cities have put people in harm's way by ignoring the imperatives of nature, and the dilemma this creates is most clearly revealed in crisis. One of the most remarkable teaching and learning experiences of my career came out of an opportunity to wrestle with exactly this problem. In 2000, I had the opportunity to co-lead a unique exercise dealing with the fragile relationship between urban settlement and the natural world on a portion of the devastated Venezuelan coastline near Caracas. Mount Ávila, which separates the Caracas Valley from the sea, rises two thousand metres above the coastal strip of towns and villages known as the Littoral Central (in the centre of the Venezuelan coast). In December 1999, the Littoral was ravaged by dramatic floods and landslides. The upper slopes were saturated by extended rainfall, and tons of debris roared down the slopes and destroyed everything in its path. In some cases, boulders the size of houses ripped up homes and literally reshaped the coastline and beaches, pushing soil into the sea. The debris created many square kilometres of new land area. Entire towns and villages were virtually eradicated in a matter of hours, and between fifteen thousand and twenty thousand lives were lost.

Less than a year later, I teamed up with Oscar Grauer and David Gouverneur, co-chairs of the Urban Design Masters Program at Universidad Metropolitana in Caracas to lead a joint urban design studio focusing on the aftermath of this catastrophe. The studio brought students from the Graduate School of Design (GSD) at Harvard University together with Oscar's and David's graduate students from Unimet.

I had already led another GSD urban design studio the previous year in Saint Paul, and one of the great attractions of this interaction was the opportunity to work with a mix of students in architecture, landscape, planning and urban design. This mix allowed us all to see complex urban problems through different disciplinary lenses. The environmental imperative at the Littoral Central clearly called for such a cross-disciplinary approach, and the cross-cultural perspective would only enhance that benefit by bringing together experiences with similar challenges in other parts of the world.

We were not starting from scratch. The Venezuelan Ministry of Science and Technology had already asked Unimet to prepare redevelopment proposals and provide tools to implement the recovery program. Oscar and David guided the Unimet study by drawing on a year's work by professionals from many different fields and about thirty-five institutions, both local and international. With that study in hand, my GSD group and the Unimet students confronted an urgent situation with severe environmental and physical challenges, all compounded by the sort of development pressures present in much of the urbanizing world. Global climactic changes are increasing the likelihood of similar events (Hurricane Katrina on the U.S. Gulf Coast; the Asian tsunamis; devastating flooding in Pakistan and China; catastrophic earthquakes in Haiti and Chile; and forest fires in portions of California, western Canada and Russia). And such catastrophes are particular threats in areas like the Littoral, where uncontrolled urban growth has taken place in high-risk areas. The joint studio focused on the portion of the coastline extending west from Macuto and including the Port of La Guaira and Simón Bolívar International Airport, both of which had been in need of re-engineering even before the floods. Sprawling *barrios* (informal neighbourhoods) ring both of these transportation facilities on surrounding hillsides that also border the historic districts. Popular beaches and proximity to the capital city had drawn people to live there, so the area examined by the joint studio was intensely urbanized. A rough estimate suggested that some twenty thousand people (four thousand households) still needed to be relocated out of the floodplain.

Given the magnitude of these challenges, the ability to step back and question fundamental "givens" with a group of bright and motivated students without the limiting constraints of politics or professional practice had great value. The fact that so much of the Littoral was damaged made it possible to imagine outcomes that were very different from what had existed before the floods. This was especially true since redevelopment on the unstable alluvial fans (the fan-shaped deposits of earth and debris left by the floodwaters) was inherently dangerous. Ecologist Steve Apfelbaum from Applied Ecological Services in Wisconsin joined our studio, as did a number of local scientists. They confirmed that while extraordinary, the flood of 1999 was not a freak event but part of an historic trend of high waters. Thinking about helping the Littoral recover from the flood raised a set of basic but intertwined questions. How could we use knowledge of the flood's natural causes to create a new, environmentally based planning framework that mitigated the dangers when another flood occurred? How could we keep residents out of harm's way and deal with flood-control issues while strengthening the recreational nature of the Littoral, creating new urban identity and attracting new investment? How could we protect the fragile ecosystems of the adjacent national park from illegal squatter occupation and create an attractive residential environment in safe zones, out of the path of future mudslides?

Shortly after arriving in Venezuela in January 2001, we visited the site of the worst damage. The Harvard students saw first-hand the conditions in the devastated coastal fringe. Along with their Venezuelan counterparts, they came to understand the relationship between the Littoral and the greater metropolitan area and gained sensitivity to the capital's geographic conditions and cultural nuances. During this first visit, the GSD and Unimet students jointly participated in design charrettes, brainstorming over maps and tracing paper. I speak Spanish but not one of my GSD group did, despite being a highly diverse group of international students, and the English of the Venezuelan students was limited. I was worried at first, but both groups used a combination of drawing, sign language and scraps of each other's languages to get past the communication barrier. Small mixed groups began to bond into flawlessly integrated teams, staking out initial hypotheses and identifying ideas to be explored in more detail later.

Once they were armed with some first hunches and hypotheses, we asked the students to deepen their knowledge of local history, geography and urban structure and to find relevant precedents for rebuilding in environmentally sensitive areas. Another way of viewing the crisis began to emerge. For example, the sixteenth-century Spanish colonial town, La Guaira, and its three imposing forts had remained intact in spite of being damaged by the 1999 floods. These forts link to the original Spanish trail over Mount Ávila to Caracas. The students speculated that a strategy of restoration and adaptive reuse and the introduction of new public spaces could reposition La Guaira and its forts as a heritage site of international importance, similar to other Caribbean sites such as Viejo San Juan in Puerto Rico, Cartagena in Colombia and Habana Vieja in Cuba, which draw international visitors.

The students identified another potential resource in the Ávila National Park, which rises abruptly from the coast. Protected reserves of undeveloped land alongside its ravines offered potential places to permanently move residents to safety, thereby making a virtue of a necessity. Installing upstream dams within the reserves' boundaries and removing impediments to river flows in times of heavy rain were necessary to allow for the rebuilding effort in the first place. The strengthening of these protections on the upstream *quebradas*—seasonal mountain streams—was an absolute necessity. If this was done, the students reasoned, the improved mountainside parklands could be turned into a new source of identity and attraction, appealing to eco-tourists, as well as producing a fitting commemoration of what had happened there.

Inspired by their visits to other parts of Venezuela, the students suggested further development of the economic and cultural dimensions of the Littoral, building on established patterns of local tourism. They were particularly taken with the beautiful resort town of Choroní, further west along the coast. Here, they saw tourists and residents enjoying local craft and food markets, festivals, cuisine and recreation, and they noticed the energy efficiency of tropical architecture and the appeal of a lush urban landscape. In an environment like this, visitors could sample the unique features and products of the country while providing the locals with a desperately needed new source of income. These observations all provided inspiration for their work on the Littoral.

Major elements of transportation infrastructure (including the airport and the port) were both on the site we were studying and needed significant upgrading. This suggested another avenue of redevelopment, and the students thought of ways to draw in visitors from one destination to many others. In particular, they imagined making connections between international air travel, which could easily be handled by the Caracas Airport, and short flights to regional destinations and cruise ships. They could exploit the Littoral's potential as a jumping-off point for other popular Venezuelan destinations such as Margarita Island and Angel Falls.

The main road along the coast, Avenida Soublette, needed substantial rebuilding after the flood. It runs on an extremely narrow strip of land that can accommodate only one main avenue and limited urban development. Even so, it could be reshaped an attractive seaside boulevard that would calm traffic and bring more visitors to the local hotels and museums. And that would allow for further redevelopment at key intersections where connections could be made to long-distance bus routes, to local jeep service up the slopes and to water shuttles, all of which would make many currently unknown local attractions more accessible.

The students took these concepts and others and worked as a team to produce an urban design framework for the Littoral. We pushed them to carefully balance the needs for both coherence and flexibility as they set the stage for future development moves by public and private actors in this large territory. This involved extensive negotiation between them in ways that mirrored the kind of real-world tensions between competing objectives that I encounter in many projects—for example, how much space should be publicly owned versus how much space should be developed by the private sector. All of this led to the preparation of an overall framework, and common principles and guidelines eventually emerged.

Next, we turned the tables. The students now had to develop proposals as individual designers, working within the framework they had created and taking on city-building roles they might one day put into practice. Their proposals ranged from the very large scale (for example, imagining the Simón Bolívar airport as a Latin American regional hub and urban core of the Littoral) to the very fine-grained (such as developing new recreational piers or designing flood-control mechanisms as cultural icons and opportunities for public art). This joint studio gave evidence of how, even among students, a range of disciplines, cultural backgrounds and individual knowledge could become a valuable combined resource in developing city-building solutions. Two of my Japanese students, for example, had backgrounds in economics. Some of the most challenging issues here involved the links and interdependencies between the formal and informal market sectors and the need to engage both. These students focused on using modest levels of investment strategically in the proposals, to find local strengths and economic niches (like growing flowers on the mountain slopes for export), to exploit those strengths and niches effectively and to devise incentives to expand on the local economies that already existed.

The landscape architecture students led the effort to protect threatened green spaces, including reconfiguring the national park. Recognizing that the potential for flooding made the current border of the park no longer meaningful in ecological terms, the students went beyond design in their proposal and recommended that the existing *barrios* in the park be legitimized by giving the State of Vargas jurisdiction over those areas of the park. The state could then implement measures to prevent future *barrio* growth. In return, the beaches east of Los Caracas would fall under the jurisdiction of the park, thus finally allowing the park to connect to the coastline and greatly enhancing its appeal as a continuous landscape. On Mount Ávila, the ravines would be redesigned as attractive green spaces with trails accessible to the urban areas and they would provide the added benefit of protecting the area from future floods through the flood control mechanisms the students were proposing. One of the most important outcomes of the studio was a rigorous environmental framework delineating clear "build" and "no-build" zones. Public policy on urbanization had to be rigorously informed by nature—as a matter of life or death.

Another critical lesson the students took from this experience—one I'd learned over twenty years earlier in Saskatchewan—was that without the political will and leadership to implement real change, the best ideas may not prevail. This "academic" studio in fact paralleled a planning process that was ongoing, and the findings of the studio, along with previous work the Venezuelan government had commissioned from the Universidad Metropolitana, were presented to the appropriate government ministers. Unfortunately, for a variety of reasons—denial, inertia, lack of committed leadership—the recommendations in the plans were followed and many people eventually moved back into harm's way.

While the outcome on the Littoral was disappointing, the good news is that almost every major city in the Western world has initiated at least one landmark project in pursuit of a more sustainable approach to city building within sensitive natural settings. Here at home, in Toronto, the city was moving aggressively ahead in 2007 with the redevelopment of a band of hundreds of acres of obsolescent industrial port lands stretching across its central waterfront. Waterfront Toronto, the revitalization corporation which had been jointly set up by all three levels of government, was now shifting its attention eastward from the central harbour to the Lower Don Lands at the mouth of the Don River. This section of the larger port lands had been land-filled in the early part of the twentieth century, obliterating what was previously the largest marshland on the Great Lakes. The area presented every conceivable challenge. It's flood prone, contaminated and deficient in services and transportation, but it was also tantalizingly close to downtown. Following the traditional silo approach, preparations for redeveloping the site would have unleashed a barrage of separate studies carried out as provincially mandated Environmental Assessments (EAs). And, in fact, a preliminary plan had already started to take shape, which anticipated discrete components: a dike-protected river channel, a large recreational

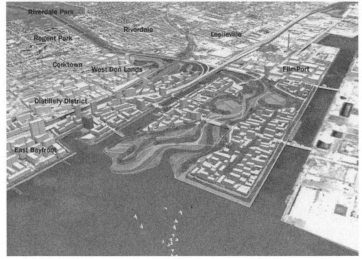

Disastrous mudslide at the Littoral on the Venezuelan coast; integrating preventive flood proofing with city building where the Don River will one day will one day enter Toronto Harbour.

area, naturalized wetlands, development areas largely for new residential use, and a new street and transit infrastructure. But by addressing these issues in isolation, all these "good things" added up to much less than the sum of their parts. What was completely missing was a vision of a shared public realm with vital synergies and overlaps.

Waterfront Toronto and city hall took a different approach and decided to hold an international design competition to tackle the entire set of challenges simultaneously: flood proofing, land reclamation, urban redevelopment, extending transportation networks and municipal infrastructure and creating parks—recognizing that these could be successfully addressed only through comprehensive design. I entered this competition as part of a team led by my colleague landscape architect Michael Van Valkenburgh, and our scheme was selected. This competition covered an unprecedented breadth of issues, which was reflected in the makeup of our wide-ranging team and the fact that "design" drew us not only into the familiar planning issues but also deeply into the hydrology and ecology of the river. Also unprecedented was our intent to move the river and naturalize its borders with expanded natural habitats. As our plan developed, we reconceived the entire Lower Don Lands as an expansive urban estuary, a sector of a sustainable "green" city and a new destination where mixed-use urban neighbourhoods, lake and river would interact. No single aspect of the plan was earth shattering. Almost every element could probably be found in plans elsewhere. But the plan was unique in that all of its ingredients were combined and layered in one space.

By shifting the Don River into a new meandering course through one hundred acres of naturalized parkland, the plan would dramatically open up critical missing links to existing neighbourhoods and to the emerging waterfront communities in the adjacent areas of the central waterfront and the port lands. Gracefully entering the harbour at centre stage once more instead of sliding through the back door, the river mouth would be marked by an elevated sloping green promontory celebrating the Don River's iconic identity as the city's place of origin. The plan has now been fully approved, and work on the Lower Don Lands will proceed in phases. Each phase is being planned to combine all the essential ingredients so that the synergies that come from the mix and overlap of living in a whole community are present from the outset. The Lower Don Lands plan has also been selected as one of seventeen founding projects for the Climate Positive Development Program, a project of former U.S. president Bill Clinton's Climate Initiative and the U.S. Green Building Council, a global undertaking to demonstrate models for sustainable urban growth. As part of the Clinton initiative, Waterfront Toronto and the other participating partners will seek to reduce the net greenhouse gas emissions of their projects to below zero through economically viable innovations in construction; the generation of clean energy through means like solar, wind power and geothermal; and innovations in waste management, water management and transportation.

In addition to the Lower Don Lands, the founding projects include projects in Victoria, British Columbia; San Francisco; Destiny, Florida; London, England; and cities in Australia, Brazil, India, Panama, South Africa, South Korea and Sweden. When the first seventeen projects are completed, nearly one million people will live and work in these climate-positive communities, which will function according to natural processes, rather than attempting to overpower them.

UNIVERSITIES AS CITY BUILDERS

In the era of urban specialization and separation, many great universities and colleges located in the hearts of cities have seemed detached from their settings. As I became involved in preparing a series of master plans for various universities, I realized that the fate of these schools was inextricably bound with their host cities. When universities and colleges compete aggressively for resources, students, faculty and research grants, the quality of life in their urban environments can be an essential asset. In return, cities increasingly see campuses as catalysts for economic development.

Linking these two perspectives has renewed our appreciation of the lively university "quarter" with its surrounding neighbourhoods, an appreciation that is slowly weaning us from the ideal of a detached and self-contained campus. I have worked on making this shift in a number places, including the University of Pennsylvania in Philadelphia; Trinity College in Hartford; Wayne State University in Detroit; Boston University in Boston and Brookline; the University of Toronto, York University and Ryerson University in Toronto; and the University of Minnesota in Minneapolis and Saint Paul.

My first involvement in the Twin Cities came when Harrison Fraker, then the dean of architecture at the University of Minnesota, was heading up a new master planning initiative for the school's twin campuses in Saint Paul and Minneapolis.

His goal was to create an updated vision for the University of Minnesota based on its evolving relationship with the two cities. My firm, Urban Strategies at the time, got the job, and our work began by digging into the rich history of plans for the school. I was impressed to find that its history included the work of two early giants—landscape architect Horace Cleveland, whose initial concept for the Knoll in the 1880s had organized the original campus buildings on an existing bluff overlooking the Mississippi, and the prominent architect Cass Gilbert, whose 1907 vision extended the campus southward along the magnificent Northrup Mall, originally intended to terminate dramatically at a bend in the river. These initial gestures had brilliantly set the stage for new opportunities. And the time was now right.

Our assignment turned out to be as much about working with the edges as with the heart of the campus. Key moves included opening up a new indoor passage through the Minneapolis campus's student centre (the Coffman Memorial Union), which had blocked Cass Gilbert's axis to the Mississippi River. We also wrestled with traffic. This was a commuter campus, where well over 50 percent of the students arrived by car. The university was also preparing for the installation of light rail transit. The route would pass through the heart of the Minneapolis campus on Washington Avenue, so we needed to orient pedestrian networks and the locations of new buildings to the anticipated rail line. Working with the Minneapolis Park Board, we proposed a renewal of the natural environment along the Mississippi River banks at the base of the bluff, which

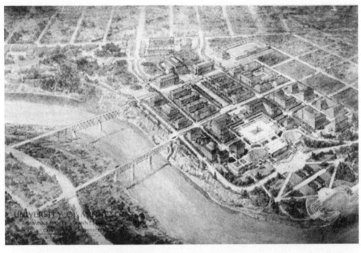

Cass Gilbert's early twentieth century vision for the University of Minnesota campus;
revisiting that city-building vision in the 1990s, when the circumstances were right.

was possible now since the heavy industry and rail activity that had encumbered the riverfront in Cass Gilbert's time had now been removed. Much of this plan, which was released in 1996, has now been implemented, and parking has since been relocated to open up further opportunities for redevelopment along the Mississippi River bluff.

Universities are emerging (along with other urban institutions such as hospitals and museums) as leaders in the move to more sustainable development practices, often drawing on their environmental research capabilities to do so. Previously hard boundaries between these institutions and their cities are rapidly giving way as mixed-use neighbourhoods form on the edges of campuses to provide students, faculty, staff and visitors with housing and access to other amenities. This benefits the universities, too, since they don't need to provide so many of these services themselves.

Mixed-use neighbourhoods also serve heterogeneous populations, including empty nesters and seniors. So a wider and year-round market exists locally for the cultural, recreational and educational facilities (libraries, theatres, fitness centres, swimming pools) that campuses provide and generate around themselves. Increasingly, campus research activities also stimulate valuable spin-offs and entrepreneurship related to their fields. They inspire knowledge-based companies to cluster, for instance, around the edges of the MIT campus in Cambridge and the University of Waterloo in Ontario, which spawned Research in Motion (RIM), the creator of the Blackberry.

In the effort to connect its downtown campus with its urban surroundings, Ryerson University in Toronto posed an

entirely different kind of challenge. This was a landlocked
university in the heart of a city core. Founded in 1852,
Ryerson had transformed itself over time from a normal
(teacher-training) school to a polytechnic institute to a university with a full complement of undergraduate and graduate programs. Led by its dynamic president, Sheldon
Levy, in 2006 the school had committed itself to developing a master plan as a framework for growth and to define
the shape and character of the university for the coming
decades. I worked with Kuwabara Payne McKenna Blumberg
Architects of Toronto, Daoust Lestage Architects of Montreal
and financial analysts at the IBI Group to prepare this plan.
Our biggest challenge was that the university owned almost
no surrounding land of its own for expansion. On the other
hand, it was right in the middle of an area that was undergoing major vertical growth. This combination of con-
straint and opportunity led us to a unique approach. We
proposed a template for codevelopment with business partners to produce an intense overlapping of campus and city
life, while bringing a new focus on design excellence.
Necessity was the mother of invention. This concept grew
out of arrangements that Ryerson had already developed
with its neighbours: a multiplex cinema, whose theatres
the school used in off hours as classrooms, and a mixed-
use building with street-level big box–style retail in the
upper floors, where Ryerson located its Ted Rogers School
of Management.

The city is quite literally Ryerson's campus, and it is
positioned as the catalyst and a principal actor in influencing
not only its own future but also the future development of a
whole neighbourhood. To improve the character of Ryerson's

public realm, the local streets are being retrofitted. This includes the pedestrianization of Gould Street to make the campus more inviting. Housing opportunities are coming from the private sector, which is keen to get involved in this exciting new development. Previously, housing students was primarily the university's domain.

By turning its limitations of space into an asset, Ryerson is affirming its unique identity as the most urban campus in the region. Its next major opportunities include the new Student Learning Centre and library expansion over retail right on Yonge Street (Toronto's main north-south corridor), giving the university a prominent new public face. It is also partnering to adapt the fabled, but long-mothballed, Maple Leaf Gardens hockey arena (former home of the NHL's Toronto Maple Leafs). Together with a major grocery chain, Ryerson is creating an athletic facility, with its varsity hockey rink sitting on top of street-level stores.

Georgia's Savannah College of Art and Design (SCAD) has taken Ryerson's model for integration with the city to the next level. Founded in 1978, it has acquired and adapted for reuse more than sixty underutilized buildings throughout Savannah's remarkable urban grid and network of twenty-four public squares, which was established almost three hundred years ago. Teaching facilities, student resources, residences and campus-run businesses have all been ingeniously housed in everything from former department stores to a theatre, warehouses and motels. The college has been recognized for its contribution to preserving Savannah's unique architectural and cultural heritage by the American Institute of Architects, the National Trust for Historic Preservation, the Historic Savannah Foundation and the Victorian Society in

America. As one of the largest art schools in the country and a major employer in the downtown, SCAD's campus is also, quite literally, the city.

BACK FROM THE ABYSS

In modern times, cities rarely disappear entirely. But there are cities that have experienced dramatic losses of jobs and population and the subsequent deterioration of the building fabric and public realm, which has tested their ability to provide the most basic municipal functions. In this category are a band of rustbelt cities in the United States from Buffalo and Rochester to Detroit and Cleveland, which have prospered in the past from their steel and auto industries. And there are others in similar circumstances in Europe from Liverpool to the Ruhr Valley. Frequently, the economic distress of these urban centres has resulted from excessive dependence on a few collapsing industries. But in the U.S., widespread layoffs, loss of office functions and plant closings have been compounded by the pervasive offshore exodus and racial and class divides.

After working in Saint Paul, I became involved in a number of cities that were in much more serious trouble than I'd faced in Minnesota—particularly Detroit, Michigan, and Hartford, Connecticut. First impressions in these places were devastating, and yet with time, I found remarkable resilience to build on. The people who brought me to these places were the committed holdouts and believers, the individuals, neighbourhood groups, institutions and businesses who either by emotional ties, inability to relocate or optimism against all odds—or some combination of all of these—were determined to turn their cities around.

232   When this kind of implosion occurs, we see how cities start to collapse and what is left when they have failed. Local stores take flight or disappear, factories sit empty, houses are boarded up and abandoned. The critical mutual dependencies and relationships that we take for granted within the built-up areas of a city are dramatically revealed by their absence as the streets become derelict and gap-toothed. On stretches of Woodward Avenue, Detroit's main thoroughfare, just north of downtown, the extent of this devastation was overwhelming. Within this corrosive pattern of decline, the few elements that remain standing become much more visible. These are often universities, hospitals, government institutions and enterprises that are heavily invested both in their physical plants and in the regions they serve and are therefore inherently less mobile. These holdouts have little choice but to lead the way toward a route to recovery. People in these institutions, many of whom have personal and family ties to their cities, often become the key drivers of new alliances between business, institutions and advocacy groups.

Propelled by crisis to step boldly across all traditional boundaries, organizations like the Greater Downtown Partnership in Detroit or the MetroHartford Alliance align their institutional leadership with embattled city governments. Local businesses; neighbourhood, environmental and cultural groups; and corporate and philanthropic leadership—often drawn from the entire city region—work together on behalf of the ailing inner city to undertake projects, restore investor confidence and advocate for support from state and federal sources. This regional solidarity reflects a growing understanding that while there may be affluent areas on the urban fringe, suburbs cannot prosper without the intensity and one-of-a-kind attractions that come only with a healthy core.

There are success stories: Pittsburgh, a postindustrial city, took full advantage of its dramatic river setting, its arts and cultural scene (including the unique Andy Warhol Museum) and new knowledge-based clusters (such as three nearby universities with their medical centres) to fuel its celebrated renaissance. Although still a work in progress, Pittsburgh has been able to achieve more than other rustbelt cities in part because it so early and completely fell into decline—its steel industry collapsed decades ago—and this collapse was so dramatic that its passionate civic leadership, demanded action.

The challenge is always to initiate the momentum that exploits the atrophied downtown and allows value to return to the core. At that point, the opportunity to purchase or lease and adaptively reuse well-built and capacious downtown structures with a great deal of character—in ways that would not be affordable in more successful cities—becomes a major asset. And this is what happened in Pittsburgh. So today, shops, offices, restaurants and entertainment venues anchor the historic riverfront site on the south shore of the Monongahela River, and Station Square, Pittsburgh's premiere attraction, generates over three-and-a-half-million visitors a year.

Rather than tackling the entire problem broadside or the hardest-hit areas first, returning life to these cities is often a matter of starting with the assets and places of greatest strength—the institutions, the great parks, waterfronts and pioneering efforts in older building stock—building on these points of life and activity and linking them together in layered new initiatives.

My own experience with this kind of problem began in Detroit. I still have vague memories of visiting what in hindsight must have been a deceptively peaceful Detroit in 1965 when I was working as an interpreter, escorting French-speaking visitors around the United States. This was just two years before the famous riots that tore the city apart and whose causes were rooted in a multitude of political, economic and social factors: economic downturn, lack of affordable housing, intrusive urban renewal projects, economic inequality, police abuse, black militancy and rapid demographic change.

When I returned to work there in the mid-1990s, Detroit had become one of the most dramatic cases of withdrawal and dis-investment in the country. Its population had dropped from over two million to less than half that. Its downtown was partially deserted, and mile after mile of neighbourhoods stood eerily half empty. Vacant lots were overgrown with weeds and houses sat abandoned. The city also suffered from an extreme racial divide and "white flight"; the population of the city was by this time largely African American. Seeing this devastation and the full impacts of flight and decay for the first time was overwhelming. I struggled to imagine a process that could rebuild this place.

My first involvement came at New Center, several miles from downtown Detroit. General Motors was planning to relocate from its historic headquarters in a collection of iconic buildings designed by the great early-twentieth-century architect Albert Kahn. They were to take over the

well-known Renaissance Center on the downtown riverfront
from their competitor the Ford Motor Company. Having
already played a lead role in the stewardship of this troubled
neighbourhood, GM was looking for an exit strategy that
would ensure that its departure from New Center would not
provoke a damaging social and economic backslide. My consultant team was brought in by the New Center Council, a
coalition led by GM, which also included the Henry Ford
Health Center, several small businesses and local residents.

Working with these combined stakeholders, we prepared
a development plan and strategy that would allow New Center
to redefine itself by introducing replacement uses and activities within and around its key asset— Albert Kahn's well-
placed, dense and solidly built ensemble of industrial buildings.
We worked closely with Development Strategies, a consulting
firm of real-estate economists, to test numerous adaptative
reuse scenarios for these structures, including the housing
of state offices, private businesses, loft housing and class-
room space. The eleven-storey, 760,000-square-foot Argonaut
Building, built in 1928 as a home for GM's design studios, for
example, now contains the Henry Ford Academy: School
for Creative Studies (middle and high school) and Detroit's
College for Creative Studies. Combining these two institutions under the generous high ceilings and abundant natural
light of these buildings has provided a unique opportunity
to introduce Detroit public school students to career paths
in art and design.

By all accounts, this transition has been successful and
the node of relative stability in New Center has been preserved (although GM itself has obviously had its own struggles). And the New Center Council continues to play a key

role in collaborative efforts to capitalize on the momentum begun by this redevelopment.

Our focus next shifted to downtown Detroit. In 1996, the broadly based Greater Downtown Partnership had been formed to accelerate revitalization. Led by CEO Larry Marantette, their comprehensive reinvestment strategy and development framework covered four areas: New Center, Downtown, Midtown and the Riverfront. Working with the staff of key remaining institutions, committed Detroiters like architect Mark Nickita, city planner Kate Beebe and a group of new downtown pioneers (who had recently moved into loft conversions or started businesses there), my staff and I led productive and sometimes emotional planning and design workshops. Through this time and effort, a remarkable consensus emerged. Downtown, we discovered, still had abundant riches to be exploited, some even tracing back to the original 1805 plan for Detroit by Judge Augustus Woodward. Taking a page from the plan for the nation's capitol—on which he had worked as a surveyor—Woodward had created a focal point in the heart of downtown Detroit where all the major arteries converged. His survey designated this "point of origin" as Campus Martius. But by the late twentieth century, this "place" existed in name only. Once the nexus of the city's streetcar lines, it had become a torturous intersection whose purpose had disappeared beneath an ever-increasing volume of cars.

We proposed redirecting the traffic, which ran awkwardly through the middle, to circulate around a significant new 1.6-acre pedestrian square. This reclaimed Campus Martius was framed by several older structures, and in a critical move, a new building was added on the north side of the square for software giant Compuware. This brought a strategic infusion of new office use and added life at street level. Campus Martius now functions as a popular new public space in the heart of the city. This success has, in turn, called attention to a set of historic structures on a band of four blocks north of Campus Martius, which have potential for reuse. We called these blocks the Necklace District because they're shaped like concentric half circles around the south end of Grand Circus Park.

We took a similar approach in Midtown. Our primary contact there was another not-for-profit: the University Cultural Center Association (UCCA), led by energetic director, Sue Mosey. UCCA was a coalition of the many great cultural institutions in the vicinity, along Woodward Avenue: Wayne State University, the Detroit Institute of Arts, the Detroit Medical Center, the Public Library, the Science Center and the Museum of African American History, among others that had come together to support the maintenance and renewal of this area. We again proposed a strategy of connecting their key assets and filling the voids. Later, I had the opportunity to work on implementing these strategies with the Michigan-based design firm SmithGroup JJR. We sought to physically link this cluster of important destinations by creating a set of appealing pedestrian amenities on the Midtown Loop, to support the daily routines of those people who regularly used this stretch of Woodward. Of course, there were the local residents, but the location was also frequented by numerous visitors and convention goers, students, staff, faculty of Wayne State, kids and school groups, as well as visitors to the medical centre and employees and clients of local businesses. A combination of public realm improvements encouraged people to extend their stay on this strip. Instead of visiting just one destination and then getting back into their cars, people began to stay for lunch or dinner, to see an exhibit or a performance or to stay in a B&B like the delightful Inn on Ferry Street. In this way, synergies are being promoted between institutions and key destinations are being psychologically linked, thus accelerating the process of renewal and infill development in this still underused area.

The initial study for the Greater Downtown Partnership had also identified opening up continuous public access to Detroit's riverfront as one of its highest priorities. So when I returned to Detroit to work with the SmithGroup JJR, we also took on the Riverwalk plan, again working with a coalition of public and private partners. This time our goal was to connect and unify a series of water's edge environments that were in a derelict state. After several years' work, the Riverwalk, a continuous public promenade with park spaces along the water's edge, now extends from downtown through to Tri-Centennial State Park, River Place, the UAW-GM building and Harbortown, the Uniroyal site, and ultimately to historic Belle Isle and the far east side. Further extensions into the surrounding neighbourhoods are in the planning and design stages.

Notwithstanding the success or partial success of these targeted efforts, the extent of the decline in cities like Detroit cannot be underestimated. While deterioration can be rapid and pitiless, the time and effort required to turn it around is prodigious. Often, the magnitude of the loss in population relative to the sheer size of these rustbelt cities, combined with their vast, underutilized capacity, is such that the best we can hope to do is to stop the hemorrhaging and then to begin a very long process of building on small pockets of strength. Only time will tell how successful these initial efforts will be in setting the stage for a larger and more sustained city renewal.

Detroit is vast and relies on an economic monoculture, but Hartford, at less than one-tenth the geographic size, is a microcosm of this same phenomenon. Its compact and complex nature brings many natural advantages but also poses particular challenges. The city occupies an ideal strategic location on the Connecticut River between prosperous New York and Boston, and logically, it should benefit from the spillover effect. This advantage would be even greater, of course, if Hartford still had reasonable rail service to these major centres, a lack which hopefully will be rectified with recent interest in upgrading regional rail service. The downtown core could be comfortably walkable (it can be measured as a ten-minute walk by a fifteen-minute walk), and it has many attractive and potentially pedestrian-friendly features like the beautiful Frederick Law Olmsted–inspired Bushnell Park at its heart.

However, like a number of cities that have what would seem to be well-positioned assets, Hartford has been hard hit. Over the course of several tumultuous decades, it has suffered severe economic shocks, with the almost simultaneous loss of key economic sectors. Once known as the "Insurance Capital of the World," with companies such as Travellers, Aetna, The Hartford and The Phoenix Companies, Inc., it lost much of its insurance sector to the suburbs and to cities in the Midwest.

Hartford was also a major manufacturing city tied to the defence industry, and many of these plants have also closed, relocated or reduced their operations. Hartford has a population of about 125,000 in a city region of over a million, but, like Detroit it lost a significant number of people to its near suburbs. Between 1990 and 1994 alone, the population dropped by over 15,000 residents.

I arrived in Hartford in the mid-1990s, when the highly reputed Trinity College on the city's south side was preparing a new master plan for the city's rejuvenation. On the way to the interview for this job, I was stunned to see the level of decay in the neighbourhoods surrounding the college. I learned that many prospective students and their parents were so discouraged when they saw the condition of the areas on the edge of the campus that they just turned around and never appeared for their appointments with the admissions office. The college had just appointed Evan Dobelle, the former mayor of Springfield, Massachusetts, as its new president, in part because he had committed to helping turn this part of the city around.

I got the job, and my firm set to work in partnership with Cooper Robertson & Partners of New York on the Campus Master Plan. Our particular role was to look outward from the campus to the city and find new ways to engage the school with its surrounding Southside neighbourhoods. With the steady decline of the city around it, the campus had become isolated. This urban setting, which should have been a competitive advantage, had become a liability.

To remain viable on its beautiful campus, Trinity College could no longer afford to retreat inside its own gates, so it linked its fate with the Southside Institutions Neighbourhood

Alliance (SINA). This partnership between the college, the Connecticut Children's Medical Center and Hartford Hospital cooperated with local residents to develop community leader- ship and to improve conditions in the adjoining neighbourhoods of Frog Hollow, Barry Square and South Green. A centrepiece of this outreach was the Learning Corridor, a $100 million campus for local primary and secondary students on the doorstep of the college. This institution, which opened its doors in 2000, had been created through a remarkable collaboration spearheaded by Trinity College, which took the lead in developing the concept and securing federal funding. SINA was also involved, along with Hartford Hospital, The Institute of Living, Connecticut Children's Medical Center, Connecticut Public Television and Radio and a host of other committed Hartford stakeholders, including the City of Hartford and the State of Connecticut.

In a series of new buildings linked around a shared quad on a property that once housed streetcar barns, the Learning Corridor combines a Montessori Magnet School, a Magnet Middle School, two Greater Hartford Academies that teach high-level math, science, and arts, the Greater Hartford Academy of the Arts and the Aetna Center for Families. By filling a dangerous void with a positive resource, our master plan had integrated the educational campus into the surrounding community and positioned it as a catalyst for neighbourhood revitalization. The Learning Corridor campus also helped to link the Frog Hollow neighbourhood on one side with Trinity College and downtown on the other.

This initial involvement with Trinity College led to a series of additional assignments, which eventually extended over the entire seventeen square miles of the city. A merchants' group on Park Street, the most important Latino shopping district in New England, asked us to help improve its pedestrian environment, encourage investment and turn around cultural perceptions of the area. Further, the city and the region enlisted our help in shaping the next wave of downtown development and linking it to these other fledgling steps in the city's neighbourhoods.

While preparing our Downtown Action Strategy, we saw that a number of incremental development initiatives already had the potential to remake downtown Hartford as a regional arts and entertainment destination and to attract a new downtown residential population. When the Action Strategy was produced in 1998, my team and I, along with the host of architects and specialists who had assisted in its preparation, found ourselves on familiar ground, challenging the importation of suburban development models and advocating against the allure of megaprojects.

In 1995, just such a project had appeared. And it called for almost all the state funding available for redeveloping Hartford. Adriaen's Landing was a proposed thirty-acre, themepark–like, all-encompassing development overhanging the highway along the Connecticut River where it cuts through downtown. Like the Bridges of Saint Paul, it ultimately collapsed under its own weight. The Capital City Economic Development Authority (CCEDA), the State of Connecticut Office of Policy and Management (OPM) and the Waterford Development Group had initially endorsed this project, but they changed their minds when it was determined that the underlying economics were unsound. The developer revised his strategy to reshape the development area, which faces the new Connecticut Convention Center and the Connecticut Science Center, into something more modest and achievable, which the city has supported. Mean-while, the city and state continued to encourage a combina-tion of small- and medium-scale initiatives with the potential to incrementally repair the city's historic fabric. Our Downtown Action Strategy had identified a band of specific opportuni-ties for new residential development, in particular around the historic Bushnell Park. Building on successes downtown, the newly formed MetroHartford Alliance, an even more broadly based business coalition working with the City of Hartford, retained me again in 2006. My frequent collaborators, Kishore Varanasi and David Nagahiro of CBT Architects in Boston, local Architect Patrick Pinnell and I led a new team in devel-oping a plan we called HARTFORD 2010. This produced a larger vision and strategic framework with a focus that expanded outside the downtown core to the near neigh-bourhoods and the surrounding region.

The framework identified strategies to encourage addi-tional private investment which (like the Learning Corridor) could fill gaps in the urban fabric by leveraging Hartford's assets, including its historic neighbourhoods and relation-ship to the Connecticut River. And we targeted clusters of public investment—resolving traffic conflicts, improving pub-lic spaces—at key entry points to the downtown where his-toric routes converged.

By this time, the decrease in Hartford's downtown population had begun a modest turnaround.

SUBURBAN TRANSFORMATIONS

244 In her book *Dark Age Ahead*, Jane Jacobs advanced an intriguing prediction about how the relentless sprawl that had contributed to gutting cities like Hartford and Detroit might ultimately be challenged. Suburbia always seemed to be the phenomenon that was most impervious to Jane's influence. Even as downtowns appeared to be newly popular with a growing cohort of the population, the advancing wave of low-density suburbs was still pushing on unabated and relatively unchanged, notwithstanding occasional heroic "new urbanist" efforts to transform it beyond the city core, like Disney's Celebration in Orlando, Florida, or Kentlands in Maryland. Jane analyzed urban sprawl as part of a longer historical trajectory. Along with slum clearance and rent control, one of the most significant housing remedies to emerge from the Depression and World War II was the availability of long-term low-interest rates. Coupled with a number of other factors, an irresistible pressure mounted for low-density housing near cities. (Among the influences that led to this pressure were, in the United States, the interstate highway program and "red lining"—a self-fulfilling prophecy described earlier, of insurance companies who both feared and caused decline by making some urban neighbourhoods ineligible for loans—and the realization by 1945 that as little as 3 percent of the population was needed for agriculture.)

Facing that influx of population, sprawl is still hard to resist. But what if it became less wasteful and suburban land were more intensively used? In other words, what if there were another evolution in urban thinking and the current first-generation suburbs (those created in the first great move outward in the post-war decades, currently under the greatest economic stress and a logical place to start) could be made denser and more sustainable in the future? In fact, Jacobs predicted that with an economic and demographic *force majeure*, the obstacles to this suburban evolution would be swept away and ingenuity and necessity would be allowed to operate. Such a force could come from the need for families to share housing when facing a drastic rise in the cost of energy or, as she presciently theorized in 2004, an economic crisis in the housing market. As she had done when examining urban "unslumming," diversification and "import replacement" in previous books, she was laying the groundwork so that when the time came, the ideas would be in place. This was a classic Jane Jacobs kind of argument. By knowing that a change might happen, we would be better prepared to direct it and respond to it with more grace and less harm. We have now, of course, reached the point where many such changes are happening in response to a number of related and sometimes conflicting pressures on individuals and suburban municipalities: "urbanization" as cities grow into their suburbs, producing increases (or in some cases decreases) in land value; obsolescence and perceived need for change; new investments in infrastructure which create opportunity; the need to grow to augment the tax base and overwhelming congestion as roads are overtaxed and commutes become unbearable.

We are currently witnessing a wave of illegal intensification as economically stressed extended families and unrelated groups are forced to share single family houses. And they are using these dwellings for both residence and business in ways that contravene zoning restrictions on living and working in the same space or dividing single-family houses into multifamily units. As it becomes more and more challenging to provide basic municipal services at affordable costs, these combined economic and environmental imperatives will be increasingly difficult to ignore in suburbia, and they are already forcing a reconsideration of currently unsustainable restrictions and practices. But while public policy and innovative developers in the suburbs have been focusing on driving a sustainable-development agenda through new individual projects on large, clear sites, the retrofitting of entire existing areas of sprawl is just as urgently needed.

In order to make first- and second-generation suburbs more economically viable and in order to reduce greenhouse gas emissions, as well as energy, water and material consumption, we will need to explore ways of introducing new types of buildings and road and block patterns. Property will also need to be reconfigured to allow for significant intensification at key transit hubs and along transit routes. And we will need to find ways to work with (and not overpower) natural systems, employ a much greater mix of land use and provide services like sewer, water and waste management more sustainably.

If and when the will to "convert" existing suburbs gains momentum, the greatest challenge will be posed by vast tracts of large, single-family houses in low-density suburbs that are almost entirely dependent on cars for personal mobility. But here, too, there is potential for adaptation and selective infill development: suburban arteries have the potential to be transformed into multipurpose urban streets, and the arterials can be converted into boulevards shared with denser buildings served by transit and cycle lanes.

Another, and somewhat related, reason to curtail sprawl has to do with the food we consume and where it comes from. As transportation costs rise, local food production in or near cities is increasing and distribution networks are having to adjust. While it is difficult to quantify the changes in consumer behavior, a 2006 Ipsos-Reid poll noted that 56 percent of Canadians "always" or "usually" check to see where their fruit and vegetables come from when they are shopping, and 42 percent regularly buy local food. This and the astonishing reappearance of seasonal farmers' markets, the popularity of organically grown produce and the focus on health concerns related to food attest to this interest. Further, consumer concerns about food origins mean that many will also want to preserve the new symbiotic relationship between the viability of cities and the protection of their agricultural hinterlands from unabated sprawl. Meanwhile, however, in the Greater Toronto Area (GTA) alone, more than 2,000 farms and 150,000 acres of farmland were lost to development between 1976 and 1996, representing the disappearance of approximately 18 percent of Ontario's best farmland.

The major impediments to making our suburbs more sustainable are cultural resistance to change, a fragmented pattern of ownership and an extraordinary tangle of intractable zoning regulations that underpinned the suburban paradigm in the first place—along with leases and covenants with, for example, long-term commitments to provide free parking in prescribed locations. I referred earlier to steps being taken to improve sprawl in Mississauga, a sizable suburban city West of Toronto, and that effort has involved modifying a thicket of such dated provisions. The strategic framework for Mississauga Downtown 2021 proposes an incremental transformation of the vast parking lots around a shopping mall into a mixed-use setting of urban streets and blocks.

If we can't overcome these barriers and these changes are not allowed to happen incrementally, they will happen anyway. And they will be cataclysmic. In the March 2008 edition of *The Atlantic Monthly*, Christopher Leinberger argued in his article "The Next Slum" that the subprime crisis is just the tip of the iceberg for the collapse of the suburbs. If more positive change does not occur, he wrote, fundamental alterations to American life may turn these neighbourhoods into what inner cities became in the 1960s and 1970s: slums characterized by poverty, crime and decay, to be inherited by the most vulnerable. Leinberger calls attention to examples from North Carolina, northwest of Charlotte, Virginia, to areas south of Sacramento, California, where vacant houses, graffiti, broken windows and other markers of decay have already appeared—not only as a reflection of the subprime mortgage crisis but of a deeper malaise.

The need to extend our focus on sustainability from the city centre to the region and the necessity of softening the blow with an early start have been recognized for some time. In the 1990s, I became involved in a series of policy studies concerning urban growth. A 1992 study for the Ontario government called *Shaping Growth in the Greater Toronto Area* took a big-picture look at the dynamics reshaping the metropolitan area. Gardner Church, an inspired civil servant who was directing the province's Office of the Greater Toronto Area, headed the group behind this study and drew upon the participation of Greater Toronto's five regional chairs and thirty mayors, as well as many affected agencies in the domains of transportation, social services and infrastructure. The study demonstrated that place-based thinking should be the foundation of our study, dealing not just with abstractions and statistics but also the visualization of actual physical settings—from natural features like the Oak Ridges Moraine, ravine systems and the Lake Ontario shoreline to the form and character of neighbourhood settings. This could help the public embrace the shift to a much denser form of mixed-use, transit-oriented suburban growth, both in retrofitting existing areas and in anticipating new regional growth.

To really be effective, these changes have to come from bottom up as well as from top down, and there are indications that communities and developers are starting to embrace them. Examples of new, more authentically urban places, as well as the urbanization of existing suburbs, are starting to appear in many maturing suburban municipalities like Markham and Oakville on the outskirts of Toronto. In some cases, the transition has been dramatic and rapid. As many regional malls decline under pressure from big box power centres and online shopping, some of them have been broken apart and reconfigured as traditional shopping streets, as has been the case in an ambitiously planned post-war garden-city suburb of Toronto called Don Mills, which is now enjoying renewed popularity.

With changes like this on the urban periphery, the dichotomy between city and suburb begins to fade and the operative scale becomes the integrated city region. This kind of transformation is not an entirely new phenomenon. Best practices elsewhere and our own history of cities absorbing earlier

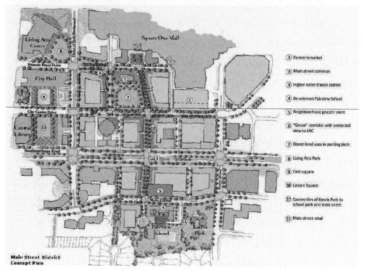

Suburban transformation; colonizing the parking lots in Mississauga to create a downtown "main street."

suburbs offer many clues. In the Netherlands, the nationally scaled physical concept for the Randstad, a ring of dense cities linked by a rail network surrounding a large, protected green area of natural systems is one possible way of urbanizing suburbs. And the Regional Plan Association (RPA) in the New York Metropolitan Area, extending into New Jersey and Connecticut, as well as regional governments like Metropolitan Portland in Oregon, have also embraced this regional approach.

With this broader view comes the potential to take on vital network issues that transcend current municipal boundaries, such as the need for regional watershed planning and effective intercity rail linked to urban transit. Recent initiatives in the Greater Toronto Area are based on the need to think and act effectively as a region. *Places to Grow*, a provincial policy document, for instance, has staked out a vast Greenbelt corridor around the city, building on previous attempts to protect the surrounding watershed going back to the 1950s. The region has also seen the creation of Metrolinx, an integrated regional transportation agency with great potential for connecting the city and suburbs to one another as increasingly sustainable parts of a smoothly functioning whole. In many North American cities, this transformation is manifesting itself in the form of new streetcar-like light rail transit in its own reserved rights-of-way on streets or on abandoned rail lines. These run from city centres into the surrounding suburbs or they link suburb to suburb. In the U.S., systems like this are being set up through the Federal Transit Administration's (FTA) New Starts program, the federal government's primary financial resource for supporting locally planned, implemented and operated transit. New Starts has also helped to make possible hundreds of new or extended fixed rail systems across the country. Similar initiatives in other countries are defining the new corridors in lower-density areas, and the next round of reinvestment in transit-oriented development can be structured around these lines.

At one time, there was a simple and obvious way to tie land use and transportation together at this scale. But for some reason we have lost sight of the need to align the vested interests of the transit operators with those of the developers; in fact, they should be one and the same. The single transit operator in Hong Kong and the Territories—for trains, subways and ferries—is also involved as the major "redeveloper" at the stations, which are virtual cities at each stop. The same integration has occurred in cities like Copenhagen and Stockholm. Historically, in North America, the developers of street railways (streetcar lines) were also the developers of the new subdivisions they served. And the transcontinental railways created opportunities for new towns and cities on their routes to provide passengers.

In the auto-dominated era, we completely separated these roles, but there is now a new opportunity to reconnect them. If we broaden the mandate of our transit authorities to optimize regional development opportunities at new and expanded transit "hubs" (especially where there are currently large surface parking lots), they, and we, will be able to measure success in terms of integrated city building and not just in terms of moving bodies and cars.

VI

RECLAIMING THE PUBLIC REALM

PUBLIC SPACE LOST AND FOUND

The mid-century crisis of confidence in cities set off a downward spiral of neglect for our public spaces: pot-holed streets, cracked sidewalks, barren parks, dying trees and previously well-used common spaces now filled with undesirable activity. Bryant Park, a ten-acre green space located one short block west of Broadway between W40th and W42nd Streets in Manhattan was a prime example. Decades ago it had been taken over by drug dealers and prostitutes and by the 1970s was nicknamed "Needle Park."

Starting in 1979 an advocacy group called the Parks Council aimed to bring life back to this valuable green space by coordinating its redesign for ease of access and greater visibility and by introducing new forms of activity with food kiosks, a book market, a flower market, cafés, landscape improvements, comfortable places to sit and periodic public

events and performances. The council's efforts are to this day
sustained by the local Business Improvement District (BID)
known as the Bryant Park Corporation.

Many urban parks went the way of Bryant Park in mid-
century, and not all have come back. Conceptually, true public
space was virtually "zoned out" of existence in post-war planning. While there was plenty of buffering green space surrounding "towers in the park," the modernists left little room
in their purely functional plans for complex, multifaceted land
use that captured the valuable social life of sidewalks and
neighbourhood parks. Consequently, the relationships that
shape and frame public space suffered. Formulas for building
setbacks, lot coverage and parking ratios were applied with
little regard for these relationships.

As cities segregated land use at ever-larger scales during
the great migration to suburbia, they robbed the parks and
plazas that did exist of the essential overlaps of people and
use to keep them occupied. Even if propped up by occasional
special events, these leftover urban voids had little chance of
success. The fertile in-between times and in-between spaces
that are the essence of public life were gone. More recently,
the virtual world of cyberspace—e-commerce, social networking on Facebook, Twitter and chat rooms—has arrived
as a new form of shared territory, along with elaborate home
entertainment and gaming centres. These technological
advances cut both ways, since they have the potential to both
further isolate us (encouraging "cocooning" in private
spaces) or to connect us in new ways (think of people using
hand-held devices to arrange meetings in parks and public
spaces) or sitting in cafés working on their laptops in the
company of others.

But most important, when we fashioned a world shaped by the car's needs, we gradually "de-spatialized" our environment. We substituted a sense of time spent in a capsule for an appreciation of physical distance thereby losing our intuitive sense of space and the connections that exist between actual places. With the lost opportunity to meet people and see things while walking from our home to a local shop, we also sacrificed critical relationships with each other. When we are encased in a rapidly moving vehicle behind a windshield, there is little opportunity for eyes to meet or for us to exchange words with strangers. A chicken-and-egg dynamic ensues: did the street become too hostile to enjoy on foot or did we make the street unfriendly by withdrawing and using it as just a way to get around in our cars? Either way, we relinquished the street as public space and turned it over to the car.

This was exacerbated by a generation of "unbundled" development that sought to completely separate vehicles and pedestrians, in order to diminish conflicts between them. But in the end, the cure was far more damaging than the problems it proposed to solve. We put pedestrians in "Plus 15" (fifteen feet above sidewalk level) skyways or tubes—Calgary, Edmonton, Minneapolis—or, conversely, in basement tunnels—Toronto, Montreal. And in doing so we replaced street-level cafés and shops that were busy at many times of the day and on weekends with basement- or upper-level food courts whose activity was largely limited to business-day lunch hours. However, parks and streets hadn't lost their foot traffic only because of cars and computers. Arguably, government could have recognized what was being lost as collateral damage a long time ago, and it could have taken measures to preserve these valuable public spaces. But at a crucial time, government turned its back and withdrew large amounts of funding.

THE REVIVAL OF THE COMMONS

Just as the movement back to the cities was gaining momentum, it was threatened and undermined by an onslaught of severe funding challenges. A widespread phenomenon of simultaneous tax cuts and withdrawal of public funding shook cities across North America and in many other parts of the world. I witnessed one example up close when, in a series of draconian moves to deal with debt and deficit in the 1980s, the government of Canada made drastic cutbacks in funding critical programs to the provinces. The provinces then did the same to their cities, which were lowest in the pecking order. Urban centres all over North America and Europe have still not recovered from this chronic underfunding—not even when economic conditions before the current recession would have allowed funding to be reinstated. This abdication was more, however, than just a reaction to larger economic forces and conditions. From Thatcherism to Reaganomics, the financial crippling of cities was the manifestation of a more profound withdrawal and detachment that emphasized drastically reduced state intervention in the public sphere and an almost complete deference to the marketplace.

In some places, like Ontario and Alberta in Canada and various U.S. states, which were also under hard-right conservative governments, the contraction of support proceeded in lockstep with highly partisan ideological attacks on the very concept of government and public services (and by implication, public spaces). There was also an exaggerated embrace of a user-pay philosophy, increased privatization and limits on public spending similar to Proposition 13 (California's infamous constitutional amendment enacted in 1978). This pullback marked the beginning of a series of disappointments for major cities and weakened many critical underpinnings of urban systems that had previously been functioning well. The collateral damage is evident in the palpable deterioration of urban infrastructure and public space. Their maintenance has been recklessly deferred, and this only postpones an inevitable, more costly and sometimes dangerous failure of their physical plants and vital services. And the public realm is just one manifestation of this broader defection from responsibility. Public school systems—bellwethers and cornerstones of urban equity—higher education, health care and housing have all suffered similarly.

While we in Toronto were once acknowledged world leaders in devising and delivering mixed-income housing solutions, we were told during this era of extreme neoconservatism that this approach was "broken." Having virtually abandoned this sector, Canada has embarrassingly become the only country in the developed world (and farther afield) without an effective national housing policy or programs for delivering affordable housing. Predictably, income polarization and homelessness have increased, as have stresses on social services, including reduced support for parks and community centres.

All of this would suggest a fairly bleak prognosis for the future of public space, let alone its ability to thrive. Still near death but stubbornly persisting, the commons (the shared public spaces in our cities) seem to be essential to our well-being as social creatures. And fortunately, with a renewed appreciation for the historic city, interest has also increased in the streets, parks, squares and trails that in combination make up approximately half of its land area. For a variety of reasons—including the economic, health and environmental benefits of walking to a park or public square to meet friends—the public realm is now back on the public agenda. It could, in fact, be argued that it has become the foundation for a new generation of city-building efforts. "Public realm" in this sense refers not only to publicly owned spaces in the city fabric. It also includes streets, small parks, squares and plazas, and the larger spaces provided by urban parks (some of which may be privately owned but publicly accessible). The correlation between the character of these spaces, the unique sense of place they provide, and the health and vitality of the city has long been identified by leading city advocates like Kevin Lynch (*The Image of the City*, 1960), who persuasively argued for comfortable human-scale and coherent relationships between streets, buildings and the landscape.

Every Sunday, Tokyo's famous Ginza shopping district is closed to vehicular traffic. The mood is festive and relaxed. Tables and chairs come out; there are vendors selling "magical" puppets that dance without strings, street music (not too loud) and other performances, and thousands of people to bump into. In places like this around the world, the pervasive desire for some form of sociability in public brings new activities into being in new ways. And the locations where these activities happen combine commerce, art and culture. On a personal level, many of us have a pent-up longing for the unscripted possibilities of being among our peers, anonymously or not. Seeing and being seen in public says something important about our place in the universe as humans and the connectedness of things. Encountering the "other" has something fundamental to do with self-actualization, and when we don't find it close to home, we seek it elsewhere. North Americans will travel great distances to experience these "exotic" qualities in Europe, Asia or Latin America (because many locales on these continents still have these everyday qualities).

We've also come to understand how critical this shared public space is for the survival of democratic societies. Cities are the places where we must learn to cope with our inevitable heterogeneity as a species. Unequal birth rates, globalization and material need have produced unprecedented migrations around the world, and many immigrants end up in cities. Immigrant societies like the United States, Canada, Australia and New Zealand, which were once the exception, are now increasingly the norm, and many traditionally homogeneous populations are looking to these societies as models for how to deal with multiculturalism. If cultural homogeneity is no longer an option, how do we live together? Cities have always been the great crucibles of cultural interaction, often to the great benefit of their citizens, notwithstanding periodic eruptions of nationalism and xenophobia. At key junctures in history, Andalucía on the Iberian Peninsula, Istanbul, Paris, London, New York, Hong Kong and now Toronto have experienced this kind of intense mixing and change.

One of the greatest challenges in contemporary city building is to get the public realm right. It is the critical compensation for the inevitable (and desirable) shrinking of private space as we return to city centres and older neighbourhoods. Successful city building is not just about the private pieces; it also requires public transportation, social services, schools, daycare, social housing and the whole range of "public" facilities. Restoring balance in this public-private dialectic and acknowledging the interdependence of the public and private spheres is fundamental to making cities work. And to do this well, enough physical space needs to be provided along with adequate resources for effective stewardship.

The most basic rationale for public space is an economic one. It counters the ultimately self-defeating prescription for neglect and withdrawal that leads to the hoarding of private wealth inside gated communities and public squalor without. There is now a broadly shared understanding among many urban economists (including all the economic consultants I work with) that cities are the principal generators of wealth, provided they can attract investment in their diverse creative economies. (This philosophy builds on some of the concepts that Jane Jacobs laid out in *The Economy of Cities* and *Cities and the Wealth of Nations*.) According to this new paradigm for economic development, value is attributed to quality of life and place as much as or more than land, labour and capital costs. Cities and regions that compete with each other primarily on cost are engaged in a losing game, since "beggar thy neighbour" policies inevitably lead to a race to the bottom and impoverishment of the very public realm and public services that generate wealth.

The project that took me back to work in the Dutch capital offers a prime example of asserting the value of the public realm. In the early 1990s, Amsterdam faced a big new challenge and opportunity on the banks of the River IJ. (The series of canal rings that define the historic city is connected to this river.) The problem at hand was how to recycle the river's valuable former industrial lands in a way that would allow the city centre to be a focus of renewal and to compete successfully with the so-called South Axis, a highway-oriented redevelopment "strip" leading to Schiphol Airport to the southwest. Seven harbour islands in the river across the entire face of the historic city centre known as the IJ Embankments (IJ Oevers) had been identified as obsolescent industrial lands and made available for new uses. I was asked by the City of Amsterdam to chair an international advisory committee for the IJ Embankments in 1992, along with an international panel of distinguished practitioners. We worked closely for over three years with the Physical Planning Department of Amsterdam (DRO) and a wide array of parties with a keen interest in this opportunity.

As the discussion unfolded, we found ourselves embroiled in a significant debate with a major consortium of Dutch companies (including banks and insurance companies) informally dubbed "Holland Inc." The consortium had hired its own design consultants to prepare plans for an ambitious commercial development program on the Amsterdam waterfront. At issue were the form of the city, the importance of pedestrian life at street level and the role of public space. These architects had proposed an extensive network of elevated roadways, walkways and tramways tied directly into major new structures at upper levels. Ironically, here were echoes of some of the aggressive and destructive elevated infrastructure that had damaged places like downtown Saint Paul, but happening in a world-famous city many times the age of the Minnesota capital.

We argued (in the end, successfully) for the primacy and independence of the public realm at sidewalk level, convinced that there was ample room here for bold, contemporary archi- 263 tecture without abandoning a clear commitment to street-level public life. Throughout Amsterdam's history the design of the densely built fabric of cheek-by-jowl seventeenth-century canal houses within the city's historic canal rings had allowed it to adapt to many roles—as residences, hotels, restaurants, shops, offices and workshops connected to a rich and varied web of public spaces. My colleagues and I were very conscious of the fact that by expanding this public realm to the River IJ there was a singular opportunity to both catalyze growth in this new area and to infuse contemporary life into the historic city and not allow it to fossilize as primarily a tourist district. And, in fact, this is what has occurred, with expansions of newly accessible public space along the water and a series of new, often dramatic, building projects serving a broad range of new needs that could not be met in the older districts.

In Quebec City, the Quartier Saint-Roch offers a prime example of improving the public realm as an economic development strategy for an area in decline. One of the oldest neighbourhoods in the city, it became a victim of sub-urban withdrawal and aggressive urban renewal. By the 1980s it was in decline, with empty storefronts and failing businesses squeezed beneath an adjacent elevated highway and the steep slopes of the Upper Town.

In the 1990s, I served as special advisor to the city and Mayor Jean-Paul L'Allier on plans to turn around this depressed area. Building on Quebec City's rich tradition of successful public squares like the Place d'Armes, we identified the creation of public space as the key catalytic ingredient to our effort. I advised that the city should both introduce new public spaces and rejuvenate some old ones to send a clear signal to the public about the city's commitment to revitlaize this area.

The first intervention was the creation of the Jardin de Saint-Roch, a new, five-acre garden forming a green oasis in the heart of the neighbourhood. On the nearby Rue Saint-Joseph, a roof that formed a suburban-style covered mall in an awkward attempt at urban renewal was torn down and the street was reopened. Investments followed, particularly from Laval University, which acquired new and renovated buildings for new facilities, including the School of Visual Arts. This, in turn, has been followed by significant investment in new housing and new businesses and retail as this historic quartier has convincingly come back to life.

As quality of place becomes a deciding factor in the location of global enterprise, sustainable public sector support for the public realm becomes a strategy for attracting and supporting effective private-sector investment. An excellent example lies in Chicago's enduring commitment to its great turn-of-the-century waterfront plan, which has consistently borne fruit. Economists like Paul Anton of the Wilder Foundation in Minnesota have quantified those benefits and demonstrated the positive impacts on property values of locating close to public green space. In his study *The Economic Value of Open Space: Implications for Land Use Decisions* (2005), he cites research he conducted in the Twin Cities, showing that many types of open spaces—from parks and nature preserves to greenways, wetlands and lakes—have a positive effect on nearby property values both initially and over time. Moreover, according to the results of referendums conducted in Minnesota, residents there value open spaces enough to raise taxes to pay for acquiring and preserving those spaces.

Of course, it's one thing to say an investment has long-term value; it's another to come up with the money. Fortunately, innovative techniques have emerged that tap the momentum and resources of the private sector, creating new funding streams both to create public realm projects and to maintain them as reinvestment occurs. Tax Increment Financing (TIF) is one such innovation, which leverages future gains in taxes, anticipated as a result of current open space improvement projects, against the debts incurred to design and build them. There is an urgent need for more initiatives like these to allow generous and welcoming open spaces to be woven again into the fabric of cities across North America as they grow denser, enabling citizens and governments to enjoy their economic and civic benefits.

BACK TO THE WATER'S EDGE

Waterfronts have become a new frontier for many cities. There is an almost universal psychological urge to be near water, and the allure of oceans, lakes and rivers is a powerful draw. And with the redevelopment of obsolescent port lands comes an extraordinary opportunity for expanded public edges. These new green spaces offer respite from the pressures of city life and an expanded or even boundless horizon. For many city dwellers, the new waterfronts become the in situ "resort," a great benefit as quality of place becomes a priority.

266

Cities that were founded on sea coasts, lakefronts and rivers were generally established there because at the time, water was the primary means of transportation and often an important source of food or, in the case of rivers, power. As these cities grew along with their ports, the waterfront zones of economic activity expanded both upland and onto water-front landfill built for warehousing, manufacturing, heavy industry and a variety of their business activities. Natural shorelines disappeared and wetlands were drained and filled as the water's edge was successively pushed out and hardened with dock wall, slips and piers that became larger as shipping technology evolved.

When rail connections and marshalling yards were added to the mix, the intensity of activity, noise and pollution and the sheer need for space caused residential and commercial life (except for port workers' housing and sailors' often red-light night life) to migrate inland. While some exceptional waterfront places like pleasure piers or ferry landings remained reachable and open, these working ports were tough, often inaccessible, workaday environments and usually *terra incognita* to the general public. By the mid-twentieth century, shipping technology and global economics had radically changed. Container shipping required larger and specialized ports, and so the maritime use of many older urban port lands diminished or disappeared. Similar technological and economic changes caused the urban nexus of rail yards, manufacturing and warehousing to fall quiet as well. As I looked over the abandoned industrial sites lining both banks of the Mississippi River through Saint Paul, Minnesota, in the mid-1990s, I first used the phrase "the retreat of the industrial glacier." As this glacier receded in

The irresistible urge to get to the water's edge fulfilled; Copenhagen Harbour and the Brooklyn Bridge Park.

city after city, new waterfront brownfields in the hearts of cities became valuable terrain. The void left behind became the driver, an expression of both potential and need, and the return to urban waterfronts has become a mainstay of twenty-first-century city building.

Along with a greater emphasis on a mix of diverse uses and a strong commitment to the public realm, the waterfront has become the testing ground for green technologies and innovations in sustainability. Reclaiming these spaces has created opportunities to develop more effective standards and innovative strategies for environmental cleanup, combining "bioremediation" (using micro-organisms, green plants or their enzymes to clean the soils through natural process), other forms of on-site treatment, and removal and capping of toxic material. These areas have also benefited from plans to tap new energy sources, innovative treatment of stormwater and new ways of handling waste. There has also been a change in city governments' mindsets toward greater flexibility in planning the rejuvenation of these large areas. In the 1970s, Battery Park City, then just a landfill site on the Hudson River in Lower Manhattan, had been proposed for redevelopment on the then-popular megastructure model of large, free-floating building clusters on super blocks. But in a trail-blazing move, the Battery Park City Authority abandoned that direction and has for over three decades been developing the district incrementally, block by block, based on a more urban streets-and-blocks plan. The intent was to emulate the best qualities of the pervasive Manhattan grid. Although Battery Park City's first buildings still somewhat stiffly and formally followed guidelines that stipulated alignment of facades with uniform cornice lines tied to that grid, the type of development and the character and variety of the architecture and open spaces has loosened up with the times. Consequently, the area is gradually becoming more of a neighbourhood.

Public access to waterfronts can have obvious economic benefits, as was the case when I became involved in the struggle for the water's edge in San Juan, Puerto Rico. In the late 1980s, the Frente Portuario was a stretch of derelict obsolescent port lands immediately adjacent to the sixteenth-century walled part of San Juan—Viejo San Juan. Cruise ship lines had been establishing the port as a point of departure, so there was a clear motivation to improve the area. San Juan demonstrated its determination and foresight when it rejected a proposed festival marketplace at the waterfront where cruise ships were docking. The city opted instead to concentrate on extending the public realm right up into the old city, hoping to draw economic benefits along with it by improving connections to the harbour. The hope was that a new, contemporary urban fabric on the waterfront would add residential population and activity to the whole area.

To this end, my team prepared an urban design plan in the form of three new *barrios* on the harbour, which reinterpreted San Juan's traditional dense blocks with buildings structured around interior courtyards. Along with architects Emilio Martínez and Andrés Mignucci, we worked with Puerto Rico's Lands Administration to issue an international request for proposals for development within this plan and to evaluate those proposals. We achieved mixed results on the development side, although the beginnings of a clearly public waterfront had been established along the Paseo de la Princesa at the base of the historic walled city.

The development was incomplete, however, and this challenge was tackled again in subsequent projects in San Juan by teams I co-led with CBT Architects and Colliers International. We produced a master plan for a convention centre district on the south side of the San Antonio Canal (much of which is now built out). We also created the San Juan Waterfront Master Plan for the Government of Puerto Rico to guide the redevelopment of an even larger band of obsolescent Port Authority lands on the historic Isleta on the north side of the San Antonio Canal. The plan sets the stage with a public "frame" for the renewal of the entire area, an interconnected network of new and renewed public spaces that provide the context for future mixed-use development. These spaces will also be connected by new light rail transportation infrastructure. Meanwhile, in the nearby Condado District, piecemeal privatization had created isolated enclaves for foreign tourists and wealthy islanders. To overcome this exclusion *ex post facto*, the city launched a program of new, pocket-sized public park and plaza spaces called *ventanas al mar* (windows to the sea).

Cities are learning from each other. By the 1990s, a series of large-scale plans for entire waterfront neighbourhoods had been created in many cities. We witnessed examples from Mission Bay (a three-hundred-acre site on San Francisco's historic waterfront) to the South Boston Waterfront (a plan that breaks up former industrial sites across an area of roughly one thousand acres). Vancouver has developed its own particular form of urban blocks by combining higher and lower buildings. And it has had great success in redeveloping its obsolescent waterfront sites as new urban neighbourhoods.

They feature a range of living choices, high-quality park space and neighbourhood vitality—most notably in the developments of Yaletown on False Creek and Coal Harbour on the Burrard Inlet. In variations on this theme, Copenhagen, Malmo and Stockholm have developed a series of remarkable new waterfront neighbourhoods, pushing the boundaries on all aspects of sustainable development.

One last example, because it's a special one. In Washington, DC, the Anacostia Waterfront Corporation is actively redeveloping new neighbourhoods on both sides of the Anacostia River using the waterfront as a powerful unifying element in a part of the city that was so divided by race and class and so neglected that it did not even appear on tourist maps. In March 2000, recognizing the enormous, untapped potential of this territory, Mayor Anthony A. Williams and over a dozen federal agencies signed a memorandum for the creation of a new vision for the Anacostia riverbank communities that would provide greater access to the waterfront from existing neighbourhoods. Access from the Mall, Capitol Hill and downtown would also be improved.

Many seminal plans—the unrealized ideas that cities once had about themselves—were swept aside in the postwar euphoria surrounding auto-oriented suburbia, but now that some of these visions are again in sync with our priorities they can be a source of new insight. For instance, while Pierre-Charles L'Enfant's famous 1791 plan for the District of Colombia envisaged a unified national capital, but essentially stopped on the north side of the Anacostia, it could be argued that his visionary grasp of the whole still has a great validity as the river becomes the city's new focus. And in some ways it is a guiding inspiration, as elements of the post-war highway infrastructure in the area straddling the Anacostia are reshaped back into avenues and boulevards.

With a $10 billion restoration and revitalization plan underway, based on a new framework that embraces the river, this massive transformation includes the Washington Nationals' new baseball stadium, 6,500 units of new housing, three million square feet of new office space, 32 acres of new parkland and a 20-mile network of riverside trails. If it succeeds, this ambitious initiative has the potential to create a waterfront made up of a series of new, mixed-income neighbourhoods that will create racially diverse waterfront areas with a range of new housing and employment opportunities on both sides of the river.

To be sure, there are enormous challenges in making these obsolescent waterfront lands accessible and opening them up for a new generation of uses—among them cleanup of soils contaminated with fuel or industrial chemicals, overcoming the physical barriers of old rail lines and highways to make these sites accessible to the public, and introducing new infrastructure and services. But because of the centrality of these waterfront places, they have the inherent capacity to produce more sustainable development by building on all the historic investment made in them, putting housing closer to existing and new workplaces, and making sure that workplaces are closer to existing housing.

Because of their often enormous size, these urban waterfronts have introduced entirely new scales of operation and ambition for city builders. Their adaptive reuse often involves transforming hundreds or even thousands of acres and presents opportunities to create entire neighbourhoods and districts. Since this move back to the water has coincided with the great collective learning curve on city building, waterfronts are frequently the places where cities are reinventing themselves.

URBAN TRAILS AND PUBLIC ACCESS

Natural features provide fertile possibilities for expanding and improving the public realm. Walking or cycling trails have become popular, as they wind through the urban fabric or along the edge of a canal, river, creek, valley or ravine to open up areas of the city that were formerly out of bounds. Old rail lines, canals and abandoned rights-of-way provide new conduits to these "forbidden" or forgotten territories. The desire to meander through the city in public space is ancient—witness the promenade, the *passeggiata* (the place for an evening stroll, a popular Italian pastime) and the *paseo* (the Spanish and Latin American equivalent). But these sinews that provide continuous links between the city's green spaces also offer something new. They respond to and facilitate walking, jogging, cycling and in-line skating (often with kids in tow) while allowing people to venture into previously undiscovered parts of the city. Every city worth its salt has multiple examples of these urban trails. The Manhattan Waterfront Greenway now extends around the island of Manhattan, the Canal Saint-Martin pathways traverse the east end of Paris and the car-free greenways of Bogotá extend throughout that city. In the heart of Buenos Aires, the conversion of Puerto Madero, a former industrial harbour, has created a bustling network of public space that incorporates artefacts of the industrial past and connects them to an adjacent Reserva Ecológica on the Rio de la Plata. And some of these urban trails were envisioned many decades ago. The remarkably far-sighted 1909 *Plan of Chicago*, produced by Daniel Burnham and Edward H. Bennett, proposed, among other things, that the city should reclaim its vast Lake Michigan waterfront for public use as a network of connected parks. This plan continues to guide the expansion of parks, trails and natural areas hugging the water's edge of this Midwestern metropolis.

The creation of these new public links has occupied an ever-greater place in my work over the years, including trail networks in New York on both sides of the East River, in Calgary at the confluence of the Bow and Elbow Rivers, in Detroit on the Riverwalk and in Boston on sites lining Boston Harbor and the Charles River. These new urban trails also provide an opportunity to reintroduce natural systems, tree canopy, naturalized areas and habitat corridors to the commons.

In Toronto, an early effort while I was working at city hall involved creating the twenty-kilometre Martin Goodman Trail, named for the publisher of the *Toronto Star* and built along the waterfront with support from that newspaper, the offices of which are prominently located on the harbour. This popular trail was painstakingly stitched together with a combination of painted lanes on existing city streets and off-street multiuse paths. The network was then extended with trails leading away from the waterfront and up the Don River Valley (through complex negotiations with the adjoining railways) and the Humber River Valley, linking to portions of existing river and ravine trails. This expanding network was, in turn, connected to the Beltline, an abandoned nineteenth-century commuter rail loop that ran through much of the city. The result is an intimate, green, somewhat magical expanding web of pedestrian and cycle paths.

In Boston and Cambridge, I became engrossed in a similar effort, the roots of which extend back to Frederick Law Olmsted's nineteenth-century plans for the renowned Emerald Necklace, a series of linked parks with connected walkways and trails that sought to tie the inland Fens and the Back Bay neighbourhoods to the Charles River. Inspired by Olmsted, a larger vision for an even broader interconnected greenway and water-based network, with links to Boston Harbor, the Charles River Basin and the new Boston Harbor Islands National Recreational Area (made of thirty harbour islands) has garnered enormous community support.

In fact, every assignment I have had in Boston and Cambridge contributes in some way to this vision, from private sector development proposals at Kendall Square and NorthPoint in Cambridge and the Fan Pier in Boston to master planning work for Boston University's Charles River campus. In each case, the opportunities to expand the public realm and connect to the water coincided with and exploited the need to retool auto-oriented infrastructure that blocked and separated the city from the water. My first involvements in extending these green space networks in Boston and Cambridge came at the invitation of investors and developers who understood the benefits of these public objectives. The site that Lyme Properties had purchased off Kendall Square had limited frontage on a short remnant stub of the Broad Canal, a waterway that had historically linked the industrial heart of Cambridge to the Charles River. We developed a plan based on two linked squares: one directly on the canal with a deck and small boat launch and the other upland with a café and, in winter, a skating rink. An unexpected opportunity also arose to incorporate a small space for boat storage and a launch for canoes and kayaks on this portion of the canal at the base of a scientific research company's head office building. Employees of companies that occupied these buildings would have the opportunity during lunch hour to paddle out to the adjoining Charles River in summer or to go skating in winter, to work in offices in a natural setting and to go to a range of eateries opening onto a public square. And the companies that occupied the buildings considered all of these things to be key competitive advantages in recruiting and retaining staff.

Further, the underground parking was designed so that people would not exit the garage directly into the buildings but would pass first through these public spaces. By designing beyond the complex itself, we had added value for the developer, the city and area residents. This, in turn, sets the stage for each new development proposal that comes forward on adjoining properties as the public realm network continues to grow out from the river.

Similar opportunities during the mid-1990s allowed other enlightened developers to enhance the value of their projects—and to succeed in gaining approvals by embracing pent-up community desire for improved access to the water. At the Fan Pier, twenty acres of former port lands adjacent to the new federal court house in South Boston, a stalemate had arisen between the city, the local community and the developers over the failure to provide real public access to Boston

Harbor. This conundrum was resolved by extending the street grid of the adjacent Fort Point Channel District to a generous promenade on the water's edge. On the Cambridge side of the Charles at NorthPoint, there was a chance to extend the Minuteman Bikeway, one of the most popular and successful rail-trails in the United States, through a new ten-acre pubic park to reach the regional trails lining the Charles River. Work on this trail is progressing in stages as development takes place along its length.

The greatest opportunity to work on the expanding green network in Boston and Cambridge came when Mayor Tom Menino and the Boston Redevelopment Authority (BRA) retained me in 2003 to advise on how the city could best take advantage of the "Big Dig"—the burying of the elevated Central Artery and the creation of the Rose Kennedy Greenway on the lands it freed up. With the goal of knitting the city back together both physically and socially, I worked with the then Chief Planner Rebecca Barnes, current Chief Planner Kairos Shen and the staff of the Boston Redevelopment Authority to develop a vision for the lands surrounding the greenway in its larger context. That context extended from the Charles River in the north to the Massachusetts Turnpike in the south and from Boston Harbor in the east to the downtown core and neighbourhoods to the west.

What emerged was the Crossroads Initiative, which focused on twelve perpendicular streets crossing the greenway (totalling over six miles in length). My initial sketch illustrated a web of improved public space on these streets to better link surrounding neighbourhoods to the greenway, to the extensive Harbor Walk (which had been extended

Design opportunities: extending the Minute Trail through NorthPoint in Cambridge to the Charles River; opening up the Crossroads at the Big Dig in Boston.

along the water's edge) and to each other. These upgraded crossroads were intended to have twenty-first-century amenities that would strengthen Boston's identity as a leading contemporary city, including improved pedestrian environments, improved signage and markers for people navigating the city and new opportunities for public art and performance. The goal was to create a convenient, comfortable, information- and activity-rich environment. (After developing the Crossroads Initiative for Boston, I was asked to serve as the city's interim chief planner during 2005 and 2006 in order to oversee its progress, among other things.) The initiative is now being put into place incrementally, and it is being funded through public-private partnerships.

On the boundaries of New York Harbor, a like-minded transformation is underway. As manufacturing and port activity diminished on the tip of Lower Manhattan after World War II, long stretches of industrial waterfront were left abandoned. Portions of this land have now been converted into mixed-use neighbourhoods, and a critical component of the transformation is the carving out of new, interconnecting public spaces. The harbor itself is becoming a kind of expansive "blue room," lined with iconic destinations: the Battery/ Castle Clinton, Battery Park City, the Brooklyn Bridge Park, East River Esplanade, Governors Island, Hudson River Park, the Statue of Liberty, Ellis Island and Liberty State Park on the New Jersey waterfront. With port lands freed up for new public facilities on Manhattan and the surrounding shores, these existing pockets of vitality—the landmarks, two-hundred-year-old forts, museums, bridges, parks and the few existing waterfront communities—have the potential to be connected by land and water to form one extraordinary and continuous public realm.

In 1999, the recently founded Brooklyn Bridge Park Development Corporation hired me as part of a larger team led by HR&A Advisors to head the urban design component of a master planning effort. The lands targeted for the park were sixty-five acres of East River waterfront that had been declared surplus by the New York Port Authority. They stretched from Atlantic Avenue, south of the Brooklyn Bridge to north of the Manhattan Bridge. The challenge was to create a great park with diverse offerings and new ways of experiencing the river on a series of obsolescent piers at the base of the Brooklyn Queens Expressway and overlooked by the famous Brooklyn Heights Promenade while extending and connecting this new public realm into the diverse communities around it, which currently had only limited access to the river. In addition, our team was to find ways of stimulating economic activity on the lands to generate a revenue stream that would support the ongoing maintenance of the park. We held extensive community meetings in venues throughout the bordering communities, and regular feedback and design possibilities were posted on the project website.

The Brooklyn Bridge Park Master Plan was soon approved and continued to evolve in the detailed designs prepared by landscape architects Michael Van Valkenburgh and his partner Matt Urbanski. In its final form, the park stretches for 1.3 miles along the East River and includes Piers 1–6, each approximately the size of Bryant Park, and their uplands. This remarkable new public space on the East River is filled with lawns, recreation, beaches, coves, restored habitats, playgrounds and beautifully landscaped areas, and it connects

visitors to the waterfront and New York Harbor with a combination of floating pathways, fishing piers, canals, paddling
waters and restored wetlands. It is the most significant park   281
development in Brooklyn since Prospect Park was built 135
years ago. Construction has begun and Pier 1 and part of Pier
6 opened in the spring of 2010 for use by a delighted public.

While working on the Brooklyn Bridge Park, I was constantly looking across the East River to Lower Manhattan
from Fulton Ferry Landing. Strangely, the distance, framed
by Roebling's magnificent Brooklyn Bridge, seemed to grow
shorter with the passage of time. But this is not so surprising. As the water re-enters the consciousness of the city,
what was inaccessible and remote becomes real and familiar.
In 2001, I had the opportunity to work with Marilyn Jordan
Taylor of the architectural firm SOM on the part of New
York City that I'd been gazing at from Brooklyn—specifically,
an East River Waterfront Plan for the area between Brooklyn
Bridge and Battery Park City. There was already a certain
magic in walking to the edge of Lower Manhattan and being
drawn to narrow slots of light between buildings, toward
where the streets end and the densely packed and bustling
verticality of the city reaches the river. Over the decades,
this shoreline has been repeatedly extended into the river—
from Water Street to Front Street to South Street and to
the current pier line. And generations of perpendicular
streets—including Dover, Peck, Fulton, John, Maiden Lane,
Wall, Old Slip, Broad, Whitehall, Broadway/State and West
Street—were lengthened to meet the ever-expanding water's
edge in order to feed commerce coming from the harbor
into the city.

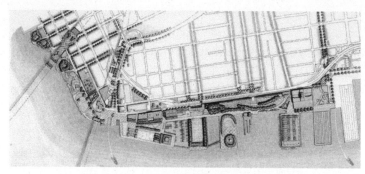

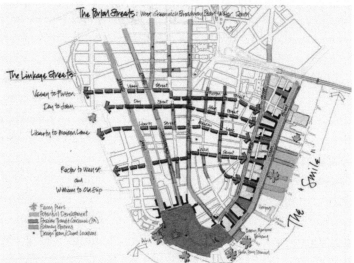

Early diagram for Brooklyn Bridge Park on the obsolescent East River piers 1–6; completing the "Smile" on the opposite side at the tip of Manhattan.

This slow growth laid the groundwork that allowed us, in 2001, to imagine an intricate web of links to the water through green vestibules, street openings, pedestrian pas- sages and public squares. In Lower Manhattan, our great challenge was to complete the "Esplanade" loop and make it possible to completely circumnavigate the Manhattan waterfront on foot. Given the limited land available, our need for open space had to be met creatively by inventive adaptation, freeing up found spaces and linking existing public spaces. We came up with a concept we dubbed the "Smile" because of the shape it made wrapping all the way around the curved edge of Lower Manhattan.

The biggest problem—or so we initially thought—was FDR Drive, the elevated highway that goes around this end of the city, right at the river's edge. After carefully evaluating a number of alternatives, we reluctantly concluded that the removal of the FDR would actually create more problems than it solved, given the tightness of the Lower Manhattan geography and the sheer volume of essential traffic that needed to be accommodated.

But seen in a new light, the elevated FDR already provided an underlying structure for public space in what appeared to be the expressway's most difficult section: from the Brooklyn Bridge to where the FDR touches down at Broad Street. The height and width of FDR (approximately thirty feet and seventy-five feet) and the rugged quality of the steel structure, all suggested an elegant, potentially beautiful found object, a great urban colonnade framing the city's opening to the river. It's potential was not immediately obvious, however, as the underside was being used for tour bus and service vehicle parking. And many of the buildings on South Street had also been

designed to effectively turn their backs to the elevated highway, with service areas and mechanical rooms at street level.
284   The area felt like a wasteland. But we realized that a bold
reconsideration and adaptive reuse could completely alter this
perception by revealing and emphasizing this two-mile colon-
naded canopy structure of extraordinary quality.

This monumental canopy defined several gateways from
Lower Manhattan to the river and destinations on the waterfront. The FDR compressed our view as we approached it
from either direction and then released us dramatically as we
passed beneath it and into the towering city. The same thing
happened if we came from the other direction, ending with
a view of the expansive riverfront vista. An FDR Colonnade
could also provide protection from rain and snow and relief
from the sun while allowing breezes off the water to pass
through. It already had the archetypal properties of the great
colonnades of ancient Rome (or early-twentieth-century
City Beautiful movement–inspired emulations of these monumental structures). And in case we designers didn't get the
hint, in the few areas that were not occupied by parking, the
space beneath the FDR was already being used by adventurous pedestrians.

Perhaps one of our most effective arguments for selling
our clients on this approach, was that the striking transformation could be accomplished with limited means. Through the
installation of a lighting scheme that highlighted the structure
and a handsome durable floor, and by the judicious placement
of furnishings and fittings, seating and kiosks, the inherent
beauty and potential of these structures and spaces could be
exposed. The combined width of the colonnade and its adjoining spaces created a corridor that could accommodate paths

and trails for strolling, cycling and in-line skating. And all along its length this winding corridor around the lower city would make cross-connections with existing and potential gateways between the river and the city.

The robust quality and length of the colonnade also fit with the dramatic juxtapositions that are Manhattan's *genius loci*. On the outboard side, pavilions for cafés and other recreational and cultural uses, grand and small, would provide a rich choice of destinations and activities. Beside these places, the character would change from busy and hard-surfaced to quiet green spaces where people could sit and enjoy the life of the river. Inboard, the backs of the buildings on South Street could create new "fronts" through renovations and additions that would take advantage of the new street life behind them.

The colonnade also provided a strong physical armature from the Marine Terminal to the Brooklyn Bridge and suggested new opportunities like the reuse of the historic Fulton Fish Market buildings and site. And traversing the South Street Seaport between Pier 17 and the historic seaport, the colonnade provided continuity and guideposts for visitors and residents alike.

Our next challenge would be to connect this new pedestrian corridor to the emerging promenades that already ran along the Hudson and East Rivers. We also wanted to connect to the pedestrian promenade across the Brooklyn Bridge, thereby providing this new space with a strong sense of belonging to New York's emerging Harbor District Park, the "blue room" described earlier. We went so far as to propose that a portion of the outside edge of the FDR surface be reclaimed as an urban balcony (still leaving active traffic lanes), serving an expanded Lower Manhattan population with new places for recreation and repose. While the "balcony" concept was not taken up by our clients, the plan at ground level did produce a consensus vision for what this area could become. It fused the cumulative impact of other public initiatives and private development patterns, including the growing importance of improved public transit (on land and water), walking and cycling. In the end the plan gained traction and by late 2006, SHoP Architects and Ken Smith Landscape Architects were retained by the city's Economic Development Corporation to take up the plan and develop landscaping and pier designs for the East River Waterfront Esplanade under the FDR Colonnade.

This strategy of opening up and expanding the urban public realm around significant natural features and cultural and historic landscapes brings to mind the great rural hiking and trekking routes of North America—such as the Appalachian Trail in the United States and the Bruce Trail in southern Ontario. More recent hybrid urban-rural trails through the Niagara Peninsula in southern Ontario traverse countryside, vineyards, villages and towns; similar trails go through the Finger Lakes District in New York State. They link viticulture, history, culture and recreation for hikers and cyclists. Venturing into uncharted territory on urban trails can be deeply satisfying, a quest combining discovery and self-discovery. Encountering others en route—friends and strangers alike—reinforces a sense that we are not alone. For me, especially from my raised vantage point of a bicycle seat, the feeling is unexpectedly reminiscent of snorkelling: like an exotic seascape seen from a fresh perspective, the city reveals itself in new ways. Self-propelled motion at relatively low speeds offers us more than exercise and a chance to commune with our neighbours. It restores an intuitive sense of direction that was weakened by the car—a feel for the real distances between things and a renewed appreciation for the connections between the parts of the city. We are able to move through barriers between neighbourhoods and city districts, heedless of traffic volume or the many limits restricting where a car can go.

David Byrne, former lead vocalist for the band Talking Heads, has been riding a bike as his principal means of transportation in New York City since the early 1980s. Two decades ago, he discovered folding bikes and started taking them with him when travelling around the world. In his book *Bicycle Diaries*, he talks about the sense of liberation, exhilaration and connection cycling provides—a magical way of opening his eyes to the inner workings and rhythms of a city's geography and population. Increasingly, the virtual world helps to guide us into the real world as these physical networks expand. Traditional paper maps are supplemented by GPS technology, and sophisticated websites provide urban travellers with detailed web-based information and online assistance. Originating in Toronto, the [murmur] project, for example, is a documentary oral history project that records stories and memories told about sites around the city. In each of these locations, a [murmur] sign is installed with a telephone number. Anyone with a mobile phone can call to listen to a story while standing in the exact spot where it happened.

One of the greatest design challenges in creating these extensions of the public realm lies in overcoming jurisdictional and bureaucratic inertia and risk aversion to allow the public into formerly off-limits territories. But these administrative and legal barriers are being broken down, driven by the public's increasing sense that they have a right to access the water's edge and other traditionally "off limits" areas of the city. In many urban jurisdictions, this right is now being enshrined in legislation and practice. For example, in Toronto, all new development in the central waterfront must now provide such unencumbered access to the lakefront and along it.

This phenomenon is still in its early stages, and it will be fascinating to see what impact it has in the long term. It's not too difficult to imagine cities traversed by extensive sociable green networks as the legacy of a post-automobile age. This increased physical and psychological access to the city may give rise to a new form of democratic public space and a powerful reversal of the post-war retreat from life in public places.

VII

MANAGING CHANGE
IN DEMOCRATIC SETTINGS

When I first read James Surowiecki's insightful book *The Wisdom of Crowds*, it struck me that while his examples were drawn from very different fields, he was also beautifully describing the creative process of city building and urban design. His thesis is that diverse groups have the most effective instincts and make the best long-range decisions. He identifies four elements required to form a wise crowd (as opposed to a mob or overheated investors in a stock market bubble). There must be (1) real diversity of opinion based on some information; (2) a measure of independence allowing opinions that are not determined by others in the group; (3) decentralization, allowing people to draw on local knowledge; and most important, (4) aggregation, a method for turning private judgments into collective decisions. These conditions are critical factors, along with what Surowiecki calls the right "table": there must be an appropriate number of people to form that wise crowd, the participants must be asked to participate in appropriate ways, and the right techniques for hearing all their voices and receiving their input must be in place. If these conditions can be met, he argues, there is potential to greatly improve the way we make collective decisions.

Without knowing the expression, I had become aware, over the years, of an extremely simple (and now widely used) tool called SWOT (Strengths, Weaknesses, Opportunities and Threats), which provides an ideal way to assemble the right table and express the wisdom of crowds. My experience using variations of SWOT in community design workshops began in Saint Paul. Instead of asking individuals or representatives to come and explain their problems with a proposed development or redevelopment or to declare their entrenched positions, this search for common ground begins with an open discussion. Participants are asked to suspend their preconceptions of one another's positions, let go of security blankets and treat the funnel as wide open (no ideas are excluded). "Noncorrelation" is the key to successfully harvesting the wisdom of crowds—that is, not overburdening the participants with briefings and too much direction about how to think about the project and the problem it's intended to solve. They have to able to draw on their own knowledge.

There is extraordinary value in allowing honestly stated tensions to be aired. If all voices are heard, no one leaves the process feeling unsatisfied with the quality of their participation. By actually listening to one another and hearing not just what the other parties' positions are but why they hold those positions, space is created for new and productive approaches to emerge. In this way, seemingly intractable conflicts can be resolved. And if done right, this process can address problems of great complexity across diverse roles, backgrounds and social and economic divides. In so doing, we can counter fatalism and the oversimplification inherent in one liners and sound bytes.

It's never easy to forge consensus among varied and passionate constituencies, especially with contentious participants—like New Yorkers with their legendary crankiness. (I know, I was born there.) To make the process even more challenging, in the case of planning Brooklyn Bridge Park, we were dealing with some of the most privileged and most disadvantaged neighbourhoods in New York. Physical topography and social distance had kept these communities isolated from one another. Contradictory claims on the turf in question were emerging though well-organized groups on all sides. The residents of Brooklyn Heights worried that new development could obscure their views of the Manhattan skyline, while the tenants in nearby public housing wanted increased recreational opportunities for their kids. From the outset, I could tell that consensus building with this group would be difficult, to say the least. We needed to quickly develop a shared dialogue that could identify some common ground and point to a bigger win for everyone.

The SWOT conversation is held in three or four rounds. I have found it important to insist on beginning with strengths to set a positive tone. This fragile initial consensus allows people to bond imperceptibly around common points of interest within their shared territory and begin to forge a sense of group solidarity. Even in the case of Brooklyn Bridge Park, identifying the initial strengths was relatively easy—the

East River itself, the extraordinary Brooklyn Heights Promenade overlooking Manhattan, the adjacent neighbourhoods, the people themselves (and, it had to be acknowledged, all the people, not just one group). Round two focuses frankly on weaknesses, and despite conflicting interest, some level of consensus usually does emerge. In the case of the Brooklyn Bridge Park, these were the impassable barrier presented by the multilevel Brooklyn-Queens Expressway (BQE), the noisy, inhospitable no man's land at its base (preventing access to the riverfront), the pressures to use the valuable vacant piers for development, fears of increased traffic congestion and potential loss of treasured views. Finally, we talked about the opportunities that development of the park offered to everyone in the room. This third and most important round builds on a new, broader understanding than any individuals originally brought into the room and is invariably the genesis of some solutions.

People from the adjacent Brooklyn neighbourhoods had many questions and divergent ideas about what the park should be: would there be vertical structures blocking views? what facilities would the new park contain and would they be monopolized by particular groups (like basketball courts for teenagers)? would the popularity of the park create more traffic in the surrounding neighbourhoods? Some preferred more active recreation; others wanted more passive and informal green spaces. But notwithstanding these sensitivities and apprehensions, the overwhelming benefits of converting a deteriorating eyesore—creating a beautiful, new, connected and accessible waterfront park—compelled everyone to stay involved. They all faced a threat larger than not getting their way because the chance to create this park would be lost entirely if the surrounding communities failed to make a unified case for public funding.

While I was initially skeptical that we could build consensus in this case, the SWOT method almost never fails to define the challenges better than any individuals (including the professionals in the room) could do. It also elicits new insights, unearths possibilities and creates a foundation in the form of a set of shared principles that that can be carried forward. This leads to future meetings in which more detailed solutions can be refined, shaped and tested through a similar process.

As I'd discovered years before at the Toronto Urban Design Group, evocative diagrams can help a process like this. By overlaying the strengths and weaknesses on the same plans and seeing that the strengths and weaknesses are often two sides of the same coin, people can begin to visualize the making of a good place—a real and tangible park with opportunities for all the amenities desired by those in the room or, in any case, some satisfying version of them. This "overlay" approach shows just how large the desired elements of the park could realistically be, and weighs costs and benefits of change, but still takes into account the participants' intuitive sense of what feels right. It's important to keep these first preliminary diagrams or sketches loose and tentative, still malleable enough to allow room for the participants to emerge with all their ideas still up for consideration. In the end, when the SWOT process works well, the "wise crowd" will be able to understand why each of their pre-conceived visions of a perfect park might have been the enemy of the common good.

GETTING TO SCALE: SUBSIDIARITY

In the 1970s and 1980s, survey after survey had identified Toronto as one of the most livable cities on the planet. It was sometimes referred to as a "city that works," and this had to do largely with a form of municipal government that had evolved to become accessible and responsive to its constituents. In order for citizens, institutions, developers and neighbourhoods to have real access to city hall, big cities need to be broken down into viable decision-making entities. The key concept in getting to the ideal size and right degree of power and responsibility is "subsidiarity," an organizing principle which holds that matters ought to be handled by the smallest, lowest or least centralized competent authority. If Toronto's government seemed to be on the right track, it was about to be derailed. And its subsequent misfortune would prove to be a cautionary tale about the value of subsidiarity to cities.

In 1998, like New York City a century before it, Toronto was amalgamated with its surrounding suburban municipalities. (In the case of Toronto, this was done by force.) The city had already been on a path to set up a new level of regional governance in response to the fact that the city region had expanded far beyond the boundaries of what was then called Metropolitan Toronto (set up in 1953). A task force led by Anne Golden was assigned to make recommendations for how this could be best accomplished. Golden, president of a major charitable foundation, understood the value of locally responsive government, and her task force advised that the province create a new "federated" system in which the thirty existing municipalities in the Greater

Toronto Area would retain their autonomy as cities but would also participate in a regional level of government. The task force also recommended that a new, enlarged metropolitan authority should oversee the GTA (combining existing Metro Toronto's territory with that of the surrounding regions). The members of that authority would be indirectly elected; some services (policing, for example) would still be provided by intermunicipal bodies while others like planning and development would remain local responsibilities within an larger regional framework. The new authority would not provide many of the services itself but would be a facilitator, broker, promoter and strategic planner. It would "steer, not row."

Disastrously, the hard-right provincial government of the time brushed aside these recommendations. Instead of the expanded model for the entire region, it forced an amalgamation of the prewar city with the inner circle of post-war suburban municipalities. This drew a hard line between the newly amalgamated city and the rapidly growing ring of outer suburban regions and municipalities, so any of the benefits foreseen by the task force's regional approach were lost. The province then deprived the newly formed "megacity" of resources through a combination of punitive uploading of tax revenues to the province and downloading of former provincial responsibilities. The enlarged city was therefore saddled with demands it could not effectively address, and it was forced to cut back drastically on maintenance and essential services.

While this move was resisted by the cities involved, rejected by 76 percent of the affected population in a referendum and strenuously fought by citizens' groups, it was nonetheless implemented. The plan had arrived out of the blue, with little or no research, study or debate. Experts in municipal affairs were virtually unanimous in opposing it, arguing that, among other failings, its purported economic savings were illusory. While the 1953 version of Metropolitan Toronto had undoubtedly been outgrown and it suffered from a need for better coordination and rationalization of resources, these problems were not solved by the amalgamation. Toronto's experience was in some ways unique, but equivalent attempts to amalgamate in other Canadian jurisdictions have met with mixed success, and some cities—notably, Montreal—have taken measures to "de-amalgamate."

The financial impacts on Toronto have been devastating. The city found itself in a structural deficit position despite provincial assistance in the form of a one-time grant of $50 million and a loan of $200 million—and it is now in a position of perennial underfunding for basic services. Property taxes as a percentage of total operating revenues have increased steadily, while provincial unconditional grants have decreased. Large property tax differentials between the City of Toronto and the rest of the Greater Toronto Area have also kept the new City of Toronto at a competitive disadvantage in the region. Deterioration of infrastructure because of deferred maintenance is now a major issue, the city is not financially self-sufficient and its debt rating was downgraded by both major bond rating organizations (because of the city's increased financial responsibilities resulting from the province's downloading of responsibilities). The current provincial government is attempting to remedy or redress many of these imbalances, but major deficiencies persist.

Disadvantaged communities within the city have been particularly hard hit by the changes induced by amalgamation. Life for these Torontonians has been marred by a perpetual lack of affordable housing and childcare spaces; homelessness; cuts to public transit, public health, community service agencies, libraries, city parks and recreation facilities. All of these trends have exacerbated the widening disparity between the rich and the poor noted in David Hulchanski's report cited earlier. But the problems caused by Toronto's amalgamation go well beyond these chronic economic stresses. The megacity is facing fundamental structural challenges. Simply put, the amalgamated city is both too big and too small.

With the increase in scale, the city lost something fundamental in terms of local vigilance and input, the *sine qua non* for livability and distinctive urban culture. Today's Toronto has jurisdiction over 632 square kilometres and a population of approximately 2.6 million, but size is not the only problem. (Toronto has only about one-third of New York's population, and New York, as I'll describe shortly, has found ways to make its amalgamation work better.) The various parts of the megacity are remote and unknowable to those tasked with running it because of a lack of meaningful local subdivisions within the municipal government.

Much of the real business of municipal government, beyond policing, transit and social services, involves making incremental judgments about building projects, parks, community facilities, and the operation and maintenance of public streets. As the city region becomes bigger and more complex, there is an even greater need for people to have a connection with meaningful representatives on matters pertaining to the local and the particular. Doing this well depends on intimate knowledge of particular neighbourhoods and the people who live in them, as well as on the ability to make real decisions on their behalf.

Part of what we have lost through amalgamation is a viable political structure for planning and managing the complex and fine-grained web of local stewardship that makes cities work. Citizens no longer have significant access to decision making, which is undertaken by a majority of councillors whose wards might have no needs or history in common with the others. While there are "community councils" (corresponding roughly to some of the former municipalities) that try to retain some local identity, they are still too big to work as local subunits. Further, they have no independent funds to spend, and they have only limited decision-making authority.

Beyond the city council itself, an enlarged bureaucracy has become inefficient, inaccessible and out of touch. Its inclination to insist on one-size-fits-all solutions is a constant problem. A recent citywide program, for example, imposed the use of oversized household garbage bins that residents in the attached or closely constructed houses typical in many downtown neighbourhoods can't really fit in their tiny front yards. The city also now has fire trucks and garbage trucks that can't safely and comfortably fit down narrow streets, as we have discovered in Regent Park—and these types of streets are common in all the older neighbourhoods. The Parks Department has organized its staff into specialized crews called "flying squads," each of which performs only one function citywide—cutting grass, pruning trees or picking up refuse. They have little or no ongoing connection to any individual park or neighbourhood and no ability to deal with any issues outside their narrowly defined assignments. What is missing is a parks employee who is accessible to neighbours, sees each park as a valuable place and a community resource, and can respond flexibly as needs arise.

"Streamlining" has also made it more difficult for citizens to have meaningful input into the city's consultation process for annual budget preparation, and this leads to costly and avoidable oversights. The ability of decision makers to understand the needs, and even the basic physical shape, of districts and neighbourhoods under their stewardship has decreased. When council members discuss an issue at the corner of X and Y Streets, very few of them have any picture or mental map of the place in question, nor do they have an accurate and informed sense of the streets and buildings in the area or of the people who live and work there. Inevitably, this leads to an increasing reliance on the abstract over the real, the standard over the particular, and an increased dependence on the most aggressive lobbyists.

Even before the megacity, there was a forty-three-year history of skirmishes between the City of Toronto and the government of Metropolitan Toronto. (Metro tended to have difficulty reconciling its suburban standards for things like roadways and public works with the city's idiosyncrasies.) But at least the city had an independent voice at that time. Today, great efforts have been made in aid of so-called "harmonization," in order to create a reduced range of zoning categories, street types and standards for all manner of municipal facilities. This centralization will harm not only the downtown but also the former suburban municipalities. Many had started to forge their own distinct identities and pride of place around their own downtowns, which included fully functioning city halls. In the core and in the suburban parts of the megacity, citizens report greater difficulties not only in becoming involved with decisions made by government but also in finding out what decisions are being made. This has produced feelings of impotence, fatalism, resentment (palpable in the most recent civic election) and loss of civic pride, the antithesis of the civic engagement that makes city building work.

During the amalgamation debate, Neil Peirce, an American commentator on urban affairs, spoke to this weakness. He suggested that as a partial antidote to the alienating nature of the megacity, each city councillor would end up functioning as the focus of a mini–city hall, and this is exactly what has begun to happen. Though this shift would seem to recapture some degree of direct accountability, it risks leading to almost total reliance on one individual. And this development lends itself to a form of balkanization in which a holistic city perspective gets lost. The situation does, however, point to a critical need for strong subentities that work within the larger scale, beyond the very limited community council model.

Other, much larger cities have successfully addressed the issue of subsidiarity—including Paris with its arrondissements and New York with its boroughs. In New York, structured community boards also help reconcile the needs of the whole city while acknowledging the importance and individuality of the boroughs and the neighbourhoods within them. I worked with several of these community boards in Lower Manhattan and Brooklyn and found them to be very effective subunits of the larger city.

As many as fifty unsalaried members and a small staff run each of the fifty-nine community boards across New York City. Board members are appointed by the borough president, with half the members nominated by the city councillors who represent the district. An effort is made to ensure that every neighbourhood is represented. Board members must reside, work or have some other significant interest in the community. They assemble locally once a month to address items of concern to the community, such as the city budget or land use matters. The meetings are open to the public, and a portion of each meeting is reserved for the board to hear from anyone in attendance. Board committees do most of the planning and they work on the issues that are raised at meetings, and their recommendations are taken very seriously by the New York's Department of City Planning, city council and the mayor. Community boards may not be the exact fix for the continued growth pains of Toronto's amalgamation—every city has its own culture and therefore it needs to tailor unique solutions to its challenges—but they have stood the test of time in New York and could suggest a practical way to start addressing some of the megacity's major flaws.

At the same time as amalgamation can leave a city struggling to cope with its large size, it can create an entity that is too small. In the case of Toronto, the megacity's borders stop far short of the Greater Toronto Area, thus making it too small in the sense that it lacks formal structures for continual dialogue and effective decision making with the broader region. And the opportunity to strengthen the city region as an effective political and operational entity—the conceptually simple two-tier system advocated in the original task force report for Toronto—has been lost. But versions of the two-tier concept recommended by the Golden task force are producing subsidiarity effectively in many other jurisdictions. Those municipalities have recognized the interdependency of the entire urban region and have also allowed for constituent municipalities to remain closer to their citizens.

"Elasticity" is a concept developed in *Cities without Suburbs* (1993) by David Rusk, former mayor of Albuquerque, New Mexico. He argues that cities should annex their suburbs in order to maintain a common frame of reference for the urban community. In many ways, the creation of Metropolitan Toronto in 1953 did this—until amalgamation derailed that agenda. The antithesis of elasticity, the megacity hardened an obsolete and arbitrary boundary at exactly the place where the large-scale issues needed to be reconciled.

What was needed and not addressed by Toronto's amalgamation were ways to move beyond the outmoded distinctions between downtown and suburbs and to reap the healthy and mutually benefits of the Greater Toronto Area, a city region with multiple centres and downtowns. These efforts could have paralleled those I've described for Metropolitan Portland or Randstad, Holland. With a regional perspective, planners would recognize that residential neighbourhoods, commerce and industry are dispersed widely throughout the entire region, and the old, gridlocked, radial commuting patterns to one primary destination for nine-to-five workers have changed radically. The cost of perpetuating this division has been a setback in facing regional challenges like land use (reducing sprawl and reliance on the car); transportation (roads, commuter rail, transit); social services; environmental issues (air quality, water quality, cleanup of contaminated sites); waste management; integrity of watersheds; common economic development strategies; and fairness in revenue allocation. Because megacities like Toronto are effectively too small, the initiative for change has been bumped back up to the provincial or state level. And when cities become more deeply dependent on the next tier of government, the gap between citizen and political power grows wider. As cities grow larger and develop more complex relationships with their surrounding regions, there is a need for government that can provide both meaningful local neighbourhood input and a big-city perspective in forging workable regional responses to common problems.

HOW THE DEVELOPMENT TABLE IS STRUCTURED

City building is a two-way street. Government plays a critical role in setting the roles and enabling change, while most direct investment comes from the private sector. But whether developers are perceived as greedy capitalists or acknowledged as constructive city builders very much depends on how the process of change is managed. Real-estate developers seek to make a profit, but as long as the parameters in which they operate are clearly defined and provide a reasonable opportunity to make money they may also operate from a perspective of enlightened self-interest. The critical role of city hall in this relationship is to ensure that public goals are advanced, defended and successfully met along the way. Developers will build; that much is inevitable. If we want them to build great cities, we need to work with them. When cities feel beleaguered, there is a real danger that any development will seem preferable to none. They may then feel that they can't negotiate for quality or advocate for the not-always-profitable things that are required to make successful communities. In a tale of two cities, the same major developer, working on major downtown sites in Toronto and Vancouver, is performing much more impressively in Vancouver (as noted by architectural critic Lisa Rochon in the *Globe and Mail*) because that city has been extremely clear about its expectations and requirements.

Yaletown sits on False Creek at the southeastern tip of downtown Vancouver. This area and a companion area, Coal Harbour on the Burrard Inlet on the north side of the peninsula, are both downtown redevelopment sites, and they have the characteristics of a particular style of high-density neighbourhood intrinsic to Vancouver. With proactive guidance by former planning director Larry Beasley and his team, Yaletown has developed in a pattern based on tall, slender towers rising from lower-scale base buildings of three to eight stories that line the streets. In combination, these provide a mix of apartments, townhouses and other housing options, along with retail, well-equipped parks and public spaces, and generous community facilities—including a former railway roundhouse converted into a community centre.

The new Yaletown features contemporary architecture employing plenty of glass and transparency. Thanks to transitions in scale, from the tall condo towers to the low- and mid-rise buildings framing the streets, it integrates skilfully with the repurposed brick industrial buildings of the adjacent

Redevelopment as effective community building: Yaletown in Vancouver, British Columbia, and a new district near the Gare d'Austerlitz in Paris.

Yaletown warehouse district. The whole project also steps down to form generous animated public spaces along the water's edge. While still exhibiting a certain sameness that comes from its buildings being developed all at once, Yaletown's design and construction does provide an excellent example of city and developer working toward high standards that are consistently applied. An effective design review panel working in support of the Planning Department helped to shape a workable, human-scale community.

Toronto's CityPlace, a project of the same developer, sits on a significant portion of former rail marshalling yards between the historic city fabric and the redeveloped edge of Toronto Harbour. The comparison to Yaletown is not flattering to Toronto. Here, too, there are tall towers, some elegant and well designed but much more closely spaced, with little daylight between them and much less attention paid to the ground-level elements. There is a preponderance of very small units, producing much less social diversity and a transient population, and residents find fewer amenities, little public realm or active street life, and few connections to the neighbourhoods to the north. At this writing, this large new area is still a work in progress, but so far it shows signs of many lost opportunities that more alert and committed city involvement might have seized upon.

Though some might like to believe that arresting growth or change is an option, we need to acknowledge frankly that development (and in most cities this means redevelopment) is an important ongoing activity. While clearly not all developers have such ambitions, increasing numbers of conscientious and highly professional developers have embraced true city-building practices and are eager to work with equally committed public partners and engaged communities. The challenge is to structure an effective process to join the interests and efforts of these different forces.

Toronto again provides the next cautionary tale, but in this case from the perspective of a challenge to the city's competence that has impeded creative planning. Almost uniquely among jurisdictions, the Province of Ontario has adopted the model of a quasijudicial tribunal, called the Ontario Municipal Board (OMB), for the adjudication and oversight of all planning matters: official plans, zoning bylaws, subdivision plans, ward boundaries and a wide range of other matters. Unfortunately, the litigious and constrained adversarial dialogue implicit in this "tribunal" model is the antithesis of the kind of informal, qualitative, multiparty dialogue that is essential to promote best practices in city building. Its decisions are final, although points of law can sometimes be appealed through the courts. Among other reasons, the OMB's role has always been controversial because of its undemocratic authority to overrule locally elected municipal councils and substitute its own decisions for municipal ones. In fact, over time this provincial oversight body has become the de facto planning board for Toronto, but it is fundamentally unsuited to this role. Because, as a tribunal, it must look at each development proposal on a one-off basis, it cannot consider the cumulative effects of multiple developments in its decision-making or seriously study how different development proposals might impact each other. And, as mentioned above, its adversarial modus operandi precludes the free-ranging multiparty discussions that are essential to building creative solutions and developing consensus among parties based on a shared understanding of the issues and places in question.

Not surprisingly, a veritable cottage industry, including lawyers, professional witnesses and handlers, has grown up around the OMB. Savvy developers will often hire lawyers even before architects. They can then select their development teams based on their abilities to perform on the stand, not on their abilities as designers. In anticipating and preparing for OMB hearings, the city's scarce planning resources are also diverted from creative design and problem solving. A former chief planner estimated that his staff was spending an estimated fourteen thousand hours annually (two thousand person-days) on preparing for and attending hearings—and this did not include time spent by legal staff and staff from other departments. All of this left few resources for integrated long-range planning, social policy planning or neighbourhood and community planning, and little time or motivation for planning staff to do their jobs. To make matters worse, because the city's decisions are frequently undermined by OMB rulings, staff and council find it difficult to take their roles seriously, knowing that they do not have the final word.

This unworkable system frustrates productive conflict resolution and has produced great uncertainty, cynicism and alienation in local communities. When the only "legal" way to address concerns about new development is for communities to engage in technical discussions (over measures of density and height, for instance) this constipated judicial model encourages the invested parties to go on the defensive, since there is little opportunity for their real concerns to be heard or to be taken seriously. In most other Canadian, American and European jurisdictions real planning decisions are actually made at the municipal level and city governments have clout. Until Ontario's system is changed, Toronto remains a poor example for cities looking to work with developers to keep and create viable, healthy communities.

There is no single best alternative to the Ontario Muncipal Board. In other cities, the responsibility to structure the dialogue and make recommendations and ultimately decisions has been vested directly with city politicians and municipal staff or entrusted to arms-length planning boards or commissions and design review panels endowed with various degrees of authority. There does seem to be real benefit in third party oversight because it removes some of the planning discussion from the immediate fray of the political arena and can therefore encourage a more balanced and thoughtful review. However, a third party with veto power (as in the case of the OMB) is not the answer. In my experience, the best versions of these arm's-length review panels have a blend of expertise—planners, urban designers, architects, landscape architects—and also a range of community members and people with development experience.

The Design Review Panel for Regent Park in Toronto (described earlier) has just this kind of mix. Panels like this can articulate the public interest, see opportunities and shed light on the choices. Invariably, this is a multistep process involving return visits by developers and their design teams to the reviewing body with refined proposals. When this process works well, as it has so far in Toronto's Regent Park, all parties come away satisfied that the project has improved greatly.

FROM NIMBY TO YIMBY

Change is inevitable—whether developers are pursuing it or not, it is being driven by external factors like changes in the economy, energy costs or lifestyle. So getting people to move from a knee-jerk "not in my back yard" (NIMBY) response to new ideas to a more well-reasoned "yes in my back yard" (YIMBY) stance is an important goal for cities seeking to evolve democratically. Increasing density, bringing in more people, more activity and larger buildings, and achieving the attributes of a growing city may sound good in the abstract, but these kinds of transformations can be frightening. Will there be more traffic and less parking, deep shadows cast by new buildings, altered and unfamiliar demographics, and noisy or unsavoury forms of assembly?

In the absence of real dialogue, people can easily find themselves wishing for less development—that is, fewer and lower buildings, and less floor area. But while self-serving and inappropriate development proposals abound and there are numerous examples of short-sighted and selfish neighbourhood obstruction, there are also many excellent examples of good projects produced when responsible redevelopment is aligned with informed neighbourhood response.

Trinity-Spadina is a downtown Toronto ward with a population of about sixty thousand people, divided roughly into fifteen neighbourhoods. This heterogeneous north-south slice through the city is undergoing a remarkable degree of change and population growth, particularly in its former industrial and railway lands and on its waterfront. In 2007, spurred by community groups, Adam Vaughan, the ward's city councillor, pioneered a method of informal, continued dialogue with his constituents about development. It's a four-way conversation engaging the neighbourhoods, the developers, the city planners and his office, which provides essential coordination. The premise is that by creating channels for early and open interaction, there is potential to tap into the momentum of change in ways that pre-empt confrontational means of settling disputes about development including the Ontario Municipal Board. The Ward 20 method uses three basic tools and techniques from which any city neighbourhood could benefit.

First, Vaughan convenes meetings in the ward's neighbourhoods to which developers and their design teams (usually without their lawyers) are invited (and invariably accept), so they can present their projects at very early stages. Developers often come several times and participate in lively and usually very positive discussions about the potential to improve the designs while addressing community concerns and achieving the city's objectives for the area. Second, his website provides access to Graphic Information System–based community mapping, which was prepared through a Ryerson University student project. This interactive mapping layers all the existing features of each neighbourhood—streets, lanes, parks, public facilities and existing structures—and then highlights where any change is proposed, with links to all the emerging relevant information. Third, adapting a technique originally developed in Ottawa, each neighbourhood prepares a "report card" (or community checklist), which sets out the neighbourhood's criteria for evaluating proposed projects.

In essence, the community is telegraphing its priorities to the developers. The report card never gives a pass-fail grade but rather provides a running record as the project evolves through several stages. It records community sentiment in the shape of feedback to the developers and to city planners. All four parties in this process have generally participated in good faith, and the results have been many well-designed buildings that fit in the neighbourhood, are commercially successful and add community amenities. Given the right conditions, there is room for creative dialogue that does not get bogged down in technicalities or litigious behaviour. This process has been remarkably successful in finding solutions and avoiding costly and unproductive referrals to the OMB.

In 2003 I found myself involved in an extraordinary effort, working with close collaborator Neil Kittredge of the architectural and urban design firm Beyer Blinder Belle to develop a vision plan and policy framework for the entire hundred square miles of the District of Columbia for Washington mayor Anthony Williams and the DC Office of Planning. Where the Brooklyn Bridge Park and the Greenway District in Boston were projects focused within a limited time frame and area, DC's physically vast undertaking was much more open ended, attempting to bridge social, economic and geographic divides in the city by also addressing the root issues of deterioration and social division. With strong involvement from the mayor's office, the project had also moved from the traditional planning realm into direct political involvement. The goal was to provide direction for a major rewriting of the district's comprehensive plan and to set the course for a number of initiatives, including the addition of a substantial new residential population. This was urban design at the largest scale, shaping a mayoral agenda with three underlying themes: restoring health to all of the city's neighbourhoods, providing greater access to education and employment, and physically reconnecting a racially divided city. The emerging ideas and concepts for DC's vision plan were presented to a public town hall gathering of over three thousand residents at the District's convention centre. Using extraordinary techniques developed by America Speaks, a company that specializes in facilitating this sort of day-long session, the mayor oversaw the day. (America Speaks had all the participants sit around numerous round-tables with computer monitors and posted continuous participant feedback on large overhead screens.) Key to this gathering was the mix of residents from across the city at each table.

From residents of the wealthy neighbourhoods of Northwest DC to the low-income areas across the Anacostia and Northeast, these sessions introduced people who would otherwise probably have had little opportunity to interact. Each table was asked to discuss a series of issues and opportunities: the division of the city into rich and poor neighbourhoods, access to education and jobs. These roundtable sessions were much like the SWOT formats that I described earlier. Each table's feedback on these topics was digitally assembled and projected onto the screens so the whole room could see it. I was initially skeptical, feeling that the issues would be oversimplified or overwhelmed by the technology. But in the end, the session provided another powerful demonstration of the wisdom of crowds—even one this big. They didn't reach definitive conclusions but took an important step in opening up the kind of dialogue that would eventually lead to more concrete steps. They set common goals for a more inclusive city by imagining ways to strengthen existing neighbourhoods and developing new ones that would overcome current physical and social barriers by targeting investments in community facilities and priority redevelopment projects in the most troubled neighbourhoods.

POLITICAL SPACE: MAYORS AND COUNCILLORS

One of the most important players in the decision making in Washington was Mayor Anthony Williams. As Joe Riley, mayor of Charleston, South Carolina, has put it, mayors are the chief urban designers of their cities. (Riley has been mayor for over thirty years and a founder of the highly influential Mayors' Institute on City Design.) Over the years, I have been privileged to work with a number of great mayors who have been critical in making political space for innovative thinking about the future of their cities and in rallying support for city-building initiatives. The challenges they face vary, since each city has its own memories of city-building successes and failures and since each city's political organization can be quite different (including some in which mayors are like peer members of the legislature—with one vote on council—and others where he or she is the head of a separate executive branch). But no matter what the political structure, looking back, great mayors taught me strategies for providing effective leadership while keeping the allegiance of the electorate.

Mayor David Crombie was in charge when I joined the City of Toronto. I've already talked about how he and his fellow reformers played a major role in reversing the destructive pattern of post-war development in their city. Although his formal powers as a mayor in the Canadian system were actually quite limited, David Crombie's persuasive powers were not and his ability to bring people together was legendary.

When he left office, he took on the leadership of what became known as the Waterfront Regeneration Trust, a civic organization dedicated to building a consensus response to community dissatisfaction with the infamous "wall of condos" along Toronto's shoreline. He reframed the entire discussion by calling attention to the vast watershed stretching from the headwaters in the Oak Ridges Moraine north of the city down to Lake Ontario. By increasing everyone's understanding of this entire lakeshore ecosystem, he rallied new coalitions to support much of the more appropriate lakeshore redevelopment that is occurring today within a precious natural setting.

As newly elected mayor of Saint Paul in the mid-1990s, Norm Coleman assumed control of a city in free fall. But he quickly took ownership of the vision for Saint Paul on the Mississippi and confidently gave voice to its power. Every opportunity that arose to make an important difference in advancing the vision was seized upon.

Evidence of his determination is still manifesting itself. In an early move, he insisted that a state highway project, the new Wabasha Bridge over the Mississippi, include ways to get down into the river valley below and also provide vertical access to Harriet Island at the bridge's midpoint. These pedestrian-oriented enhancements are part of that bridge today. Resources were limited, but Norm Coleman was extremely effective in using civil society as an important sounding board, reaching out to community leaders and drawing in philanthropic and private sector resources to create support for the city's vision.

Change occurs both through changes in policy that reflect new thinking and through examples of how that new thinking could look when applied: in other words, pilot projects. Two notable U.S. mayors have distinguished themselves and their cities with this sort of project and with bold examples of new thinking. In doing so, they have effectively marketed their cities as successful innovators. In 2005, I was on a panel at MIT that bestowed the prestigious Kevin Lynch Award for leadership in innovation on Chicago mayor Richard Daley. Many of Chicago's remarkable recent achievements can be attributed to his adminstration: converting nearly all of the city's twenty-six miles of lakefront to public use, a "greening" that does not stop at the lakefront but extends inland to the neighbourhoods; planting 1.6 million square feet of gardens on the roofs of schools, city hall, parking garages and museums (and encouraging stores like Target and Walmart to do likewise), thus lowering building temperatures and cooling costs; transforming brownfield sites into new industrial facilities, affordable housing and green spaces (and in doing so generating thousands of "green" industry jobs); and creating environmentally progressive construction standards, including the use of recycled materials and solar panels, for all public buildings while helping private enterprises achieve similar standards.

Key to Daley's success and, by extension, Chicago's success, is the fact that the power of these varied initiatives lies in their accumulation. The more they succeed, the more momentum the city brings to further initiatives for innovation and change.

New York City Mayor Michael Bloomberg is another American mayor who proves that leadership in innovation doesn't *have* to come from the top, but it sure helps to have the full weight of the chief magistrate behind new initiatives. He has been leading efforts to make the city's streets reflect a new balance between drivers, pedestrians and cyclists, and to facilitate this, his administration has issued the city's first street-design manual. By providing what the mayor calls "a single framework and playbook" for creating shared space on New York's roadways, this manual provides direction to simplify the design process and reduce costs for city agencies, urban planners, developers and community groups. It offers detailed guidance on how to design the street spaces in public rights-of-way, including specifications for paving materials, lighting and street furniture treatments. It provides descriptions and benefits of applications, including separated bike lanes between the sidewalk and parked cars, exclusive bus lanes, raised speed reducers, greening of medians and new sidewalk designs. Presented in straightforward language, the manual also provides a glossary for many technical planning terms, so community groups and the general public will find the manual accessible. By supporting the initiatives described in the manual, Mayor Bloomberg has significantly accelerated the evolution of his city and welcomed a broad spectrum of New Yorkers and their invaluable perspectives into the process.

In a completely different environment, outside Paris on the Plateau de Saclay, an area near Versailles, I encountered another powerful example of a mayor overcoming the handicap of bureaucratic and political silos. The *commune* is the lowest administrative level in the French Republic, roughly equivalent to incorporated municipalities or cities in North America. Robert Trimbach, mayor of Gif-sur-Yvette, one of the *communes* surrounding the five-thousand-hectare Plateau de Saclay, had stepped forward in the mid-1990s to organize a voluntary planning district, the District du Plateau de Saclay. This was a new vehicle that would allow all the small *communes* sharing the plateau to use their combined governing powers to protect this valuable natural feature and agricultural resource by responding together to development pressures from nearby Paris.

There was a great temptation for each *commune* to individually seek the economic benefits of development through a piecemeal, low-density erosion of the plateau's character. But under Trimbach's leadership, the participating *communes* sought to concentrate urban growth in a limited area, allowing them to be better served by transit and to avoid sprawl. Sharing tax benefits of the increased population among the *communes* would also provide the financing necessary to coordinate decision making in the district.

Trimbach and his peers organized a competition for the urbanization of the selected area, and Parisian architect Antoine Grumbach and I won with our collaborative entry. The design challenges in this area included accommodating the expansion plans of the adjacent Paris XI campus of the Université de Paris, which required new faculty buildings, student housing and campus amenities. We also found and exploited opportunities for other mixed-use development, new parks and open spaces, as well as an expanded street network in compact urban form—all on the limited site. Working and living in Antoine's office in Paris, I experienced first-hand the operations of a completely different planning culture and tradition, encountering the highly ordered French system of the ZAC (Concentrated Development Zone), which could be used to develop guidelines to implement our plan, and the impressive power of the French state in planning matters. There was little risk of second guessing by anything resembling the Ontario Municipal Board. The French planning culture is a highly circumscribed one, but impressively, it is also one in which Mayor Trimbach and his colleagues had been able to create the voluntary planning district—something new and ideally suited to the kinds of planning challenges he and his fellow mayors on the plateau were facing.

Since then, events have overtaken this original initiative. The Plateau de Saclay, extending over a much larger area than originally targeted, is to be served by important new transportation infrastructure and has been identified as a major scientific and research pole in the emerging plans for the "Grand Paris" of the twenty-first century (a new initiative of the French state). But as these plans have evolved, the shared vision to protect the plateau and ensure a sustainable development pattern has endured.

When supported and guided by strong political leadership, the municipal civil service (aka the "bureaucracy" when we are feeling frustrated) can add to a mayor's and city council's efforts and play a positive role in city building. But in undertaking transformative projects, staff need encouragement and permission from their elected bosses to be proactive in making change, to become creative problem solvers and not just prudent regulators, and to accomplish new things, not just ensure that no harm is done.

I have seen this first-hand in some of the finest civil services I've worked with: the Boston Redevelopment Authority; Amsterdam's DRO, the city's physical planning department;

and the City of Vancouver Planning Department, each of
which have long maintained a proud tradition of excellence.
When morale is high and fresh thinking is encouraged—as
when Vancouver planners were assigned a key role in the creation of the Olympic Village for the 2010 Winter Games—cities
are great places to work and attract real talent. When staff are
held back, stressed and given little direction, they become the
bureaucracy we complain about when bogged down in red
tape, a dead hand impeding positive city building.

In difficult times, when the city's own resources are
painfully stretched, there is an increasing tendency to call
upon resources beyond city hall. This has led to new kinds
of roles and involvement for community-based and philanthropic groups, foundations, universities, business, and
social and cultural organizations.

In 2000 (shortly after Ontarians had voted their neoconserva-
tive government out of office), I spoke at the Canadian Studies
Center at Bowling Green State University to Americans studying Canadian cities. I explained that the painful withdrawal
of government support for cities at federal and provincial
levels made Canadians who had always counted on the availability of effective public services look with much greater
interest to a new energy that was already in play in the U.S. If
government was getting out of constructive city building, perhaps the active engagement of civil society and the not-for-
profit and philanthropic sectors could partially fill that void.

Even where government is willing but incapable of providing and maintaining city parks and public spaces (common
rallying points for civil society's involvement), communities,
individuals, the private sector and institutions have generated

a groundswell of support for the commons. Some of this help has come from high-profile efforts like New York's Central Park Conservancy to hundreds of more modest "friends of" organizations. Betsy Barlow Rogers, the founder and first director of the Central Park Conservancy, became a great friend and mentor on the new and changing role of the private and philanthropic sector in paying for, managing and maintaining public space. The Central Park Conservancy's Youth Education and Service programs, for example, provide groups and individual youth with hands-on opportunities to learn about Central Park and help preserve and maintain its landscapes. Through activities that are both educational and fun (such as gardening alongside Parks Department employees), students develop a sense of stewardship for Central Park and, by extension, other natural environments.

These public-private partnerships (or P3s) have become a critically important vehicle for accomplishing what government could no longer manage alone. And a visionary philanthropist or community leader, for example, may outlast many mayors. This redefining of public and private roles has many benefits, but just like government, civil society needs to be accountable in clearly defined roles. Betsy Barlow Rogers' organization, the Cityscape Institute (founded in part to share the conservancy's experiences in Central Park beyond New York City), has played a vital role in developing a range of models and partnership options for civil society to follow from—P3s to conservancies to informal associations—when looking to build effective stewardship organizations for public spaces.

The Greater Toronto CivicAction Alliance provides a shining example of what civil society can do for a city that has been hit hard by loss of government funding. Founded in 2002 as the Toronto City Summit Alliance, and initially chaired by visionary civic leader David Pecaut, the Alliance brings together leading figures from business, organized labour, the health sector, the sciences, arts and culture, social agencies and Toronto's many communities. It has mobilized over six thousand volunteers.

Across the city and region, the Alliance has realized a range of programs including Greening Greater Toronto, the Emerging Leaders Network and DiverseCity. This last program seeks to engage the full resources of the city's diverse population in addressing a range of challenges critical to the future of Toronto, such as expanding the knowledge-based industry, improving the economic integration of immigrants, updating decayed infrastructure and creating affordable housing. Its strictly nonpartisan modus operandi is to work with governments and an array of community partners, but to date the reception at city hall to this growing civic resurgence has been somewhat guarded, although there are signs that this may be changing.

Civic actors like the Greater Toronto CivicAction Alliance can dramatically enhance the capacity of city government to facilitate and guide change. Broader involvement in city building will not only enable cities to do more with less but will greatly enhance their capacity for honest discussion about difficult issues and encourage thoughtful risk taking where elected officials may fear to tread.

David Pecaut's contributions to his adopted city (he had immigrated from Iowa thirty years earlier) were many and varied. He exemplified the best sort of city builder that civil society can produce. Unfortunately, on December 14, 2009, he succumbed to cancer at the age of fifty-four after a two-year battle. His loss was an enormous blow for Toronto. Over six hundred guests assembled to pay tribute at his funeral, including federal and provincial politicians, mayors, academics, labour leaders, business leaders, social activists, major figures in the arts, family and friends, representing a spectrum of people of all ages and walks of life.

In hours of heartfelt tributes, it became evident that two things in particular make civic actors like David so valuable to all city builders and urban dwellers: a special love for his city and the ability to see in it great things that others did not fully appreciate. He had set something vitally important in motion, beyond formal politics. He developed and inspired a form of creative community building by civil society that draws on all available resources and talents to make the city the best that it can be—in his words the most vibrant, economically viable and socially responsible city in North America.

In particular, he had zeroed in on Toronto as the immigrant city par excellence, and he had launched the special efforts that were required to fully tap the human potential of that unique cultural diversity. He was convinced that Toronto's best years were ahead, and his unshakable optimism and quest for solutions were infectious. It's tempting to say that David Pecaut was one of a kind, but because of the many extraordinary city builders I've met in my work around the world I am grateful to be able to say that there are more like him in other urban centres. Nonetheless, David is one of the most extraordinary examples of a visionary city steward.

VIII

REDEEMING THE PROMISE
OF CITIES

TURNING THE CORNER

When I began my work as Director of Architecture and Urban Design at the City of Toronto over thirty years ago, what we would now call sustainable city building was a really hard thing to sell. If I met with a developer, I had to start from scratch, explaining why walkable, mixed-use, transit-oriented neighbourhoods mattered and how such an approach could possibly work, so deeply engrained was conventional anticity thinking.

Fortunately, there has been a sea change in city building, echoing the bigger shift in consciousness from the postwar decades to the beginning of this new century. In rejecting the deeply rooted traditions of city building in the mid-twentieth century, we didn't appreciate the historic skills and knowledge we possessed. But now a powerful set of imperatives—from the economics of living in close quarters to our increasing consciousness of environmental stress and degradation, commuter fatigue, inconvenience and social isolation—is compelling us to learn these all again.

In August 2009, my wife, Eti, and I made a visit to Copenhagen, Malmö and Stockholm to see some of the innovative projects and areas I described earlier and were enormously impressed by what we saw. These northern cities have some of the same conditions that we have in Canada and the northern United States: long winters with short days, large land areas with a relatively small population, and a complex mix of free enterprise and social democratic traditions. With our cheaper fuel, vast natural resources and geographic isolation, North Americans sometimes myopically think that we live in a bubble of immunity to larger forces, but that illusion is fading. By looking abroad to see how cities elsewhere are transforming themselves in response to these new pressures, we were hoping to find inspiration and maybe a chance to kick the tires to see how well these Scandinavian responses to the changing world were working. In Stockholm, we visited the neighbourhood of Hammarby Sjöstad, which has set a high standard (though Stockholm's next leading-edge project, in the Royal Harbour district, is on course to exceed it). While Scandinavia's important innovations in green technologies are becoming increasingly well known, more impressive yet are the ways in which many types of technologies are being linked together. The label SymbioCity (a trademarked term used for Sweden's approach to sustainable urban development) is used by the developers at Hammarby to express this integration of sustainable practices in water supply and sanitation, traffic and transport,

Trailblazing: Hammarby Sjöstad; from industrial squatters to a complete new neighbourhood, raising the bar for sustainable cities.

energy, land uses, architecture, waste management and landscape design.

But these functional categories are too limited to capture the full accomplishment of Hammarby's innovations—the strings of interconnected consequences. While nearly every one of them may be in use in other places, in Hammarby their overlap unlocks many new possibilities and optimistically points to new ways of living in cities.

From the requirement to use new, commercially available, low-energy appliances to the extremely tight and well-designed building envelopes, no stone has been left unturned in Hammarby's efforts to reduce energy consumption. Every conceivable source of energy is being tapped: geothermal heating and cooling, district heating, cogeneration using biofuels from organic waste, and using biogas from wastewater to produce power and heating (and to fuel buses). Hammarby also draws energy from ubiquitous wind farms, solar panels for hot water and photovoltaics for power. These new sources, along with education programs targeting adults and children in the matters of recycling, water consumption and daily travel patterns, have encouraged residents to further reduce their own environmental footprints. In combination these measures demonstrate ways to drastically reduce the city's reliance on fossil fuels (and, by extension, its economic vulnerability to volatile political situations around the world).

The combined effects of environmental cleanup are palpable. The air feels cleaner, and people are now swimming and fishing in previously polluted waters. Innovations in stormwater management, like treating water in naturalized ponds closer to the source instead of transporting it long distances, have produced attractive and accessible new urban waterscapes incorporating ponds, fountains and naturalized plantings. In new projects, underground vacuum systems are used for waste management, like one in Hammarby made by Envac. Collection points are found inside communal areas of apartment blocks and in public areas. All users have to do is lift a small, colour-coded lid and drop their rubbish into one of three different kinds of chute: combustible waste, organic waste and paper. The rubbish collects at the bottom of each chute until a sensor indicates that the storage space is full, and then the system kicks into action. The waste material travels through underground pipes at seventy kilometres an hour to a small, centralized collection point for recycling and use as fuel for cogeneration. Not only is the system cost effective and clean but there are also no garbage trucks making the rounds, and builders have no need to provide garbage rooms, loading bays or the intrusive, space-consuming bins that clutter our streets in North America.

Getting around without a car in all the cities we visited is easy, comfortable and efficient, and can be done in several ways. Schedules for subways, trams and buses are reliable, with short waiting times. Effective alternatives to auto use are increasing as the convenience of transit, cycling, walking and ferries reverse the tidal pull to the suburbs and the allure of commuting by car.

The city-building benefit comes not just from the use of transit but also from the way new neighbourhoods are forming around the stops. Light rail tracks are easily crossed by pedestrians; shelter is generous, as are the amenities at important stations: cafés, restaurants, grocery shopping and social services. As more people use these alternatives, the need for parking decreases and new housing projects

From new innovations, like vacuum-powered waste removal, to old solutions, like streets safe enough for kids to bike to school.

require fewer expensive and space-consuming garages (parking stalls cost in the tens of thousands of dollars at the outset and produce ongoing maintenance costs). Instead, a smaller number of shared spaces is made available for rented or car-share vehicles.

Achieving mixed land use is one of the hardest nuts to crack in establishing new neighbourhoods. Newly built areas often feel sterile and lack the interweaving of living, working and shopping that developed organically in older parts of cities. For decades, the rigid specialization in concept, form, financing and delivery that characterized post-war development has worked against this kind of hybridization. Nevertheless, Scandinavian cities have made impressive strides here, too, increasing the mix and moving away from the isolating and underperforming monocultures of residential enclaves, no matter how well designed they might have been.

The new projects we visited in Copenhagen, Malmö and Stockholm now mix housing with jobs, and in some cases the number of employees roughly equals the number of residents. That combination brings life to the streets and makes districts more sustainable. Residents and workers take transit to and from work or other destinations, allowing more steady use of the transit system throughout the day for more than just commuting. Solutions for accommodating this mix ranged from the conventional—dedicating entire blocks to either residential or office buildings, thereby forming mini–office clusters—to an intricate intermingling of buildings and purposes on the same blocks or even in the same buildings.

Scandinavia already has a tradition of courtyard housing that allows for relatively quiet green spaces in the interiors of larger blocks, and the newer projects reflect this. Because they can easily incorporate play spaces for young children, this housing form is especially appealing for young families. Balconies slightly larger than the North American norm make wonderful outdoor rooms that compensate for typically smaller interior living spaces. It also helps that European barbeques are not the super-sized variety that North Americans use.

333

Affordability is critical for a broad demographic to actually live in these central locations, and this is made possible through the generous social structures that provide support across income levels for daycare, education, health care and housing. While there are exclusive areas in these cities, the difference in income and the disparities in the quality in the housing stock seem much less pronounced than elsewhere. In Sweden, for example, there is no public housing per se. Rent subsidies are applied not to buildings, but to individuals and households based on need, allowing them to choose where to live.

Not everything we found in these northern European cities worked as well as the places and systems I've described so far. The incorporation of street-level retail into the mix was uneven. Some new areas in Copenhagen had clearly been tempted to include a shopping mall in the plan, depriving the streets of life and vitality, whereas retail stores successfully lined the new tramway street in Hammerby Sjöstad and restaurants and cafés were sprinkled throughout the neighbourhood. In the older neighbourhoods, the adaptations were subtle reworkings of long-established traditions. Attractive street markets were located in older squares and along newly carved-out pedestrian streets.

In Copenhagen, the dominant grocery chain, Irma, had created a category of downtown-scaled "mini" Irmas, which had cropped up everywhere. We were impressed that there was still also a wide variety of traditional, nonchain specialized establishments: bakeries and delicatessens and even tiny cafés with only two or three tables, demonstrating that with enough density and overlap, these kinds of small, unique businesses can thrive.

Scandinavians compensate for living in smaller interior spaces with the incredible richness and variety of their public realm. Within the Hammarby Sjöstad neighbourhood, there are recreational spaces for all ages and levels of energy and fitness. It has a preserved grove of huge, mature oak trees; a ski hill; spots for skating, fishing and playing sports; places where you can stroll along the water on boardwalks over marshes; and beautifully designed pedestrian bridges. The city has become its own resort. There are tiny squares where people can meet and take in the scene and big parks where people can be more active—places to be together in public and intimate places to be alone.

In the centre of Copenhagen, swimming pool barges are docked along the harbour and there are new recreational areas like the beautiful Amager Strandpark Beach, which looks east across the Öresund Sound facing toward Malmö, Sweden. To someone raised in New York, Amager Strandpark felt like a twenty-first-century Jones Beach (one of Robert Moses' great accomplishments, which gave post-war New Yorkers a place on Long Island to go for family outings in their new cars). But Denmark's version featured parking lots for bicycles, not cars. Everywhere, we

saw changes in the design of streets to reflect a new hierarchy: first pedestrians, then cyclists and transit, followed
by cars and trucks. The treatment of spaces for walking was
obviously a high priority, with well-designed places to
gather and sit and a visible commitment to ongoing maintenance. This prioritizing also came across in the city's
safety efforts through the use of highly visible pedestrian
and traffic signals—such as crosswalks clearly delineated by
colour and road-surface texture.

In each city, we found expanding pedestrian-only zones.
With a population of over one million, Copenhagen has created the famous Strøget, a 3.2-kilometre-long, car-free zone
in the narrow streets of the city's fine-grained medieval
heart. Strøget (literally "the stroke") was created in 1962 at
a time when cars were beginning to overwhelm the centre.
The idea was at first controversial, since some thought that
Danes didn't have the taste for the "public life" of such a
street, and many local merchants feared that the move would
scare away business. However, success proved them wrong
and the network has continued to expand. About 250,000
people use Strøget every day in the summer and about
120,000 on a winter day.

Periodically, the main pedestrian spines have spawned
perpendicular offshoots in the form of other pedestrian
streets, which lead into small interior passages and courtyards or widen out into squares. These were obviously
popular places for all ages to see and be seen, and the markets and cafés lining them seemed to be prospering. The
pedestrian networks were still surrounded by, and pene-
trated by, shared-use vehicular streets that provided basic
access especially for transit and for servicing restaurants

A neighbourhood for all seasons, with ample opportunities for recreation in its heart; the city becomes its own resort.

and other businesses. But the feeling they conveyed was nonetheless informal and inviting, liberated from the need to "fight" with cars.

Cyclists in the Scandanavian cities we visited have a privileged place on streets, and their already high numbers are increasing. (Copenhagen is aiming for bike trips to make up 50 percent of all trips in that city.) As a result, efforts are continuing to increase the number of separated bike lanes and to provide traffic signals and safer markings for turning at intersections. Bicycles can also be easily rented on the street. In Stockholm and Copenhagen, stands are located all over the city with bicycles that can be returned at another location.

Most impressive for us was the fact that many younger kids in the elementary school in Hammarby safely and comfortably ride their bikes to school—reminiscent of the independence we enjoyed in my childhood in Brooklyn. This was remarkable to me, since it would be impossible for children to cycle safely for any significant distance in the auto-dominated heart of almost any other city.

When we took to exploring Copenhagen on bicycle, we rode the separate bike lanes almost everywhere. They kept us on the inboard side of parked cars or even separated from moving traffic by a raised curb, providing a secure space where drivers' doors wouldn't unpredictably open and put cyclists at risk of the infamous "door prize." We were also relieved to find traffic signals and consistently painted or textured delineations in the pavement to help cyclists turn safely. In North American cities, there is constant ambiguity about where cyclists should ride and a dangerous lack of clarity about how to accomplish basic moves like a left turn: should

I turn in the traffic lanes or with the pedestrians? Here, the rules were clear and practical, so it was not surprising to find that everyone generally followed them. Interestingly, parked bicycles were not chained up to fixed objects but simply had modest locks blocking their spokes. Theft is obviously not the same kind of problem as it is in North America, and that is a very good thing. Because with the number of bicycles on a Scandinavian street, North American–style hitching posts would be impossible to accommodate.

The newly designed buildings and commons in these Scandinavian cities take many cues from the adaptive reuse of the historic settings. And every new public building and a number of the private ones that we saw on the newly accessible harbour in Copenhagen contributed a public facility, a café or restaurant to the waterfront. The Black Diamond, an elegant addition to the National Library, extended this sense of "publicness" and invitation with its magnificent interior atrium overlooking the river and the unfixed, comfortable chairs on the water's edge promenade. The promenade's broad edges and beautifully simple pedestrian and cycle bridges provided a deep sense of the public realm extending from the historic inland districts into these previously under-developed territories on the water.

The water is becoming cleaner here too, and with its newly developed accessible borders is safer for recreation. It's also becoming central to the changing self-image of this historic city. The sense of green refuge within the city is an old idea in Copenhagen. The famous Assistens Cemetery, for instance, has long doubled as a park. But a literal "green-ness" is now extending from the softened old industrial edges of the waterfront back toward the interior of the city, where more park and forest-like spaces are being created. And some green spaces offer the added benefit of doubling as conveyances of stormwater.

In Stockholm, we were impressed by the health of the street trees and simple measures being taken to keep them healthy—like slow-release water bags placed around their trunks to carry them through dry spells. We were also struck by the presence of kids and young families everywhere we went. The city centres are extremely child friendly, both in the older neighbourhoods and especially in the new ones like Hammarby Sjöstad or Västra Hamnen in Malmö. Play spaces, daycare facilities and schools are available in many places. A large number of the residential courtyards also have imaginative play sculptures instead of the standard-issue, off-the-shelf playgrounds that many municipalities have settled for in North America, often through a combination of penny pinching and risk aversion. The cities themselves are playful, offering many examples of whimsical public art, from poetry embedded in bronze characters in the streets and sidewalks to the preservation of a harbour crane as sculpture.

Each of these cities has areas (often, but not always, on the water) where obsolescence allows for great change, and they are efficiently mining this potential, upgrading the infrastructure and using much of the stock of industrial buildings for cultural uses—celebrating their history while densely infilling vacant sites with new urban fabric. In Copenhagen, for instance, the schools of architecture, dance and theatre now occupy wonderfully adapted heritage structures in the former navy yard. In some cases, major surgery has been necessary to realize a site's potential—such as the introduction of new subways or a major new tunnel to expand the rail network under the centre of Stockholm. Through this interconnected set of moves at many scales, these old cities are getting a completely new lease on life.

Copenhagen, Malmö and Stockholm are achieving their greatest successes by orchestrating a shift into a new way of living in cities. Innovative architectural and landscape design that is unashamedly contemporary makes it clear that what is new is of this time, but in each case there is obvious respect for the city's long relationship with its history. Significant buildings like the new opera house in Copenhagen deserve to stand out, but most residential and commercial buildings— both old and new—play more modest, supporting roles by providing a continuous and comfortable edge to public spaces. To promote diversity in style and expression in a single area, the city limits how much a single developer or architect may design or build. This creates many opportunities for young design firms to land contracts in the city centre, increasing the richness and variety of new structures. With much attention paid in residential areas to the entrances, stoops and gardens of individual units, many of these designs are breaking down the barriers between indoors and outdoors. Some buildings have effectively become vertical gardens, with plantings that climb their facades and grace their rooftops.

These Scandinavian examples are offered here not as templates for the rest of us to follow but as indications of how other societies are coping with the same issues we face. But they do offer models that we might adapt and particularize to our own cities. These societies have clearly made city building a high priority and see it as the key to achieving sustainability. Copenhagen, Malmö and Stockholm work well, they are reasonably funded by their national and regional governments, and they have effective self-governing powers that they use wisely. With a strong commitment to the benefits of collective action, they have demonstrated the value of formulating large-scale strategic plans and sticking to them over time. But they still face challenges. These once culturally homogeneous cities are becoming much more mixed, and in many ways, they now look for guidance from immigrant societies like Canada that have been relatively successful at integrating new populations. The ongoing challenges of dealing with an aging population, tapping entrepreneurial energy and talent while protecting social equity, among many others, are shared by cities everywhere.

Ultimately, we all need to make a fundamental shift to a more sustainable way of life. The notion of a quick technological fix is just fantasy. There are some who think our current, sprawling, auto based, high-energy-consuming way of life can proceed unchanged if we find a magic new fuel source like hydrogen fuel cells or a solution for climate change like solar energy reflected back from space. But all of these purported solutions come with their own serious limitations and high costs. The way out of our dilemma starts with the frank and unequivocal acknowledgement that we are facing serious problems. From that understanding flows the knowledge that we all need a similar rebalancing in our urban world and that we will have to summon the leadership, the will and the resources to make hard course-changing decisions.

341

THE CASE FOR EMPOWERING CITIES

At the very time when cities are faced with the urgent need to absorb more people and adopt more sustainable practices, recent economic stress has revealed their vulnerability. The phenomenon is especially pronounced in Canada, where roughly 80 percent of the population already lives in major urban centres—and that number is increasing. Unfortunately, according to the British North America Act, cities were made the virtually powerless "creatures of the provinces" at a time when 10 percent of the population lived in urban areas and the major issues were public drunkenness and profanity, running of cattle or poultry in public places, itinerant salespeople and the repair and maintenance of local roads. It's obvious that cities need greater and different powers to realize their full potential, but it has proven to be extremely difficult to remedy this situation. And cities in many other countries, including the United States, face similar issues. (Regarding the U.S., though, it's encouraging to observe that in 2009, for the first time in American history, the president appointed a White House Director of Urban Affairs.)

In jurisdictions everywhere there needs to be greater recognition of the crucial roles that cities are called upon to play and the need to address the long-festering radical disconnect between these responsibilities and the powers and financial resources they have at their disposal. As major generators of wealth and prosperity, why should big cities be so hobbled in their ability to invest in the future and the lives of their citizens? Adequate support for the creation and maintenance of urban infrastructure and the public realm is a strategic investment in quality of life, but it is also an investment in a nation's competitiveness on the world stage, as city regions play vital new roles in anchoring their nation-states. For decades, we have been heavily subsidizing unending, unsustainable sprawl onto greenfields on the urban fringe. This investment urgently needs to be redirected toward densifying and redeveloping urbanized areas that already exist: city centres, brownfield sites, older neighbourhoods and existing suburbs. While respecting the principle of subsidiarity, we need to let cities do what they alone can do. And this means getting resources closer to the people who use them in order to develop solutions in problem areas like urban transportation and infrastructure.

This means that reliable financial support is needed, not just sporadic pre-election handouts from higher levels of government that don't allow for long-term planning. It is impossible to do effective city building when relying on unpredictable election goodies and one-time stimulus handouts or when tapping only the market-driven interest of the private sector. Cities need dependable funding streams and programs and the ability to structure borrowing in order to make the kinds of long-term investments needed to sustain dense populations—investments in physical and social infrastructure, housing programs, transportation, education, health and waste management.

Clearly, cities desperately need a new deal. But herein lies a dilemma. When faced with their cities' demands for greater support (meaning, quite possibly, new sources of tax revenue), citizens may look with deep skepticism at the way many municipal governments actually function. They often appear to be locked in inefficient and wasteful practices, trapped in contracts with employees that seem to preclude best practices, reluctant to make use of available new technologies and unwilling to enter new partnerships for service delivery. These observations are valid. Cities also have to earn the trust of the public and do a better job with the resources they have, even as they ask for more. The onus is on civic leadership to demonstrate its readiness and competence to use scarce resources wisely, to innovate in service delivery and to make the hard changes that will provide future gains.

It is tempting to imagine how the future might play out if cities really did have the resources they need and if they really did get their acts together. Predictions can be a hazardous business, but in this case a glimpse into the future does not require such a huge leap of the imagination. In many respects, cities in the years to come may resemble what we have already begun to see in the more forward-looking examples I discussed earlier. It's interesting and helpful to extrapolate from those models and reflect on the possibilities they suggest. What might life in our cities look like if we aggressively filled in the obsolescent rail yards and port lands, cleaned and remediated their polluted soils and built denser, more walkable neighbhourhoods? What if the suburbs also began to thicken, diversify and densify, becoming cities in their own right? What if we were able to move toward zero carbon footprint communities or even "net plus" energy (meeting all of own energy requirements and creating a substantial amount of additional electricity) by creating energy from our waste and from renewable sources where we live and work? The places we envision might in some ways take us back to forks in the road that North America confronted in the heady days of post-war euphoria. Following the same path is no longer an option. However, the other path will lead us not to a tabula rasa or another brave new world but rather to a complex intertwining of old and new. Much would be familiar, much would be recycled and hybridized, but this new, twenty-first-century city would not be a facsimile of any other time or place.

345

A future rooted in practicality would combine emerging technologies with some very old low-tech and passive solutions. With recreation, shopping and cultural life much closer to hand, proximity would replace speed to help solve the problem of access. Many of us would still be using cars— or whatever the next version of personal mobility will look like—but perhaps not vehicles we own. And we would likely get around using a greater choice of methods, including more walking, cycling and transit. Our living spaces might be smaller, but that would be compensated for by a greater variety of public spaces, amenities and necessities close at hand, so we will likely spend less time in our own private places anyway.

By accommodating an increasingly diversified urban society and economy, neighbourhoods would be home to people of all origins, ages and stages in life. (It is tempting again to think that cities would even contribute to prospects for peaceful coexistence in the world by demonstrating the benefits of tolerance.) Great natural features in the heart of cities—lakefronts, riverfronts, seafronts and harbours— would become important public gathering spaces and amenities, interconnected by networks of trails that would enhance the presence and functions of nature in the city. As suburbs coalesced around new transit hubs, more people would be attracted to these evolving urban centres, allowing for a more balanced combination of smaller and larger cities. If it is possible to imagine this kind of shift for cities in the Western world, is it possible that cities in the developing world will move directly toward these sustainable patterns, exploiting advantages and qualities that many of their older cities already possess? Will they avoid the grievous missteps the "developed" nations made in the twentieth century?

Is it also possible to conceive of a new form of politics in which the needs and potential of cities are acknowledged? Despite the fact that most Canadians live in a handful of urban regions, Canada's national politics is still defined by competition between the regions. Similar divisions exist in the United States between the "blue states" and "red states," reinforced by deep-seated mythologies and a persistent and strident anticity rhetoric. "Inner city" has become a code for "problem districts" even when the reality of these neighbourhoods does not bear this description out. But if larger forces can inspire us to move beyond the urban-suburban political divide and if we acknowledge that the suburbs are part of emerging urban regions with problems and opportunities similar to (and connected with) those of the cities they surround, the demographics start to look different. The red state–blue state divide and divisions between provinces become misleading when we understand that residents of Toronto, Montreal, Vancouver and Calgary or New York, Chicago, Denver and Los Angeles already have more in common with each other than they do with their respective hinterlands. At the same time, though, it will be vital for planners and politicians to link the urban fabric to those hinterlands—the agricultural lands and other green spaces near the city—in sustainable and productive ways that promote local economic development. It is not difficult to imagine that North American political structures could evolve to replace old-style regionalism with a new politics based on the city-region or that political parties could emerge that acknowledge the changing demographics by championing pro-city policies. However, despite such optimistic prognostications, there is no guarantee of a smooth ride. Inevitably, new pitfalls and challenges will arise as unanticipated events and trends surface and upheavals like the recent financial crisis occur.

We live in an impatient world that seeks to avoid complexity. But city building is complicated work that requires a great deal of patience. Still, cities do not have to face a "dark age ahead" if we rise to the challenges now. To avoid repeating one another's errors, we need to share and build on the success stories—stories like the ones I've been telling in this book. The best defence against inertia is the development of a strong, deep culture of the city with a widely shared web of relationships, a deep bench of committed city champions and a long collective memory. If we can marshal these resources, we can build great places to live, and the coming decades may indeed be the decades of healthy, vibrant, sustainable cities.

II THE CITY REBOUNDING

ACTION-REACTION: THE EMPEROR HAS NO CLOTHES

Team X included noted architects Jaap Bakema, Georges Candilis, Giancarlo De Carlo, Aldo van Eyck, Alison and Peter Smithson and Shadrach Woods.

José Luis Sert invited an impressive group of leading architects and urban thinkers to his 1956 conference at Harvard University. These included Hideo Sasaki, Richard Neutra, Jacqueline Tyrwhitt, Victor Gruen, Eduard Sekler, Gyorgy Kepes, Garrett Eckbo, Lewis Mumford, Jerzy Soltan and Edmund Bacon.

THE STREAMS MERGE

The deep immersion in our studios cemented by the shared experience of the strike was a powerful bonding experience which formed the basis for many life long relationships including my great friendship and continued exchange over many decades with Tony Schuman, a professor in architecture at New Jersey Institute of Technology, in Newark, NJ.

ARRIVING IN TORONTO: A SECOND CHANCE

The emergence of the Reform Council in Toronto grew out of these diverse strands of civic engagement gaining momentum over the course of several municipal elections. In 1972, former Ryerson Professor David Crombie would become the first mayor to lead this reform coalition supported by a strong cohort of newly elected councillors like John Sewell, Karl Jaffary, William Kilbourn, Michael Goldrick, Colin Vaughan, Dan Heap, Dorothy Thomas and Allan Sparrow. They were united in their advocacy of another path for the city, and many had been inspired to temporarily leave distinguished and active careers in other fields.

JANE JACOBS' IDEAS RESONATE

While living in Toronto, Jane continued her life's work as an author and followed *The Death and Life of Great American Cities* with a series of other books: explorations of the economic underpinnings of cities, trade, import replacement and the generation of wealth in *The Economy of Cities* (1969) and *Cities and the Wealth of Nations: Principles of Economic Life* (1984); the ethical underpinnings of the commercial and guardian structures in *Systems of Survival: A Dialogue on the Moral Foundations of Commerce and Politics* (1992); and the great synthesis of economic, social and natural systems in *The Nature of Economies* (2000) and *Dark Age Ahead* (2004).

A TIPPING POINT

The role of a critical talent pool in driving the new creative economy has been extensively documented by Richard Florida and Meric Gertler in *The Rise of the Creative Class* (2004) and other works.

III THE ELUSIVE ART/SCIENCE OF CITY BUILDING
WE SHAPE OUR CITIES AND THEY SHAPE US

Real leadership in Regent Park was provided by Derek Ballantyne then the CEO of the Toronto Community Housing Corporation. I enjoyed a close collaboration with city planner John Gladki and architect Ronji Borooah.

IV NEW TOOLS AND TEAMS

TESTING A METHOD IN TORONTO

350 At different times and overlapping during this period, the planning team engaged by the Reform Council included highly motivated individuals like Ray Spaxman, Tony Coombes, Steve McLauglin, Ron Soskolne, Howard Cohen, Peter Tomlinson, Ken Whitwell, Greg Stewart, David Weinberg and John Gladki, among others.

Previously commissioned studies like *On Foot Downtown* (1970) and *On Building Downtown* (1974) had provided Toronto City Council with important pieces of a conceptual framework for a new approach to city building.

Key early collaborators within the Toronto Urban Design Group were Mary Lynn Reimer, David Dennis, Mark Hewitt, Lee Jacobson, Robert Packham, Graham Moore, Robert Davies, Eric Pederson, Frank Vajda, Elizabeth Sabourin and Mary Jakoi.

The revitalization of Yonge Street was guided by City Councillor Allan Sparrow, with economic advisor Barry Lyon as liaison to the local business community.

TAKING IT ON THE ROAD TO SAINT PAUL

Currently led by landscape architect Tim Griffin, the Saint Paul on the Mississippi Design Center Team has included many key members over the years including Gregory Page, Lucy Thompson, Nancy Holt, Leon Pearson, Tim Agness and Tom Eggum, all of whom have worked very closely with Patrick Seeb, the CEO of the Riverfront Corporation.

NEW KINDS OF COLLABORATION

The adventurous spirit of the Lyme Property team and their commitment to design really made the Kendall Square project possible, especially David Clem and his associate Dan Winny.

Buildings and landscapes in the Lyme Properties project in Kendall Square were produced by Behnisch and Behnisch of Stuttgart, Stephen Erlich and Anschen and Allen of Los Angeles, CBT of Boston and Michael Van Valkenburgh

Associates of Cambridge among others, including the LEED Platinum–rated Genzyme headquarters.

A NEW TOOL KIT

Another strong developer team committed to design and innovation made NorthPoint work including Spaulding and Slye partners, Dan O'Connell and Kyle Warwick, along with my close and frequent collaborators at CBT Architects, David Nagahiro and Kishore Varanasi.

The Innovation Team for Rockcliffe included the key collaborators who joined me in making up the "gang of 4": architects Bruce Kuwabara and Barry Padolsky and landscape architect Greg Smallenberg.

V CITIES PERPETUALLY RE-INVENT THEMSELVES

SHAPING FORCES IN OUR TIME

The great potential and efficacy of urban boulevards was chronicled by Allan Jacobs and Elizabeth McDonald of UC Berkeley in *Great Streets* (1995) and *The Boulevard Book* (2003, with Yodan Rofé) Allan Jacobs.

Our Lower Don Lands team was led by Michael Van Valkenburgh Architects with a great range of collaborators in many related fields including myself as urban designer; the MMM Group Ltd. and GHK International Consulting, urban planners; Limno Tech. Inc., river hydrologist; Applied Ecological Services, Inc., regional ecologist; Transsolar Energietechnik GmbH, climate engineer; MSME Architects, architect; AECOM, civil and marine engineer; Arup, traffic and transportation engineer; RFR Engineering, bridge engineer; Carpenter Norris Consulting, sustainability consultant.

The members of the International Advisory Committee for the IJ Embankments in Amsterdam included Tjeerd Dijkstra (the State Architect for the Netherlands), Wim Crouwel (award-winning designer, NL), Antoine Grumbach (Grand Prix D'urbanisme, Paris), and Peter Butenschøn, (Director of the Design Institute, Oslo).

The fact that New York City residents have a lower per capita environmental footprint (which by almost all measures is a fraction of the national

average) is confirmed in studies by the Brookings Institution and the New York
Regional Plan Association. A report, which sought to quantify the amount of
carbon emitted from transportation and from residential energy use in the
nation's hundred largest metro regions in 2000 and in 2005, found that in 2005,
the average New York resident emitted 0.825 tons of carbon from highway
transportation, the lowest amount among the metro areas while the average
American emitted 1.44 tons.

CITIES IN NATURE

The restoration of the Lower Don River mouth had been a long-standing goal
of groups like Bring Back the Don, who had been advocating it for decades and
who played a vital role in the elaboration and refinement of the plan for the
Lower Don Lands development.

BACK FROM THE ABYSS

The work at New Center in Detroit was led by senior staff at the New Center
Council Ann Lang and Kurt Weigle, and General Motors Vice-President for
Real Estate Matt Cullen.

VI RECLAIMING THE PUBLIC REALM
THE REVIVAL OF THE COMMONS

In the 1980's, contemporary observers like Danish architect Jan Gehl (*New City
Life*, 2006 with co-authors Gemzøe, Kirkness and Søndergaard), have deepened
the understanding of the social roles that public spaces play from the essential
(such as walking to work or school), to the optional (such as recreational activities) and enriched the combinations of the two.

BACK TO THE WATER'S EDGE

Over the years, I have worked on the whole of the Anacostia waterfront and
many of its parts, the SE Federal Center, and the Southwest waterfront with
many professional colleagues, including John Alschuler of HR&A, Neil
Kittredge of Beyer Blinder Belle and Alex Krieger of Chan Krieger &
Associates, and then-DC Chief Planner Andy Altman and his team. The
Anacostia Waterfront Initiative Framework Plan received the 2005 Boston
Society of Architects/AIA New York Chapter Urban Design Awards Jury
Special Citation for a Physical Plan.

URBAN TRAILS AND PUBLIC ACCESS

The Brooklyn Bridge Park Planning Team was led by economic strategist
John Alschuler of HR&A and included landscape architect Michael Van
Valkenburgh, whose firm Michael Van Valkenburgh Associates went on to
implement the design and construction of the new Brooklyn Bridge Park,
which is currently underway.

VIII REDEEMING THE PROMISE OF CITIES

THE CASE FOR EMPOWERING CITIES

Alan Broadbent has argued persuasively in his recent book, *Urban Nation*, that
this new economic reality of diverse cities as economic drivers and the dramatically altered demographics of Canada (an immigrant society which now has
eighty percent of its citizens, and the vast majority of recent arrivals, living in
a few major urban regions) poses major challenges to the traditional conception
of Canada as a country whose economy is based on resource extraction and
traditional manufacturing.

ACKNOWLEDGEMENTS

Writing this book has been both greatly challenging and immensely satisfying. Without the constant support of my wife, Eti, who has read every draft and has given much useful advice, and that of many other friends, family and colleagues, who have contributed ideas and encouragement, it would not have been possible. I want to offer special thanks to a group of generous readers who provided important constructive criticism and suggestions at a critical juncture, including Alan Broadbent, Tony Schuman, David Gouverneur, Oscar Grauer and Kishore Varanasi. I am immensely grateful to the many collaborators in many places who have shared this journey of over three decades with me and from whom I have learned so much. Due to the limitations of space and lapses in memory, I have obviously not been able to mention them all, and to those I have regrettably overlooked, I ask forgiveness in advance. I have worked from my recollection of events over a long period of time and many places, trying to capture the highlights, but I am certain there will be some errors and omissions. I particularly want to express my gratitude to my publisher, Anne Collins, at Random House Canada for her faith and support, and to my editor, Craig Pyette, who constantly forced me to be clear and concise and avoid jargon in making these ideas accessible to a broad public. With his help I hope I have achieved some modest success. During this writing, my father, Martin Greenberg, passed away, and I am sorry he will not get to read *Walking Home*, but I want to thank him and my mother, Gertrude, for taking me on the first crucial steps of this walk.

IMAGE CREDITS

ii   Image is property of the author.

4, 5   Images are property of the author.

19   Top image is property of the author; bottom image is by Kishore Varanasi, used with permission.

59   Top image is property of the author; bottom image is © Vincenzo Pietropaolo, used with permission.

95   Top image is property of Toronto Community Housing, used with permission; bottom image is property of Diamond + Schmitt Architects, used with permission.

136   Top image by Saint Paul design team, used with permission of University of Minnesota Archives; bottom image is property of the Saint Paul Riverfront Corporation, used with permission.

157   Images produced by the Rockcliffe design team, used with permission.

182   Top image by Eti Greenberg, used with permission; bottom image is property of the author.

198   Top and bottom images are property of the New York City Department of Transportation, used with permission.

202   Top image is property of the Lower Don design team, used with permission; bottom image is property of the author.

222   Top image is property of Oscar Grauer and David Gouverneur, used with permission; bottom image is property of the Lower Don Team, used with permission.

227   Top image by Cass Gilbert is used with permission of Northwest Architectural Archives Special Collections, Rare Books & Manuscripts Division University of Minnesota Libraries; bottom image by University of Minnesota design team, image is used with permission of KPMB Architects.

250   Top image is property of City of Mississauga, used with permission; bottom image produced by Mississauga 2021 Design Team, used with permission of Glatting Jackson Planners.

267   Top image is property of the author; bottom image is by Elizabeth Felicella, used with permission.

278   Top image is property of the NorthPoint design team, used with permission; bottom image is property of the author.

282   Top image by Brooklyn Bridge Park design team, used with permission; bottom image by East River Lower Manhattan design team, used with permission.

306   Top and bottom images are property of the author.

328   Top and bottom images are property of Lennart Johansson, Infobild, Stockholm, used with permission.

336   Top image is property of Erik Freudenthal, used with permission; bottom image is property of Lennart Johansson, Infobild, Stockholm, used with permission.

INDEX

Page numbers in italics refer to illustrations.

aboriginal peoples, 112
accessibility, 2, 8, 23, 25, 32, 63–64,
    90, 91, 100, 101, 124, 125, 135,
    138, 151, 160, 175, 177, 194,
    220, 228, 238, 254, 259, 263,
    266, 269, 271, 272, 273, 276,
    280, 281, 288, 293, 295, 299,
    300, 314, 316, 329–30, 335–36,
    338, 345
adaptability, 55–56, 58, 60, 62,
    75–76, 82, 184
Adriaen's Landing (Hartford), 242–43
advertising, 6, 32
Aetna (insurance co), 239
affordable housing, 61, 69, 177–78,
    183, 191, 209, 234, 258, 317,
    333, 234, 298

African Americans, 35
aggregation, wise crowd concept,
    290
aging population, 91, 176, 193, 341
Agnew, Spiro, 57
agriculture, 174, 189, 191, 244, 247,
    319, 347
air quality, 92–93, 186, 193, 213,
    304, 329
Alaskan Way Viaduct (Seattle), 200
Albert Lambert Galleria (Toronto),
    70
Alexandra Park (Toronto), 210
allotment gardens, 189
Amager Strandpark Beach
    (Copenhagen), 334
amalgamation, 295–301, 302–4

America Speaks, 314
American Institute of Architects, 230
Amsterdam, 29, 54–56, 196–97, 201, 206, 261–63, 320
Anacostia River, 271–72
Anacostia Waterfront Corporation, 271–72
Andalucía (Spain), 260
Andrews, John, 56, 93, 94
Andy Warhol Museum, 233
Angel Falls (Venezuela), 218
anticity thinking, 25–27, 31, 36–37, 48, 49, 326, 332, 346
anti-Semitism, 81
Anton, Paul, 264–65
AOL Time Warner Center (NYC), 82
Apfelbaum, Steve, 13, 215
Appalachian Trail, 286
appliances, 30, 86, 329
Applied Ecological Services, 215
architects, self-critique, 52–54
architectsAlliance, 184
Architectural Forum, 48
architectural photography, 55
architecture in isolation vs. architecture of the city, 50–52
Architecture without Architects (Rudofsky), 45
Argonaut Building (Detroit), 235
Art Gallery of Ontario, 83
art. *See* public art
artists, 162, 184
arts & culture, 28, 82, 175, 242 (*See also* entertainment)
as-of-right development, 165
aspirational change, minimum compliance to, 181, 183
Assistens Cemetery (Copenhagen), 338–39

Ataratiri project (Toronto), 154–55
Athens Charter, 24–25, 46–47
Athletes' Village (Pan Am Games), 155
Atlanta, 37, 88
Atlantic Monthly, The, 248
Australia, 224, 260
autobahns, 32
avant-garde schemes, 98–99
Avenida Soublette (Venezuela), 218
Ávila, Mount, 217, 220, 213
Ávila National Park, 217

baby boomers, 193
balconies, 189, 333
Barcelona, 101, 170, 197
Barker, Dennis, 116
Barnes, Rebecca, 277
Barnett, Jonathan, 89, 116
Barnum, P.T., 119
Barooah, Ronji, 90
barrios, 215, 220, 269
Barry Square (Hartford), 241
Battery Park City (Manhattan), 268–69, 279, 281
Battery Park City Authority, 268
Bauhaus, 29
Beach neighbourhood (Toronto), 63
beaches, 213, 215, 220, 280, 334
Beasley, Larry, 305
Bedford, Paul, 164
Beebe, Kate, 236
Belle Island (Detroit), 238
Beltline (Toronto), 274–75
Bennett, Edward H., 274
Berczy Park (Toronto), 122, 123
Berlage, Hendrik Petrus, 29
Berlin, 93, 170, 197
Berridge Lewinberg Greenberg (BLG), 131–32
Berridge, Joe, 131

Besant, Derek, 13
Beyer Blinder Belle, 313
Bicycle Diaries (Byrne), 287
big bang option, 144, 147
big box stores, 7, 184
Big Dig (Boston), 199, 277, *278*
bike lanes, 181, 197, 247, 337
bike parking, 338
bike paths, 148
bike rentals, 197, 337
bike theft, 338
bike-sharing programs, 197
billboards, 6
biofuels, 329
biogas, 329
biomass energy, 191
bioremediation, 268
birth rate, 176, 260
BIXI (public bike) system (Montreal), 197
Bloomberg, Michael, 317–18
Bloor Street (Toronto), 180
boardwalks, 204, 267, 334
body rub parlors, 125, 126
Bogotá (Colombia), 197, 212, 273
Bois de Boulogne (Paris), 212
Bois de Vincennes (Paris), 83
Borneo Sporenburg and Java Islands development, 206
Bosch, Theo, 47–48
Boston Harbor Islands National Recreational Area, 275
Boston Harbour, 150, 275, 276–77
Boston Redevelopment Authority (BRA), 277, 320
Boston University, 154, 201, 225, 275
Boston, 18, 37, 80–81, 102–3, 105, 149, 176, 179, 199, 212, 270, 274, 275–77, *278*, 279, 313
Boulevard Péripherique (Paris), 83

boulevards, 1, 34, 167, 201, 247
Bourgeois Utopias (Fishman), 34
Bow River (AB), 274
Bowling Green State University, 321
Brand, Stewart, 91
Brazil, 191–92, 224
Bridges of Saint Paul project, 143–46, 242
bridges, 75, 242, 279, 316, 334, 338 (*See also* elevated infrastructure)
Broad Canal (MA), 275–76
Broadacre City concept, 26, 44
Broadway, 197, *198*, 201
Broeker, Dick, 132, 158
Brookings Institution, 72
Brooklyn Bridge Park Development Corp, 280
Brooklyn Bridge Park, 267, 279–81, *282*, 292–94, 313
Brooklyn Bridge, 281, 283, 285
Brooklyn Heights Promenade, 280, 293
Brooklyn Heights, 292
Brooklyn, 14–16, *19*, 20–21, 39, 292–94
Brooklyn–Queens Expressway (BQE), 280, 293
Brown, Catherine, 133
brownfields, 153, 268, 343
Bruce Trail (ON), 286
Brundtland Commission, 74
Brush Creek Boulevard (Kansas City), 17
Bryant Park (NYC), 254–55
Bryant Park Corporation, 255
Buchbinder, David, 81
budget cycles. *See* capital budget cycles
Buenos Aires, 88, 273
Buffalo, 231
building codes, 160 (*See also* zoning)

building design/city design,
difference, 96
building envelopes, 162, 165, 168,
209, 329
building longevity, elements, 183
building programs, 97–98
bureaucratic inertia, 287–88
Burnham, Daniel, 274
Burrard Inlet (BC), 271, 305
buses, 20, 92, 101, 126, 176, 204,
329, 330
Bushnell Park (Hartford), 239, 243
Business Improvement Areas (BIAS),
86
Business Improvement Districts
(BIDS), 255
Byrne, David, 287

Cabbagetown (Toronto), 61
Cabrini-Green (Chicago), 28
CADD (Computer-Assisted Drafting
and Design), 128
cafés, 86, 92, 123, 149, 255, 256,
333, 334, 335, 338
Calgary, 256, 274, 346
California, 13, 215
Cambridge (MA), 161–62, 176, 205,
275–77, 278
Cambridge Planning Board, 161
Campo dei Fiori (Rome), 148
Campus Martius (Detroit), 236–237
Canada Post, 106
Canadian National Railways, 93,
161
Canadian Pacific Railway, 93
canal houses, 263
Canal Saint-Martin pathways (Paris),
273
canals, 262, 263, 273, 275–76, 281
Candilis-Josic-Woods, 93
capital budget cycles, 129–30

Capital City Economic Development
Authority (CCEPA), 242
Capital City Partnership, 141
car pooling 195, 196
car shares, 195, 332
car
advertising, 32
alternatives to ownership, 175
allure of, 35–36
alternatives to, 194–97, 330–31
and economic competitiveness,
196–97
and New Urbanism movement,
98
catalyst for change, 31–33, 35
dependence on, 17–18, 21, 205,
246
hegemony of, 8, 24, 51, 256
negative impact of, 37, 193
predictions, 345
(*See also* car-free zones)
Caracas (Venezuela), 213
Caracas Airport, 218
Caracas, 88, 213, 214, 217
carcass houses, 55–56
car-free zones, 335, 337
Carson, Rachel, 44
Cartegena (Colombia), 217
Carter Greenberg Architects, 64–65,
110
Carter, Phil, 64, 65
"Case for Saving Toronto's Old
Houses, A" (article), 58
Casino Nova Scotia, 101
Cass, Sam, 33
CBT Architects, 161, 243, 270
Central Business Districts, 38, 135,
209
Central Freeway (San Francisco),
200
Central Park (NYC), 82, 212

Central Park Conservancy (NYC), 211, 322

Central Waterfront (Toronto), 63

centrifugal shift, 174–75

centripetal shift, 174, 176

CFB Rockcliffe, 156, *157*, 158

Chain of Lakes and Grand Rounds Scenic Byway (Minneapolis–Saint Paul), 212

change
  and pilot projects, 317
  and time frames, 183–84
  demographic pattern,176–77
  management, 304–10
  perpetual nature of, 96–97
  resistance to, 162–63, 247–48, 311
  sense of urgency for, 182–83
  talent-driven, 82–83

Chapultepec Park (Mexico City), 212

Charles River, 153, 274, 275, 276, 277, *278*

Charleston (SC), 315

Charlotte (VA), 248

chat rooms, 255

Chelsea (Manhattan), 104, 178

Cheonggyecheon Highway (Seoul), 200

Chicago Housing Authority, 28

Chicago, 28–29, 37, 57, 170, 176, 264, 274, 317, 346

child-friendly city centres, 339 (*See also* daycares; play spaces; playgrounds)

Chile, 215

China, 192, 214

Chinatown (Toronto), 82, 83

Choroní (Venezuela), 218

Christie Pits riot, 81

Church Street (Toronto), 124

Church, Gardner, 248–49

CIAM (Congrès International d'Architecture Moderne), 55, 78, 93
  and urban renewal, 27–28
  Athens Charter, 24–25
  founding declaration, 23
  four functions, 37
  principles, 24, 31
  (*See also* modernist urban planning; Team X)

Cincinnati, 200

Cities and the Wealth of Nations (Jacobs), 261

Cities Centre (U of T), 177

Cities Without Suburbs (Rusk), 303

cities
  as resort, 334–35, *336*, 337
  compared with Internet, 97
  complexity/heterogeneity of, 96–97
  creative momentum of, 169–71
  defined, 78
  developers' relationship with, 304–9
  dynamic nature of, 78–79
  European model, 1–2, 18, 20
  exodus from. *See* suburbs
  expression of ongoing process, 96
  in crisis, 231–43
  in developing world, 346
  in nature, 43, 211–25
  inherent capacities of, 10
  interconnectedness of forces, 67, 68
  move back to, 72–73
  organic vs. mechanistic model, 78–79
  philosophical divide, 34–45
  predictions, 344–47
  relationship with developers, 304–9

replacement models, 23–27
reshaping forces, 174–75
resources, sustainability, 75–76
syntax of, 86–87, 89
transformation of, 1–3, *4*, 5–9
  (*See also* medieval cities; rustbelt
  cities; seacoast cities)
citizen/political power gap, 304
City Beautiful movement, 284
city building, 9, 10–11
city council, 320
City Form and Natural Process
  (Hough), 212
City in a Park/Park in the City
  concept, 143
City of Toronto/Metro Toronto,
  comparisons, 300
City Parent Network, 209–10
City Place (Toronto), 307
City Planning Dept (NYC), 301
City Planning Dept (Vancouver), 321
City Planning Dept (San Francisco),
  201
City Property Dept (Toronto), 129
Cityscape Institute, 322
city-street grid, elegance/efficiency,
  94, 96
civic design, 116
civic engagement, loss of, 299, 300,
  301
civic pride, 20, 90, 301
civil rights movement, 52, 57, 82
civil society, 141–42, 149, 321–24
civility, 87–88
Clem, David, 205–6
Cleveland, 231
Cleveland, Horace, 212, 226
climate change, 214–15, 341
Climate Initiative (US), 224
Climate Positive Development
  Program, 224

climate-positive communities,
  224–25
Clinton, Bill, 224
Close, Bob, 134
CN Tower, 94, 160
CO_2 emissions, 186–88
Coal Harbour (BC), 305, 271
cocooning, 255
cogeneration, 187, 329
Coleman, Norm, 132, 133, 138, 140,
  146, 316
collaborations, 11, 133–34, 140,
  152–58, 232 (*See also* participatory planning; public/private
  partnerships)
collective building traditions, 47
collective decision making, wise
  crowd concept, 290–91
collective memory, 347
College for Creative Studies
  (Detroit), 235
Colliers International, 270
Colombia, 212, 217
colonnades, 124, 284–85
Columbia University, 48–52, 76
command-and-control model, 99
commons, the, 258–59 (*See also*
  public spaces)
Commonwealth Ave (Boston), 1, 201
communes (France), 318–19
communications technologies,
  153–54
community boards, 301–2
community centres, 106, 191, 258,
  305
community councils, 299
Community Improvement Plans,
  166
community report card, 312–13
commuter campuses, 226
commuter fatigue, 40, 72, 327

commuter rail, 200, 304 (*See also* light-rail transit)

complete streets, 201, 202, 203

computers, 255

Compuware, 237

Concentrated Development Zone. *See* ZAC

Condado District (Puerto Rico), 270

condos, 63, 69, 100, 210, 316

Coney Island, 51

conflict resolution, 309, 312–13 (*See also* consensus building)

connectedness, sense of, 260, 286 (*See also* civic pride)

Connecticut Children's Medical Center, 241

Connecticut Convention Center, 243

Connecticut Public Television and Radio, 241

Connecticut River, 242

Connecticut Science Center, 243

Connecticut, 251

consensus building, 292–94, 316

Constitution Plaza (Hartford), 179

construction standards, downtown, 317

consumption vs. sustainability, 75

context/fit issues, 150–52

Cooper Robertson & Partners, 241

co-ops, 64–65, 71, 184, 210

Copenhagen Harbour, 267

Copenhagen, 86, 170, 175, 197, 201, 202, 206, 252, 271, 317–28, 332, 333, 334–35, 337–40, 341

Corneil, Carmen, 63

courtyards, 91, 122, 124, 190, 211, 269, 332–33, 335, 339

creativity, 72, 107, 168

crime, 23, 30, 31, 94, 126, 148, 167, 248, 249

Crombie, David, 69, 114, 115, 124, 315–16

cross-disciplinary teamwork. *See* collaborations

Crossroads Initiative, 277, 278, 279

crosswalks, 130, 335

Cuba, 206, 217

cultural diversity, 80, 87, 260, 324

cultural entrepreneurship, 175–76

cultural fusion, 80–81

cultural memory, 179–80

cultural norms, and shared space, 87–88

curbs, 3, 149, 203

Curitiba (Paraná, Brazil), 191–92

cyberspace, 255

cycling, 2, 6, 18–19, 55, 148, 166, 175, 180, 188, 194, 196, 197, 204, 273, 275, 277, 285, 286–87, 330, *331*, 334, 337–38, 345

Daley, Richard, 317

dams, 217

Daoust Lestage Architects, 229

Dark Age Ahead (Jacobs), 244

daycare, 167, 209, 261, 298, 333, 339

Deadmalls.com, 100–1

Death and Life of Great American Cities (Jacobs), 36, 42–45, 48, 49, 67

decentralization, wise crowd concept, 290

Delirious New York (Koolhaas), 83

Democratic National Convention (Chicago), 57

Denmark, 334–35

Denver, 178, 346

design charrettes, 134, 216

design competitions, 62, 153, 170–71, 223, 319

design review panels, 310

design talent, attracting, 170–71
Design with Nature (McHarg), 212
de-spatialization, 256
Destiny (Florida), 224
Detroit Institute of Arts, 237
Detroit Medical Center, 237
Detroit, 28–29, 101, 225, 231–32,
    234–39, 244, 274
developers/city relationship, 304–9
Development Strategies (firm), 235
diabetes, rise of, 193
disabled pedestrians, 3
disorganized complexity, 44 (*See also*
    organized complexity)
Distillery District (Toronto), 124,
    176, 207, 209
distributed transportation systems,
    195
District du Plateau de Saclay, 319
district energy, 191, 329
District of Columbia project, 313–15
diversity of opinion, wise crowd
    concept, 290
Dobbin, Jim, 154–55
Dobelle, Evan, 240
Dockside Green (Victoria, BC), 190
dog legs, 3, 6
domestic migration, 14–18
Don Mills (ON), 249
Don River Valley (Toronto), 71, 274
Don River, 221, 222, 223–24
Douglas, Frederick, 119
Downtown Action Strategy
    (Hartford), 242, 243
DRD (Amsterdam), 320
drug scene, 125, 126, 148, 167, 254
Dubai, 99
Dundas Square (Toronto), 127
Dundas Street (Toronto), 180
Durán, Hilario, 81

earthquakes, 214–15
East Bayfront (Toronto), 124
East Cambridge (MA), 153
East River Waterfront Esplanade,
    279, 286
East River Waterfront Plan, 281, 283
East River, 274, 280–81, 282, 285,
    293 (*See also* Piers 1–6)
East Village (NYC), 206
Eastern Harbour redevelopment
    (Amsterdam) 206
Economic Development Corp
    (NYC), 286
economic development
    and access to waterfronts, 269
    and quality of place, 261–64
    and role of city, 79
    and sustainability, 75–76
    and urban design, 11
    and waterfronts, 280
    predictions, 346–47
    universities and, 225
economic downturn (2008), 99, 146
economic inequality. *See* income
    polarization; rich/poor divide
Economic Value of Open Space . . .
    (Anton), 264–65
Economy of Cities (Jacobs), 261
ecotone concept, 205–6
Edmonton, 256
Eisenberg, Bob, 164
Eisenhower, Dwight, 32, 38
elasticity concept, 303–4
Elbow River (AB), 274
elevated infrastructure, 33, 199–200,
    148, 262, 277, 283–84
elevated linear park, 83–84
elevated walkways, 93
Ellis Island, 279
Emaracadero (San Francisco), 33,
    199–200

Emerald Necklace (Boston), 212, 275

Empire State Building, 29

empty nesters, 185, 228

energy, 8, 10, 73, 75, 92–93, 107,
175, 176, 181, 183, 186–88,
200, 245, 327, 329, 344

entertainment, 28, 82, 103, 165,
167–68, 187, 206, 233, 242,
255 (*See also* arts & culture)

entrepreneurial sector, 99–100

Envac, 330

envelopes. *See* building envelopes

Environmental Assessments (EAs),
221

environmental cleanup, 268, 272,
329–30, 344

environmental footprint, 186–91

environmental industries, 183

environmental movement, 52

environmental protection, 131 (*See
also* habitat protection)

environmental stress/degradation,
327

Europe, early modern expressions,
29

expressways, 33, 44, 68–69, 114, 199,
293

eye contact, 2, 3, 149, 175, 190, 204,
256

Facebook, 255

False Creek (Vancouver), 271, 305

family businesses, 137

Fan Pier (Boston), 275, 276–77

Fannie Mae Foundation, 72

Farewell to Oak Street (film), 30–31

farmers' markets, 189, 247 (*See also*
street markets)

fast-food structures, 184

FDR Colonnade (Manhattan),
284–86

FDR Drive (Manhattan), 283–85

Federal Transit Administration
(FTA), 251

Federal-Aid Highway Act, 32

ferries, 252, 330

festival marketplaces, 102–3, 269

Fillmore, Millard, 142–43

Finger Lakes (NY), 286

Finland, 189

fires, 119, 160, 215

Firestone, 29

Fishman, Robert, 34

Flatiron Building. *See* Gooderham
Flatiron Building

Flint (MI), 103

floods, 141, 154, 155, 183, 212,
213–21, 222, 223

Florida, 224

"flying squads" (Parks Dept,
Toronto), 299–300

food courts, 38, 103, 256

food distribution networks, 189

food safety, 73, 247

Fort Mason Center (San Francisco),
176

Fort Point Channel District
(Boston), 105, 178, 277

Fort Washington Way (Cincinnati),
200

forts, 279

fossil fuels, 329

Fraker, Harrison, 225–26

France, 20

franchise monopolies, 38

Free University (Berlin), 93

Freiburg (Germany), 189

Frente Portuario (Puerto Rico), 269

Fresh Meadows (Queens, NYC), 17

Frog Hollow (Hartford), 241

Front Door Organics, 189

Front Street (Toronto), 122–23, 124

frontier thesis migration, 33–34
Fulton Ferry landing, 281
Fulton Fish Market, 285
Functional City concept, 24, 28 (*See also* Athens Charter)
funding
    banks, 97–98
    corporate, 142
    government, 257–58, 321–22, 342–44
    innovations, 265
    non-profits, 141–42
    private donations, 123, 129, 137, 265
    private sector investment, 304
Futurama, 32
futurism (exhibits), 35–36

Galleria Italia (Toronto), 83
galleries, 104, 121
Gans, Herbert 39, 45
Garden City movement, 27
Garden City, 28, 43
Garden Club of Toronto, 123
garden suburbs, 34
gardens. *See* allotment gardens; rooftop gardens; vertical gardens
Gardiner Expressway, 33, 200
Gardiner, Fred, 33
Gare d'Austerlitz (Paris), 306
Garnier, Tony, 29
gasoline, 31, 88
gated communities, 261
gay pride parades, 81–82
General Motors, 29, 31–32, 234–35
Geneva, 18, 20, 39, 55
gentrification, 65, 177
geothermal energy, 73, 187, 224, 329
Germany, 32, 183, 189, 189
Gif-sur-Yvette (France), 318–19

Gilbert, Cass 226, 227
Ginza shopping district (Tokyo), 259
Gladki, John, 90
global migration, 176–77
global peace, 345
global warming, 10, 74
globalization, 260, 266
Globe and Mail, 58, 59, 63, 305
Golden, Anne, 295–96
Good Egg (Kensington Market), 86
good life concept, 8
Gooderham and Worts distillery, 207 (*See also* Distillery District)
Gooderham Flatiron Building (Toronto), 120, 122, 123
Gouverneur, David, 214
Graduate School of Design (GSD; Harvard), 214, 216–21
Grand Circus Park (Detroit), 237
Grand Paris plans, 170, 320
Granite Garden, The (Spirn), 212
Granville Island (BC), 206
Graphic Information System, 312
Grauer, Oscar, 214
Great Depression, 32, 80, 244
Great Fire (1849), 119
Great River Park, The (watercolour), 133, 135
Greater Downtown Partnership (Detroit), 232, 236, 238
Greater Hartford Academy of the Arts, 241
Greater Toronto Area (GTA), 247, 248–49, 251, 295–96, 297, 302, 303
Greater Toronto CivicAction Alliance, 322–23
green industry jobs, 317
Green Metropolis (Owen), 187
green roof, 186, 191 (*See also* rooftop gardens)

green spaces, 90–91, 317, 338–39, 347
green technologies, 327
green walls, 211
greenbelts, 24–25, 27, 251
Greenberg Consultants Inc.,155
Greene, Lorne, 30
greenfields, 343
greenhouse gas emissions, 187, 224, 246
Greenway District (Boston), 313
greenways, 190, 264, 273
Greenwich Village, 42
Greer, Bill, 121
grey water, 188–89
ground-floor uses, 124, 137–38, 190, 230
Grumbach, Antoine, 79, 319

Habana Vieja (Cuba), 206, 217
habitat protection, 211, 213, 223, 274, 280 (*See also* nature, cities in)
Habraken, John, 56
Haiti, 214
Halifax, 101
Hall, Barbara, 70, 162–63
Hammarby Sjöstad (Stockholm), 327, *328*, 329–31, 333, 334, 337, 339
Hanover Street (Boston), 149
Harbor District Park (NYC), 285
Harbor Drive (Portland), 200
Harbor Walk (Boston), 277, 279
Harbortown (Detroit), 238
Harbourfront Centre (Toronto), 176
Harbourfront Passage (Toronto), 63
Harlem, 53, 54, 76
harmonization, 300
HARTFORD 2010 plan, 243
Hartford Hospital, 241

Hartford, 179, 212, 231–32, 239–43, 244
Hartford, The (firm), 239
Harvard University, 48, 214, 216–21
Harvard Urban Design, 53
Haussmann, Georges-Eugène, 34
health care, 176, 258, 333
heat recovery, 73
heating innovations, 329
Helsinki, 189
Henry Ford Academy (Detroit), 235
Henry Ford Health Center (Detroit), 235
heritage easements, 208–9
Héritage Montréal, 64
heritage preservation, 29–30, 114, 118–20, 131, 137, 207–9, 339–40 (*See also* historic city)
Hertzberger, Herman, 54, 55, 56
High Line (NYC), 84, 170
high-rises, 10, 15, 26, 69, 88, 90, 115, 123–24, 186–87, 190, 207
highway rest stop design, 51
highways, 16, 32–33, 36, 46, 48, 66, 133, 134–35, 174, 195, 197, 199–205, 244, 316
historic city, 2, 24, 25–26, 33, 160, 259, 262–63, 307
Historic Savannah Foundation, 230
historical preservation. *See* heritage preservation
historicist approach, urban development, 21–22
Holland Inc., 262
homelessness, 258, 298
Hong Kong, 194–95, 252, 260
hospitals, 135, 228, 232
hotels, 118, 206, 218, 263
Hough, Michael, 212
House Form and Culture (Rapoport), 87

housing. *See* affordable housing;
    specific types
How Buildings Learn (Brand), 91
Howard, Sir Ebenezer, 27, 43–44, 78
HR & A Advisors, 280
Hudson River, 268, 285
Hulchanski, David, 177, 298
human ecology, 74
Humber River Bike and Pedestrian
    Bridge, 70–71
Humber River Valley, 274
Hurricane Hazel, 212
Hurricane Katrina, 214
hybridization, 179
hydrogen fuel cells, 341

IBI Group, 229
"Ideas that Matter" event, 70
IJ Embankments (Amsterdam),
    262–63
Image of the City, The (Lynch), 259
immigration/immigrants, 57, 80–81,
    176–77, 181, *182*, 260, 323, 341
impact fees, 209
import replacement concept, 244
in-between places, 179
income polarization, 177–78, 258
    (*See also* rich/poor divide)
incremental growth, 144 (*See also* big
    bang option)
independent thinking, wise crowd
    concept, 290
India, 71, 192, 204, 206, 224
individualism, 28, 34
industrial lands/structures, 69, 70,
    164–67, 180, 190, 210, 221,
    223–25, 261–63, 266–67,
    273–74, 311, 339–40
Industrial Revolution 21–22
infill development, 69, 124, 180,
    207, 238, 246, 339

"Infilling the Toronto Block System"
    (thesis), 60–61, 64
infrastructure renewal, 129–31, 197,
    199–205 (*See also* elevated
    infrastructure)
inner city, 30, 232, 248, 346
Innovation Team, 156
Institute of Living (Hartford), 241
insurance sector, 36, 244, 239
integrated fare cards, 195
iterative method, 155–56, *157* (*See
    also* maps)
intercity rail, 200, 251 (*See also*
    light-rail systems)
interior/exterior synergy, 83
International Style, 29, 30
Internet, 97
interstate highway program, 244
Isleta (San Antonio Canal), 270
Israel, 29–30
Istanbul, 260
iterative method, 155, 158

Jacob K. Javits Convention Center
    (NYC), 84
Jacobs, Allan, 201
Jacobs, Jane, 10, 36, 39, 42–45, 48,
    57–58, *59*, 60, 66–71, 79, 113,
    164, 178, 244, 261
Jacques, Emanuel, 126
James, Scott, 121
Jane's Walk program, 71
Jeanneret-Gris, Charles-Edouard.
    See Le Corbusier
job creation, 164, 165–66, 176, 317
job loss, rustbed cities, 231
Jones Beach (Long Island), 334
juxtapositions, 82–84

Kahn, Albert, 234, 235
Kansas City, 17

Ken Smith Landscape Architects, 286
Kendall Square (Cambridge), 205, 275–76
Kennedy, Robert F., 57
Kensington High Street (London), 204
Kensington Market (Toronto), 61, 80, 86, 92, 105, 206
Kevin Lynch Award, 317
King Street (Toronto), 180
King Street East (Toronto), 104, 118
King, Martin Luther, Jr., 57
King-Parliament district (Toronto), 164
Kings Regeneration Initiative (Toronto), 70
Kings, the (Toronto), 148, 167–69
King-Spadina district (Toronto), 166, 167–68, 207
Kittredge, Neil, 313
knowledge sector, 161, 175, 233
knowledge-based design, 82
Koolhaas, Rem, 83
Kulash, Walter, 134
Kuwabara Payne McKenna Blumberg Architects, 229
Kuwabara, Bruce, 156

L'Enfant, Pierre-Charles, 171
La Guaira (Venezuela), 215, 217
Labour Council Development Foundation, 65
laissez-faire model, 99
land use, 36, 75, 167–68, 304, 329
land value, 16, 81, 115, 245
landscape design, 123, 152, 220, 329
landslides, 213, 216, 222
laneways, 61, 69, 180, 211, 259, 318
language, and cultural fusion, 81
lateral thinking, 155–56

Latino Americans, 242
Laval University, 264
lawyers, 118, 159, 309, 312
Le Corbusier, 23, 25, 26–27, 44, 78
Le Marais (Paris), 80–81, 206
learned systems concept, 91–92
Learning Corridor (Hartford), 241, 243
LEED (Leadership in Energy and Environmental Design), 187
LEED-ND (LEED for Neighbourhood Development), 188–89, 191
Leinberger, Christopher, 248
Lerner, Jaime, 192
Leslie Street Spit (Toronto), 212
Levitt & Sons, Inc., 36
Levittown (Long Island), 36
Levy, Sheldon, 229
Lewinberg, Frank, 131
Liberty State Park (NJ), 279
Liberty Village (Toronto), 210
Lifchez, Ray, 49
life sciences, 44–45
lighting, 86, 130, 167, 284, 318
light-rail transit, 200, 226, 251–52, 270, 330
Lind, Jenny, 119
Lindsay, John, 116
linear thinking, 156
Linn, Leo, 110, 111
Littoral Central (Venezuela), 213–15, 222
Liverpool (UK), 231
local food production, 247
LoDo (Denver), 178
lofts, 69, 180, 236
London (UK), 34, 170, 195, 204, 206, 224, 260
Long Island (NY), 16, 36, 334
Longoria, Paco, 50

Los Angeles, 28–29, 346
Los Caracas (Venezuela), 220
Lower Don Lands (Toronto), 71, 159, 202, 221
Lower Manhattan Expressway, 42
Lower Manhattan, 268–69, 281, 283–85
Lowertown (Saint Paul), 132, 178
low-rise structures, 60, 210
Lu, Weiming, 132
Lyme Properties, 153, 275–76
Lynch, Kevin, 259
Lyon (France), 203

Macdonald, Elizabeth, 201
Macuto (Venezuela), 215
mail delivery, 106
malls, 6, 37, 38, 100–1, 111, 112, 181, *182*, 248, 249, 264, 333
Malmö (Sweden), 189–90, 271, 327, 332, 334, 339, 340, 341
Manhattan Bridge, 280
Manhattan Waterfront Greenway, 273
Manhattan, 20, 21, 29, 43, 83, 84, 102, 103, 104, 116, 203, 254–55, 279, 293
manufacturing sector, 175, 176
Maple Leaf Gardens, 230
maps, 120–21, 128, 137, 312
Marantette, Larry, 236
Margarita Island (Venezuela), 218
market forces, 99–100, 116, 160, 176
Market Gallery (Toronto), 121
Market Square (Toronto), 124
markets. *See* farmers' markets; festival marketplaces; street markets
Markham (ON), 249
Markson, Jerome, 124

Martin Goodman Trail (Toronto), 274–75
Martínez, Emilio, 269
mass production, 23
Massachusetts Institute of Technology (MIT), 153, 317
Massachusetts Turnpike, 277
Massey Harris factory, 210
mayors, 315–20
Mayors' Institute on City Design, 315
McHarg, Ian, 212
McKnight Foundation, 142
Meatpacking District (NYC), 84
mechanistic view, 22–23 (*See also* modernist urban planning)
media & technology sector, 82
medieval cities, 104–5
megacity, 296, 298 (*See also* amalgamation)
megaprojects, 102, 242
megastructures, 53, 96, 268
Menino, Tom, 227
Merrens, Roy, 63
MetroHartford Alliance, 232, 243
Metrolinx (Toronto), 251
Metropolitan Toronto (1953), 127, 303
mews housing, 61, 203
Mexico City, 212
Michigan, Lake, 274
mid-rise buildings, 186–87, 190, 207, 210
Midtown Loop (Detroit), 237–38
Mignucci, Andrés, 269
Milan, 195
military, 53, 96, 118, 159, 189, 240, 309, 312
Millard Fillmore dinners, 142–43
Millennium Park (San Francisco), 176

Milton Keynes (UK), 27
Minneapolis Park Board, 226, 228
Minneapolis, 37, 133, 141, 143, 256
Minneapolis–Saint Paul
    International Airport, 141
Minneapolis–St. Paul, 212, 225–27
Minute Trail, *278*
Minuteman Bikeway, 277
Miss Behav'N (Kensington Mkt), 86
missed-use neighbourhoods, 228
Mission Bay (San Francisco), 180, 270
Mississauga (ON), 88, 247–48, *250*
Mississippi River, 26, 132, 133, 134,
    135, 138–39, 142–46, 212, 228,
    316
mixed-income neighbourhoods, 65,
    69, 89, 90, 91, *95*, 124–25, 208
mixed-use development, *95*, 115,
    117, 137, 148, 228
modernist urban planning, 7–8,
    17–18, 21–31, 42–48, 255 (*See
    also* CIAM)
monster homes, 104
Montreal, 64, 81, 105, 197, 206, 256,
    346, 297
monumental structures, 75
Morningside Heights gym, 54
Morningside Park (NYC), 53–54
Morrish, Bill, 133
Moses, Robert, 33, 43, 334
Mosey, Sue, 237
mudslides. *See* landslides
multiculturalism, 260
multifamily dwellings, 209–10,
    245–46
multigenerational households, 60, 210
multimodel street design, 201–4
municipal engineers 8
municipal government, 129–30, 295,
    298–99, 308–10, 320–21,
    343–44

murals, 123
[murmur] project, 287
Museum of African American
    History (Detroit), 237
Museum of Modern Art (NYC), 83
museums, 35, 83, 138–39, 149, 228,
    237, 279
music, cultural fusion, 81

Nagahiro, David, 243
naked streets, 204
National Film Board, 30
National Great River Park (Saint
    Paul), 143
national housing policy (Canada),
    lack of, 25
National Museum of American
    History, 35
National Trust for Historic
    Preservation, 230
nature, cities in, 211–25
Neal's Yard (London), 206
Necklace District (Detroit), 237
Needle Park (NYC), 254
neighbourhoods
    and immigration, 57
    downtown, 69
    racially divided
    shift in priorities, 72–74
    succession, 184–85
    valuable, rankings, 206
    (*See also* old neighbourhoods)
neo-conservatism, 257–58
net plus energy, 344
Netherlands, 50, 54, 190, 251
New Amsterdam, 179
New Center (Detroit), 234–36
New Center Council, 235, 236
New Jersey, 21, 251, 279
New Orleans, 103
New Starts program, 251–52

New Town movement, 27

New Urbanism movement, 98

New York City (*See also* Lower Manhattan; Manhattan; specific boroughs)

New York City Planning Commission, 45

New York City, 14–17, 20–21, 51, 52, 57, 81, 82–83, 179, 197, 206, 274, 287, 295, 298, 301–1, 318 (*See also* Lower Manhattan; Manhattan; specific boroughs and structures)

New York Harbor, 279, 281

New York Life Insurance, 17

New York Port Authority, 280

New York Public Library, 50

New York World's Fair (1939), 31–32

New Zealand, 260

Newton (MA), 18, *19*

Nickita, Mark, 236

nightclubs, 148, 167–68

NIMBY response, 311

Nixon, Richard, 57

no-competition leases, 104

noise, 15, 22, 148, 266

non-conventional auto options, 195–96

noncorrelation, 29

Norfolk (VA), 103

North American Convention of Colored Freemen (1851), 119

North Beach (San Francisco), 206

North Carolina, 248

North End, Boston, 80–81, 149

NorthPoint (Cambridge), 161–62, 275, 277, *278*

nostalgia, 97–98

Oak Ridges Moraine (ON), 249, 316

Oakville (ON), 249

occupancy above stores, 2, 3

Octavia Boulevard (San Francisco), 201

Odessa/Havana (band), 81

Odette, Louis, 123

Office and Policy Management (OPM) (Conn), 242

offices, 7, 37, 69, 115, 178–79, 332

Official Plans, 121

oil supply, 40, 175, 193

Old Delhi (India), 206

old neighbourhoods

  qualities of, 14–16

  pattern of succession, 184

  narrow streets, 299

  and immigration, 57

  and sustainability, 75

  capacity to absorb change, 183–84

  clearance & demolition, 58, 60, 63

  open-ended design strategy, 60–61

  organic growth of, 97

  popularity of, 65

  value of, 72

Olmstead, Frederick Law, 211–12, 239, 275

Olympics, 101, 190–91, 321

online shopping, 249, 255

Ontario Municipal Board (OMB), 308–10, 312, 313, 320

Ontario, Lake, 249, 316

open-ended design strategies, 56, 57, 58, 60–61

Opéra Bastille (Paris), 83

Opportunities for Youth, 65

oral history project, 287

organic foods, 92

Organization Man, The (Whyte), 45

organized complexity concept, 44–45, 68, 79, 155

Ottawa River, 156

Ottawa, 312
overspecialization, 148–49
Owen, David, 187

374

P2P communications, 195
packaged development formula,
    98–99, 102–4
Padolsky, Barry, 156
Pakistan, 214, 224
Paris, 1, 25–26, 34, 53, 80–81,
    83–84, 92, 104, 170, 197, 206,
    212, 260, 273, 301, 306, 318,
    319
Park Street (Hartford), 242
parking lots, 3, 5, 17, 37, 111, 115,
    118, 135, 136, 148, 164, 188,
    250, 252
parking, 3, 6, 7, 100, 196, 247, 248,
    276, 330, 332, 334
Parks Council (NYC), 254–55
Parks Dept (Toronto), 299–300
parks, 15, 75, 83–84, 91, 122, 136,
    183, 209, 211, 212–13, 220,
    223, 233, 255, 256, 258, 259,
    270, 271, 274, 279–81,
    299–300, 321, 334, 338–39
participatory planning, 62, 63–64,
    73, 89–90, 113–14, 117, 120,
    132, 147 (See also civil society
    initiatives; collaboration)
Paseo de la Princesa (Puerto Rico),
    269–70
paseos, 273
passeggiata, 273
pastoralism, 26–27, 34, 35
pavement delineations, 6, 86, 337
PCBs, 155
peace movement, 52, 57
Pecaut, David, 323–24
pedestrian bridges, 338 (See also
    elevated infrastructure)

Pedestrian Center (Copenhagen),
    206
pedestrian malls, 125–26, 198
pedestrian-only zones. See car-free
    zones; pedestrian malls
pedestrian-vehicle conflicts, 196–97
peer-review panels, 168
Pei, I.M., 178
Peirce, Neil, 301
Penn Station (NYC), 29
People's Guide to the Toronto
    Waterfront, A, 63–64
Périphérique (Paris), 1
Philadelphia, 225
philanthropic organizations, 321–24
Phoenix Companies, 239
photovoltaics, 329
Physical Planning Dept
    (Amsterdam), 262
Piers 1–6 (East River), 280–81, 282
piers, 219, 266, 280–81, 282, 293
Pike Place Market (Seattle), 92
Pinnell, Patrick, 243
Pittsburgh (PA), 233
place vs function concept, 39
place, sense of, 259 (See also civic
    pride; connectedness, sense of)
Places to Grow (document), 251
Plan of Chicago (1909), 274
Plan Voisin pour Paris (Le Corbusier),
    25–26
Plan Zuid, 29
planned obsolescence, 75
Planning Dept (Vancouver), 321
Planning and Development Dept
    (Toronto), 114, 115–18
Planning Office (DC), 313
Plateau (Montreal), 80–81, 105
Plateau de Saclay (France), 318–20
Plateau, the (Montreal), 206
play spaces, 91

playgrounds, 15, 167, 196, 209, 211, 280, 333, 339
plazas, 6, 45, 181, 203, 259, 270
Plus 15 approach, 256
pollution, 22, 193, 266 (*See also* air quality; water quality)
ponds, 18, 229, 230, 329–30
Popular Mechanics, 35
Popular Science, 35
population bubble, 193 (*See also* aging population)
porches, 106
port lands. *See* waterfronts
Portland (OR), 175, 197, 200, 251, 303
post-war modernist development. *See* modernist urban planning
Potsdamer Platz (Berlin), 170
poverty, 31, 94, 177, 248 (*See also* income polarization; rich/poor divide)
power stations, 75
Prangnell, Peter 49
pride of place. *See* civic pride
Prince Albert (SK), 110–14, 117, 127
Prince Albert Arts Centre, 110
private judgments/collective decisions. *See* aggregation
privatization, 258, 270
Progressive Conservative Party 57
Project for Public Spaces, 206
Promenade Plantée (Paris), 83
promenades, 83, 238, 273
property tax, 156, 164, 297
property value, 37, 72, 121, 122, 162, 166, 264–65 (*See also* land value)
Proposition 13, 258
Prospect Park (NYC), 212, 281
prostitution, 125, 126, 266

provincial oversight. *See* tribunal model
Provincial Planning Act, 121
Prudential Center complex (Boston), 179
Pruitt-Igoe project, 94
public art, 123, 129, 131, 219, 279
public education, reinvestment in, 210
public events/performances, 254–55
public housing. *See* specific projects
Public Improvement Plan, 122
public realm, 259, 261–64
public sector support, 264–65
public spaces, 86–88
    and role of street, 25
    and survival of democratic societies, 260, 288
    components of successful, 45–46
    deterioration of, 254–58
    loss of, 6
    moving inside, or up, 93–94
    pedestrian oriented, 201–4
    revival of, 259–60
    tax revenues devoted to upgrading, 209
public transit, 194–95, 286, 330–31, 345 (*See also* specific types)
Public Works (Toronto), 106, 129, 130
public/private
    dialectic, 260–61
    dichotomies, 67
    partnerships, 149–50, 279 (*See also* collaborations)
Puerto Madero (Buenos Aires), 273
Puerto Rico, 269–70

quality of life, 131, 159, 162, 175–76, 196, 197, 225, 261–64, 343
quality of place, 261–64

Quartier des Etats-Unis (Lyon), 29
Quebec City, 263–64
Queen Street (Toronto), 180
Queens (NYC), 16, 17, 39
quick fixes, 101–3
Quincy Market Faneuil Hall, 102–3

racial/class divide, 231
racism, 35, 57, 81
Radiant City, 26, 30, 44
Radio City Music Hall, 83
rail lands, 94, 75, 83–84, 160–61,
    175, 251, 273, 274, 275, 305,
    307, 311, 344, 340
rail yards/manufacturing/warehousing
    nexus, 266
rainwater, 188, 211
Randstad (Netherlands), 251, 303
Rapoport, Amos, 87
ravines, 212, 217, 220, 249, 273, 274
real-estate investment trusts
    (REITs), 97
recreation, 24, 28, 36, 143, 187, 211,
    216, 218, 219, 221–22, 228,
    275, 280, 285, 286–88, 292,
    293, 298, 334–35, 336
recycling, 73, 183, 244, 317, 329,
    330
red lining, 36
red state–blue state divide, 346
red-light districts, 266
Regent Park Public Housing Project,
    30–31, 46, 65, 89–91, 92, 95,
    105–7, 210, 299, 310
regional perspective. See elasticity
    concept
Regional Plan Association (RPA;
    NYC), 251
regionalism, 232–33, 342–47, 249,
    251
regulatory infrastructure, 105–7

Renaissance Project (Saint Paul),
    137
renewable energy, 73
rent control, 244
rent subsidies, 333
rental housing, 61, 65, 180, 191, 210
report card. See community report
    card
Requests for Proposals (RFPs), 155
Reserva Ecológica, 274
resort, city as, 334–35, 336, 337
respect, 10, 29, 64, 87, 89, 340
responsible redevelopment/informed
    neighbourhood response,
    311–15
restaurants, 2, 38, 82, 103, 118, 145,
    203, 206, 233, 263, 330, 333,
    335–36, 338
Revell, Viljo, 62
reverse frontages, 7
rich/poor divide, 34, 234, 298, 313,
    333 (See also income polariza-
    tion; racial/class divide)
right table concept, 290–91
right-turn traffic. See dog legs
Riley, Joe, 315
Rio de la Plata (NYC), 274
riots, 81
Rise in Downtown Living, A (report),
    72
risk aversion, 287–88, 339
risk management, 147
River IJ (Amsterdam), 261–63
Riverfront Corp, 140, 141
Riverwalk (Detroit), 238, 274
roads, 5, 75, 101, 188, 195, 199,
    200–1, 304 (See also highways;
    traffic)
Robertson, Jaquelin, 116
Rochester (NY), 231
Rochon, Lisa, 305

Rockcliffe Military Base. *See* CFB Rockcliffe
Rockefeller Center, 83
Roebling, John A., 84, 281
Roger and Me (film), 103
Rogers, Betsy Barlow, 211, 322
Rome, 148
rooftop farming, 189
rooftop gardens, 124, 211, 317, 340
Rose Kennedy Greenway, 277
Rouse Corporation, 102
Rubin, Jeff, 176
Rudofsky, Bernard, 45
Rue du Temple (Paris), 104
Rue Mouffetard market (Paris), 92
Ruhr Valley (Germany), 231
rush hour, 148
Rusk, David, 303
Russia, 215
rustbelt cities, 231–43
Ryerson University, 127, 225, 229–30, 312

Sacramento (CA), 248
safety/security, 2, 3, 6, 16, 46, 86, 87, 88, 91, 92–93, 193, 204, *331*, 335, 337–38 (*See also* food safety)
Saint Louis (MO), 94
Saint Paul Bridges project, 143–46
Saint Paul Foundation, 142
Saint Paul on the Mississippi Design Center, 140–41
Saint Paul on the Mississippi Development Framework, 135, 136, 137–43
Saint Paul Port Authority, 141
Saint Paul Riverfront Corp, 133–34, 144
Saint Paul, 132–58, 214, 231, 262, 266, 291, 316

Saint Paul, Great River Park initiative, 142–43
Saint Paul-Minnesota, 264–65
Salem Street (Boston), 149
San Antonio Canal (Puerto Rico), 270
San Francisco, 33, 180, 197, 200, 201, 206, 224, 270
San Juan (Puerto Rico), 269–70
San Juan Waterfront Master Plan, 270
sanitation, 22, 23, 30, 246, 327
Savannah College of Art and Design (SCAD), 230–31
Scandinavia, 183, 327, 327–41
Scarborough College (U of T), 93, 94
Schiphol Airport (Amsterdam), 262
schools, 185, 209, 210, 258, 338 (*See also* universities/colleges)
Science Museum of Minnesota, 138–39
sculpture, 123, 124, 339
sea levels, 74
seacoast cities, 266
Seattle, 92, 200
security. *See* safety/security
sedentary lifestyle, 193
Seeb, Patrick, 132
segregated land use policies, 167–68
segregation, 94
self-actualization, 35, 51, 79–80
self-discovery, 286
self-guided vehicles, 195
self-organizing survival mechanisms, 43
seniors, 3, 65, 91, 228
Seoul (South Korea), 200
Sert, José Luis, 48, 49, 53
sewage, energy from, 191 (*See also* wastewater)

Sewell, John, 62
Shaping Growth in the Greater Toronto Area (study), 248–49
share vehicles, 195, 195
shared culture, 170
"sharing" software, 153–54
Shen, Kairos, 277
Shepard Road (Saint Paul), 141
shipping, 266
SHoP Architects, 286
shopfronts, 149
shopping, 2, 17, 194, 196, 230, 247, 249, 259–60, 317, 330, 332, 333, 334
signage, 2, 3, 6, 86, 149, 204, 279
Silent Spring (Carson), 44
silo thinking, 99, 163, 221
Simcoe, John Graves, 208
Simón Bolívar International Airport, 215, 219
Singapore, 195
single-family housing market, 72
Sketchup (software) 154
skyways, 135, 138, 256
slum clearance, 23, 244
Smile concept, *282*, 283
SmithGroup JJR, 237, 238
Smithsonian Institution Traveling Exhibition Service (SITES), 35
sociability, 7, 15, 43, 72, 255, 256, 259–60
social arrangements, and sustainability, 75
social diversity, designing for, 209–10
social dynamics, balancing, 211
social equity, 18, 27–28, 177–78
social gravity, removal of, 35–36
social housing, 64–65 (*See also* specific projects)
social isolation, 31, 255

Social Life of Small Urban Spaces (Whyte), 45
social networking, 255
social services, 177, 192, 249, 258, 261, 298, 304, 330
social sustainability, 209–10
soft infrastructure, 167
Soho (NYC), 178
soil quality/remediation, 92–93, 154–55, 183, 268, 272, 304, 344
solar energy, 73, 183, 191, 224, 317, 341
SOM (architects), 281
South Africa, 53, 224
South Axis (Amsterdam), 261
South Boston Seaport Plan, 150
South Boston Waterfront, 270
South Boston, 276
South Green (Hartford), 241
South Korea, 200, 224
South Orange (NJ), 21
South Street Seaport (NYC), 103, 285
Southeast False Creek (Vancouver), 190
Southside Institutions Neighbourhood Alliance (SINA), 241
Spadina Avenue (Toronto), 82
Spadina Expressway, 66
Spain, 50, 260
special financing districts, 209
specialization, 7–8, 11, 17, 38, 128, 147–48, 152, 225, 332
Spirn, Ann, 212
sports, 15, 24, 102, 334, 150 (*See also* Olympics)
Springfield (MA), 240
squares, 127, 164, 203 211, 230, 259, 333, 335

St. George Street (Toronto), 70, 201

St. James Anglican Cathedral (Toronto), 123, 124

St. James Park (Toronto), 123

St. Lawrence Hall (Toronto), 118

St. Lawrence Historic District (Toronto), 127, 129

St. Lawrence Historic District Coalition, 120–22

St. Lawrence Market (Toronto), 118, 119, 121

St. Lawrence Neighbourhood (Toronto), 69, 124, 185

stadiums, 101, 272

Stamm, Gary, 164

Standard Oil, 29

starchitects, 98–99

Station Square (Pittsburgh), 233

Statue of Liberty, 279

steel industry, 233

Stinson, Jeff, 63

Stockholm, 271, 327–32, 337, 339, 340, 341

Stop Spadina movement, 68–69

storefronts, 6, 86, 117, 128–29 (See also shopping)

storm sewers, 188

stormwater, 190, 268, 329–30, 339

streamlining, 300

street furnishings, 86, 126, 203, 284, 318

Street Life Project, 45

street markets, 2, 80, 86, 92–93, 104, 333, 335

streetcars, 66, 71, 236, 252

street-level retail, 38, 229, 256, 333 (See also ground-level uses)

streets

  and demise of city, 7–8

  as traffic artery, 6

  in the air, 94

  modernist vision. See modernist urban planning

  modifying, 200–5

  narrow, 2, 6, 105, 179, 299, 335

  pedestrian-oriented, 1–2

  pedestrian-unfriendly, 3, 6–7

  roles of, 25

  sawtooth effect, 17

  wide/widening, 2, 33, 112, 118–19, 123, 126, 127–28, 130, 135, 148, 190

  (See also complete streets; curbless streets; multimodel street design; naked streets)

streets-and-blocks plan, 268–69

stripped-down style, 93

Strøget (Copenhagen), 335, 337

student housing, 228, 230, 319

studios, 69

subprime mortgage crisis, 245, 248

subsidiarity, 295, 301–4, 243 (See also amalgamation)

suburbs

  and dependence on car, 17–18, 73, 81

  and modernist vision, 28

  and New Urbanism movement, 98

  and subsidiarity concept, 303

  archetype, 36

  challenges to, 38–40

  characteristics of, 17

  collapse of, 248

  densification/diversification, 344

  exodus to cities, 72–73

  flight to, 10, 15–16, 31–39, 255

  frontier yeoman idiom, 28

  growth of, 174–75

  immigrant population, 81, 181

  impact of, 36–39, 48

  in crisis, 244–45, 248

malls, failed, 100–1
move away from, 72
population, 21, 75
predictions, 346
roots of, 10, 15–16, 31–36
slowdown in development, 72
social equity issues, 177–78
transplants, 103–4
urbanization of, 246–49, 250,
  251–52
(*See also* pastoralism)
subways, 151, 192, 194, 200, 252,
  330, 340
suites within suites, 180
summer-camp plan, 50–51
super blocks, 17, 27, 89, 166, 268
supermarkets, 92
support and fill concept, 55, 56
Surowiecki, James, 290–91
sustainability, 10, 43, 73, 74–76, 149,
  150, 176, 186–93, 268, 271,
  326–27, *328*, 329–41
Sustainable Model City District, 189
Sweden, 224, 327–28, 333
SWOT (Strengths, Weaknesses,
  Opportunities and Threats),
  291–94, 314
SymbioCity, 327
systems analysis, 96
Systems of Survival (Jacobs), 67, 149

Talking Heads (band), 287
Tampa, 103
Target, 317
Tax Investment Financing (TIF),
  265
taxes, 131, 209, 245, 257, 343 (*See
  also* property tax)
Taylor, Marilyn Jordan, 281
Team X Primer, 47
Team X, 46–49, 55, 93–94

technological advances, 255
Ted Rogers School of Management,
  229
Tel Aviv, 29–30
temperature moderation, 213
"the other" concept, 260
third party oversight, 310
Thompson, Ben, 133, 135, 139, 142
Three Cities within Toronto, The …
  (Hulchanski), 177
Tokyo, 179, 259
Toledo (OH), 103
tolerance, 72, 87, 345
Toronto City Hall, 62
Toronto City Summit Alliance, 323
Toronto Community Housing Corp,
  210
Toronto Harbour, 222, 307
Toronto Historical Board, 121
Toronto Hydro, 129
Toronto Islands, 212
Toronto Port Lands, 150
Toronto Sculpture Garden, 123, 124
Toronto Star, 274
Toronto Transit Commission
  (TTC), 129
Toronto Urban Design Group, 294
Toronto, 62, 206, 256, 260, 346
  amalgamation, 295–301, 302
  bureaucracy, 300
  Central Area Plan, 115, 117–20,
    185–86
  cultural diversity, 80, 81, 323, 324
  cycling in, 204–5
  downtown redevelopment, 72,
    114–22
  economic stresses, 297–98
  harmonization, 300–1
  immigration to, 57
  Jacobs's contribution to, 66–71
  juxtapositions, 82, 83

municipal govt, 295
Official Plan (1969), 114
population, 298
public improvement program,
    123–25
reform council, 114–15, 124
size, 298, 302, 304
subsidiarity, 303–4
tribunal model, 308–9
urban design in, 69–70
waterfront redevelopment, 63–64,
    150–52, 203–4, 221, 223–25,
    288
–Yaletown comparisons, 307
(*See also* Greater Toronto Area;
    Metropolitan Toronto (1953))
Touchstone, 52
tourism, 102–3, 217–18, 233, 260,
    269, 270, 279
towers in the park, 30, 45, 117, 255
towers in the plaza, 117
town hall gatherings, 314–15
townhouses, 105–6
traboules (hidden passages), 203
traffic, 23, 195, 327
    congestion pricing, 195
    dog legs, 3, 6
    engineering, 8, 37, 169, 200–1
    forlorn arteries, 5, 6–7
    left-turn lanes, 3, 6, 337–38
    rights-of-way, 222, 251–52, 273,
        318
    signals, 2, 335, 337
    suburbs, 17–18
    one-way streets, 33, 111, 135, 148
trails, 259, 272, 273–79, 286–88, 345
transit hubs, 252
transit malls, 126
transit options, 200
transit planners, 8
transit shelters, 127

transit stops, 8, 195
transit system, 251–52, 332
Transportation Dept (Toronto), 106
transportation, 327, 343
    and Athens Charter, 24
    and sustainability, 75
    cost of, and choice of neighbour-
        hood, 72
    paradigm shift, 196–97
    predictions, 345
    progressive strategies, 192
    tied to land use, 251–52
    (*See also* cars; expressways;
        highways; roads; transit
        [heading])
Travellers (insurance co), 239
trees, 6, 122, 126, 130, 142, 148,
    149, 334, 339
Trefann Court Heights (Toronto), 62
triangulation, 46
tribunal model, 308–10
Tri-Centennial State Park (Detroit),
    238
Trimbach, Robert, 318–20
Trinity College (Hartford), 225,
    240–41
Trinity-Spadina (Toronto), 311–13
Trudeau, Pierre Elliott, 57
tsunamis, 214
tunnels, 256, 340
Twin Cities. *See* Minneapolis–St. Paul
Twitter, 255

U.S. Green Building Council, 187,
    224
U.S. Interstate Highway System, 32
unbundled development, 256
universal accessibility, 91
Universidad Metropolitana
    (Unimet), 214, 216
Université de Paris, 319

universities/colleges, 9, 149, 225–26, 227, 228–31, 233, 275
University Cultural Center Association (UCCA), 237
University of Minnesota Design Center for the American Landscape, 133
University of Minnesota, 132, 140, 225–26, 227
University of Pennsylvania, 225
University of Toronto, 56, 70, 93, 94, 177, 201
Upper Landing (Saint Paul), 141, 146
urban balcony concept, 285–86
urban agriculture, 189 (*See also* rooftop gardens)
Urban Design Awards, 70
Urban Design Group (NYC), 116, 151
Urban Design Group (Toronto), 116, 118, 120–31, 137
urban design, 9
    economic development tool, 131
    integrating role, 131
    origin of, 47–48
Urban Fare (Vancouver), 92
urban forests, 186
urban renewal, 23, 46, 47, 49, 51, 57, 60, 62, 66, 69, 118, 123, 132, 178–79, 207, 234, 244–47, 263, 264
Urban Ring, 176
urban sprawl, 343
Urban Strategies (firm), 131, 226
urban village, 18, 139, 145
Urban Villagers, The (Gans), 45
Urbanski, Matt, 280
urban-suburban political divide, 246
user-pay philosophy, 258
utopian theories/visions, 22–25

vacuum-powered waste removal, 330, *331*
van Eych, Aldo, 47–48, 49, 55
Van Valkenburgh, Michael, 223, 280
Vancouver, 61, 92, 180, 190, 206, 270–71, 305–6, 346
Vander Rohe, Mies, 178
Varanasi, Kishore, 243
Vargas state (Venezuela), 220
Västra Hamnen (Malmö), 339
Vaughan, Adam, 311–12
Venezuela, 218, 220, 213–18, 222
Venezuelan Ministry of Science and Technology, 214
vertical gardens, 340
Victoria (BC), 190, 224
Victoria Memorial Square (Toronto), 207, 208
Victorian Garden (Toronto), 123
Victorian Society in America, 230–31
Viejo San Juan (Puerto Rico), 217
Vietnam War, 52, 54, 57
views, 292, 293
Viikki (Helsinki), 189
voluntary planning district, 320

Wabasha Bridge, 316
Wacouta Commons (Saint Paul), 141
walking tours, 71
walking, 83–84, 175, 193, 194, 273, 286, 330, 334, 335
walkways, 63, 90, 93, 122–23, 275
Wall Street Journal, 100
Walmart, 317
Ward 20 method (Toronto), 311–13
Ward, Samuel Ringgold, 119
Warehouse redevelopment, 82, 118, 132, 164, 178, 181, 183–84, 208, 266
Washington (DC), 271

waste management, 73–74, 75, 92–93, 106, 181, 188, 224, 268, 246, 299, 330, 343

wastewater, 188, 189, 329

water consumption, 329

water filtration, 213

water levels, 92–93

water quality, 92–93, 143, 304, 329, 338

water supply, 327, 329

Waterford Development Group, 242

Waterfront Design Review Panel, 151

Waterfront Regeneration Trust, 316

Waterfront Toronto, 151, 221–22

waterfront redevelopment, 9, 63–64, 101, 143–47, 150–52, 189–90, 203–4, 221, 223–25, 233, 261–63, 265–66, 267, 268–77, 288, 311, 316, 338, 344

watershed planning, 251

water-use practices, 188–89

Wayne State University, 237

weather protection, 6, 112, 138, 186, 284

Weaver, Warren, 44

Weinstein, Richard, 116

Wellington Place (Toronto), 208

West Africa, 47

West Don Lands project (Toronto), 155

West Side Flats (Saint Paul), 144–46

West Side Highway (NYC), 199–200

West Side Yard (Manhattan), 102

Westchester (NY), 16

western alienation, 112

wetlands, 44, 71, 223, 264, 266, 281

White City (Tel Aviv), 29–30

white flight, 35

Why Your World Is About to Get a Whole Lot Smaller (Rubin), 176

Whyte, William H. "Holly," 39, 45–46

Wilder Foundation, 264

Williams, Anthony A., 271, 313, 315

wind energy, 73, 183, 224

window displays, 2, 3, 86

Wisconsin, 215

wisdom of crowds concept, 290–91, 314–15

Wisdom of Crowds, The (Surowiecki), 290–91

women's movement, 52, 82

Woodward Ave (Detroit), 1, 232, 237

Woodward, Augustus, 236

woonerfs (curbless streets), 137

workplace, living close to, 165, 166, 196, 272, 276, 332

World Cultural Heritage sites, 29–30

World Trade Center, 52, 94

World War II, 7, 8, 10, 16, 17, 21, 23, 35, 174, 178, 179, 244, 279

Wright, Frank Lloyd, 26, 43–44, 78

Wurman, Richard Saul, 63

xenophobia, 260

Yaletown (Vancouver), 271, 305, *306*

Yamaski, Minoru, 94

Yesterday's Tomorrows (exhibit), 35–36

YIMBY response, 311

YMCA (Toronto), 70

Yonge Street (Toronto), 118, 125–28, 129, 230

York University (Toronto), 63, 225

young families, 185, 210, 211, 333

ZAC (Concentrated Development
    Zone), 319–20
zero carbon footprint communities,
    344
zoning
    and harmonization, 300–1
    and historical preservation, 208–9
    and resistance to change
        (suburbs), 247–48
by land use, 36–37
deregulation, 164–67
French planning culture, 319–20
impact of CIAM on, 31
inclusive, 177
language of, 159
maps, 121
principles, 165
residence/business, 245–46

KEN GREENBERG is an architect and urban designer. For over three decades, he has played a pivotal role on public and private design assignments in urban settings throughout North America and Europe, focusing on the rejuvenation of downtowns, waterfronts, neighbourhoods and university campuses, from the scale of the city region to that of the city block. Cities as diverse as Toronto, Hartford, Amsterdam, New York, Boston, Montréal, Washington, DC, Paris, Detroit, Saint Paul and San Juan, Puerto Rico, have benefited from his advocacy and passion for restoring the vitality and relevance of cities as key to a more sustainable, prosperous and equitable future. Former Director of Urban Design and Architecture for the City of Toronto and Principal of Greenberg Consultants, he is the recipient of the 2010 American Institute of Architects Thomas Jefferson Award for public design excellence. He lives in Toronto.